D1605948

The Territorial Peace

There is continued discussion in International Relations surrounding the existence (or not) of the "Democratic Peace" – the idea that democracies do not fight each other. This book argues that threats to homeland territories force centralization within the state, for three reasons. First, territorial threats are highly salient to individuals, and leaders must respond by promoting the security of the state. Second, threatened territories must be defended by large, standing land armies, and these armies can then be used as forces for repression during times of peace. Finally, domestic political bargaining is dramatically altered during times of territorial threat, with government opponents joining the leader in promoting the security of the state. Leaders therefore have a favorable environment in which to institutionalize greater executive power. These forces explain why conflicts are associated with centralized states, and in turn why peace is associated with democracy.

DOUGLAS M. GIBLER is Professor of Political Science at the University of Alabama. He has published articles in journals including the *American Journal of Political Science*, *Comparative Political Studies*, *International Studies Quarterly*, the *Journal of Conflict Resolution*, the *Journal of Peace Research*, and the *Journal of Politics*. His research has been funded by the US National Science Foundation and the Folke Bernadotte Academy, and in 2008 he was named a fellow by the H.F. Guggenheim Foundation.

The Territorial Peace

Borders, State Development, and International Conflict

DOUGLAS M. GIBLER

CAMBRIDGE
UNIVERSITY PRESS

CAMBRIDGE UNIVERSITY PRESS
Cambridge, New York, Melbourne, Madrid, Cape Town,
Singapore, São Paulo, Delhi, Mexico City

Cambridge University Press
The Edinburgh Building, Cambridge CB2 8RU, UK

Published in the United States of America by Cambridge University Press, New York

www.cambridge.org
Information on this title: www.cambridge.org/9781107016217

First published 2012

Printed and bound in the United Kingdom by the MPG Books Group

A catalog record for this publication is available from the British Library

Library of Congress Cataloging in Publication data
Gibler, Douglas M.
The territorial peace : borders, state development, and international conflict /
Douglas M. Gibler.
p.   cm.
Includes bibliographical references and index.
ISBN 978-1-107-01621-7 (hardback)
1. Boundary disputes.   2. Boundaries.   3. Borderlands.   I. Title.
JC323.G469 2012
320.1′2–dc23   2012016087

ISBN 978-1-107-01621-7 Hardback

For Julia,
"a summer love for spring, fall and winter…"

Contents

List of illustrations   *page* x
List of tables   xi
Acknowledgments   xii

1 **Introduction**   1
   1.1 Introduction   1
   1.2 Issues raised in this book   3
   1.3 Plan of the book   5

   PART I   INTERNATIONAL BORDERS   7

2 **Territorial issues and international conflict**   9
   2.1 Introduction   9
   2.2 Territorial issues, disputes, and wars   10
   2.3 Territorial issues and the steps to war   14
   2.4 Regime type, dyadic conflict and cooperation,
        and territorial issues   16
   2.5 When are territorial issues salient?   17
   2.6 Conclusions   23

3 **Individual, state, and territorial issues**   25
   3.1 Introduction   25
   3.2 Territorial issues and the individual   26
   3.3 Territorial issues and the state   31
   3.4 Territorial issues and democracy   36
   3.5 Territorial issues and international conflict   40
   3.6 Conclusions   44

PART II   STATE DEVELOPMENT   47

4   **Territorial threats and political behavior**   **49**
     4.1   Introduction   49
     4.2   Territorial threat and political tolerance   50
     4.3   Sample and variable descriptions   54
     4.4   Predicting political tolerance   60
     4.5   Some caveats, with a note on other political behaviors 65
     4.6   Conclusions   68

5   **Territorial threats, standing armies, and state repression** **69**
     5.1   Introduction   69
     5.2   The quest for preparedness   70
     5.3   External threat, standing armies, and repression   74
     5.4   The effects of territorial threat on army size   77
     5.5   Predicting state repression   82
     5.6   Conclusions   88

6   **Territorial threats and domestic institutions**   **89**
     6.1   Introduction   89
     6.2   External conflict and the domestic opposition   90
     6.3   Centralizing political power   95
     6.4   Identifying opposition party effects   96
     6.5   Identifying institutional changes   101
     6.6   A note on the role of judiciaries   106
     6.7   Conclusions   107

PART III   THE TERRITORIAL PEACE   109

7   **Territorial peace among neighbors**   **111**
     7.1   Introduction   111
     7.2   The democratic peace and territorial issues   112
     7.3   Operationalizing border stability   117
     7.4   International borders and joint democracy   125
     7.5   International borders, joint democracy, and
            international conflict   128
     7.6   A note on alternate specifications   132
     7.7   Conclusions   133

8   **Territorial peace and negotiated compromises**   **135**
     8.1   Introduction   135
     8.2   Democracies and peaceful dispute settlement   136

8.3	Territorial issues and negotiation	139
8.4	Modeling choices and variable definition	141
8.5	Predicting negotiated compromises	144
8.6	Confirming the role of issues	146
8.7	Conclusions	148
9	**Territorial peace and victory in conflict**	**149**
9.1	Introduction	149
9.2	Democracy and conflict selection	150
9.3	Territorial peace and conflict selection	151
9.4	Modeling choices and variable definition	154
9.5	Victory in conflict	157
9.6	A note on conflict duration	162
9.7	Conclusions	164
10	**Final thoughts**	**165**
10.1	Summary of findings	165
10.2	Additional issues raised by this book	169
References		175
Index		188

Illustrations

7.1   Omitted variable bias in the democratic peace   *page* 124

Tables

4.1	Aggregate political tolerance levels in 36 countries	*page* 57
4.2	Multi-level models of political tolerance	61
5.1	Predicting army size with militarized dispute involvement	78
5.2	Substantive effects of militarized disputes on army size	80
5.3	Predicting repression with army size changes	85
5.4	Substantive effects of army size changes on repression	87
6.1	Non-democracies, party polarization, and territorial threat	94
6.2	Party polarization in the state, 1975–2000	99
6.3	The number of veto players in the state, 1975–2000	103
7.1	Predicting joint democracy with territorial threat	126
7.2	International borders and fatal militarized disputes	129
8.1	Predicting negotiation in militarized disputes, 1816–2000	145
9.1	Predicting victory in militarized disputes, 1816–2000	158

Acknowledgments

Any book of this kind cannot be written alone. I have benefited from the help of many friends who have taken their time to provide comments at different stages of this project. Among those who have commented on the work described here, I especially thank Chuck Boehmer, Alex Braithwaite, Bruce Bueno de Mesquita, Margit Bussmann, Kathleen Cunningham, Paul Diehl, Cédric Dupont, Erik Gartzke, Scott Gates, Gary Goertz, Henry Hale, Paul Hensel, Marc Hutchison, Paul Huth, Pat James, Charles Lipson, Sara Mitchell, Jim Morrow, John Mueller, Brian Pollins, Karen Rasler, James Lee Ray, Toby Rider, Randy Schweller, John Stephenson, Cameron Thies, Bill Thompson, Joe Walsh, and Scott Wolford. I have also benefitted greatly from the many discussions I have had with current and former colleagues. Barbara Chotiner, Ellen Cutrone, Karl DeRouen, Mike Desch, Rich Fording, Eugene Gholz, David Lanoue, Mark Peffley, Kirk Randazzo, and Emily Ritter, have all been very willing to share their time with me, and I greatly appreciate their help. Finally, much of this book presents a challenge to democratic peace scholarship. Nevertheless, John Oneal, one of the pioneers of democratic peace theory, encouraged me to come to Alabama and has always been gracious and supportive of my work. I can think of no better colleague or scientist.

Three of the chapters are based on work that I have written with former students. I thank Marc Hutchison and Steve Miller for their willingness to allow me to build from our earlier work together. I also thank my friends, Alex Braithwaite and Jaroslav Tir, for their help on several related pieces and, more generally, for helping me think more deeply about many of the mechanisms in what has become the "Territorial Peace."

I have also presented various pieces of this project at several universities, received excellent feedback, and made many friends. This book is much better for the comments made by those seminar participants. My thanks to the political science departments at Columbia University, Louisiana State University, the

University of Chicago, the University of Illinois, and the University of Iowa; my thanks also to the Mershon Center at the Ohio State University, the Lyndon B. Johnson School at the University of Texas, and the Graduate Institute of International Studies, in Geneva, Switzerland.

Much of the analyses used in this book rely on data that is publicly available. I think much of our great progress in uncovering the causes and effects of conflict has been due to scholars agreeing to post and disseminate the data they collect. I know this book would have been tremendously more difficult, and much less developed as well, were it not for the work and graciousness of Paul Huth and Todd Allee; Adam Przeworski; Bruce Russett and John Oneal; Wittold Henisz; Alex Braithwaite; and Doug Stinnett, Jaroslav Tir, Phil Schafer, Paul Diehl, and Chuck Gochman. Thank you.

I have received funding for various aspects of this project. Fellowship money from the Harry Frank Guggenheim Foundation allowed release from classes and also research assistance. The National Science Foundation (Grant #SES-0923406) provided both summer money and research support for two years. Finally, the Dean of Arts and Science at the University of Alabama generously provided funds to host a conference related to this work. I thank Bob Olin for his support.

Cambridge University Press have been incredibly helpful as well. They provided an excellent, informative review process for the initial manuscript, and they were understanding when I needed more time to work on the final draft of the book. I thank John Haslam and Carrie Parkinson and all of the Cambridge University Press team.

My remaining acknowledgments are more personal. First, I have always relied heavily on the advice and instruction of John Vasquez. He is an inspiration. As you will read in the pages that follow, his work has played a prominent role in my thinking about politics. More than that though, John has always been my vision of what a scholar should be – always thoughtful, always engaging, and always curious. He continues to be the perfect mentor.

Finally, I thank my wonderful family. Doug, Mary, Sam, and Audrey, each in their own and many ways, have made me the proudest and happiest father imaginable. I cannot believe how very lucky I am to be part of their lives. They remind me every day about what is truly important.

For my wife, Julia, thank you is just not adequate. She has read just about every word of this manuscript, as well as those many words she made me cut. I actually now write with one over-arching purpose: to avoid one of her sit-down, writing conferences! But of course that is just a small part of the thanks I need to give. She has made a family, she has made a home, and she has filled it with joy, laughter, and understanding. I owe and love her so much, and I thank her for my happiness. This book is dedicated to her.

1

Introduction

1.1 Introduction

India and Pakistan were long-time colonies of Great Britain. In 1947, British rule ended and the territories of the empire were partitioned into the Union of India and the Dominion of Pakistan based largely on the religious characteristics of the population in the territories. While most Muslim territories were quickly incorporated into Pakistan, the maharajah of Kashmir, Hari Singh, hesitated instead of joining the new state, even though his territory was 77 percent Muslim. Pakistani forces immediately tried to force the maharajah into accession with guerrilla violence. Singh then appealed to Louis Mountbatten, the last viceroy of India for the British, and he agreed to assist, so long as the Kashmiri territory became part of India. Singh agreed, and Indian forces pushed the Pakistani irregulars from the area (Stein and Arnold 2010). The war that followed lasted into the next year and claimed thousands of lives. Unresolved, the dispute recurred multiple times, resulting in deadly wars between Pakistan and India in 1965 and 1999. They fought a related war in 1971, and China and India actually fought over territory in the area in 1962. The sensitivity of the region is one reason why the floodlights along the border can be seen from space at night, as the photo on the book jacket shows.

Why does it really matter to both India and Pakistan which state Kashmir joined in 1947? The land itself, though breathtakingly beautiful, provides little in the way of resources or raw materials for manufacturing. Its economy has not developed much beyond agriculture and textiles. Although predominantly Muslim, there has not really been large-scale repression of the population by the Hindus to the south. The land itself also provides no overwhelming strategic advantage to any of the states involved. So, then, why is Kashmir important for both leaders and publics?

These are certainly not idle questions since Kashmir is just one example of many contentious borders in the world. In fact, territorial issues are numerous and usually conflict-prone. Almost every single study that controls for issue type finds that territorial issues lead to international disputes and wars, tend to recur, and are difficult to resolve. Still, though the conflict-proneness of these issues has been well documented, we still do not know much about *why* territorial issues are so different from other types of international issues. We do not know why Kashmir matters so much for India and Pakistan. I wrote this book to begin an answer to this question.

I argue that the characteristics of Kashmir or other disputed territories are often less important than what the issue itself represents. For India or Pakistan, an attack over the issue of Kashmir also becomes a conflict for homeland territories, against a neighboring state, with the goal of territorial occupation. These types of conflicts of course engage the average individual in both states as occupation and fear of land-based conflict supplant other issues of importance in their daily lives. This salience also empowers leaders by creating a favorable environment for the centralization of their power; the populace looks to their leader to provide security for the state. When coupled with the increase in military manpower necessary to defend or conquer these lands, leaders in territorially threatened states become quite powerful domestically and often oversee highly centralized institutions.

The domestic political effects of these issues have important implications for international conflict as well. Since centralization often follows territorial threat, it makes sense that non-democracies are more likely to be associated with conflict. India is actually among the rare exceptions in this regard. Most states are like Pakistan, with regimes that are army-backed and elite-governed variations of non-democratic rule. Indeed, territorial threat and centralized governance most often tend to covary.

The presence of territorial issues in a dyad imposes constraints on the leaders involved. Though powerful domestically, leaders must prosecute the international conflicts that the public now fears, and this encourages dispute recurrence until the issue is resolved. Meanwhile, the leaders of states at territorial peace suffer no such constraints and can choose among those issues which they wish to negotiate or escalate to war. This is also why democracies, at territorial peace, are more likely to find negotiated compromises and win the wars they choose to fight.

1.2 Issues raised in this book

Though I focus on two quite familiar topics in the conflict literature – territorial issues and democracy – I argue that their interconnectedness is far greater than we might initially realize. Developing this argument highlights several key issues in international relations.

This book is first an argument about the importance of territorial issues. As I describe in Chapter 2, as a field we know that territorial issues are related to conflict. Less understood is why. I develop this argument by examining how territorial issues affect public opinion and political bargaining within the state. Note, however, that I do not provide an all-encompassing theory of why states fight over territory. One single explanation probably does not exist. Instead, I focus on the domestic salience of these issues and the opportunities and constraints this provides leaders involved in domestic and international bargaining.

I believe this book presents one of the only attempts to fully develop a "second-image-reversed" explanation of domestic politics that is also then used to re-examine observed patterns of international behavior (see Gourevitch 1978). That advancement is important because it highlights an underlying heterogeneity across dyads that has only occasionally been recognized. Most dyads are not equal, and ignoring this fact imperils both our theories and our empirical tests. If my argument is correct, there is a complicated, interdependent relationship between the international and domestic politics of conflict. It is not recursive in the now popular sense that democracy causes peace and peace causes democracy (Russett and Oneal 2001). Instead, international politics affects the structure of domestic politics, as territorial issues shape individual attitudes and the institutions of the state. This, in turn, also controls the constraints placed upon leaders engaged in international politics.

Methodologically, most examinations of the effects of conflict on regime type have relied exclusively on conflict involvement. The focus has been on whether wars prevent democratization. However, conflict involvement is usually the last stage in a long process. Much state centralization is likely to have occurred in anticipation of conflict involvement, and this is missed with such crude measures. I focus instead on identifying territorial threats to the state, which may include the unanticipated dispute or war. Military personnel increases by neighboring states, territorial claims, and even a past history of territorial conflict, all make the outbreak and recurrence of territorial conflict likely. This is especially true when states have no existing mechanisms to arbitrate or discuss their differences. By incorporating these factors into a more complex description of the territorial threat environment for states, I am able to also capture the long-term effects that territorial threats have on the domestic politics of the state.

This book is not intentionally about democracy. I offer no theory of democratization. I offer no theory of democratic stability. Democratization is a rare event, and we have few good models identifying the states likely to transition. As a field we also tend to rely on wealth, the middle class, income inequality, and other economic factors as the best predictors of the occurrence of these regimes (Moore 1966; Przeworski *et al.* 1996; Przeworski 2000; Boix 2003). Instead, I develop a theory of political centralization. I argue that the centralization of institutions, and even of domestic public opinion, depends heavily on the regional threat environment of the state. Domestic political centralization, which most often advantages the leader, is likely to occur as a by-product of the state being targeted by territorial issues. This is true even among democracies, and this theory of territorial threat provides a nice way of linking conflict to regime dynamics that goes well beyond the democracy/non-democracy dichotomy. Regime type may affect how quickly states respond to threats, how informative their signals can be, and how their leaders are held accountable, but territorial conflict controls their foreign policy. The removal of these threats provides the freedom to pursue other interests.

Finally, I believe that the importance of territorial issues should shape how we understand international relations theory more generally. Traditionally, our theories have been guided by a realist paradigm that reifies power at the expense of issues. What states fight over has mattered little compared to variations in their ability to fight. This does not make sense, though, when one considers how different relations between India and Pakistan are from most other dyads across time and across the globe. After all, most leaders are not always trying to conquer their neighbors, and it is important to remember this when trying to explain those rare, conflict-prone exceptions.

The most cogent response to realism – liberalism and the rising focus on democratic peace and cooperation – remains limited in its informative power. Joint democracies have only recently comprised as much as 20 percent of the international system, and the relative number of these dyads has historically been much, much smaller. Democratic theory also provides few answers for why states fight, relying instead on explanations of peace for what are, relatively, a very small number of dyads. This narrowing of focus has made us miss the larger context in which states compete. If democracy is a by-product of territorial peace, a more general theory of conflict can be had, and the wealth of findings associated with democracies is likely to be explained better by democracies' placement amid a larger group of states at territorial peace. I hope this book encourages a productive path away from traditional theories of conflict by demonstrating that the issues of contention do indeed matter and by making domestic political behavior and institutions more important parts of general international relations theories.

1.3 Plan of the book

The book is divided into three parts. Chapter 2 begins by describing the importance of territorial issues for studies of international conflict and outlines different ways that territorial issues have been identified. My theoretical chapter follows in which I develop the domestic salience of territorial issues, outlining how these threats to the state affect domestic political bargaining. The next two parts of the book test expectations derived from my theory of the effects of territorial threat and peace. The first set of empirical examinations assesses my individual-level and state-level predictions for domestic bargaining. The second set is dedicated to dyadic-level conflicts.

The argument I develop in Chapter 3 is really a theory of state development. Territorial conflicts, past and present, will lead a state to possess a citizenry that is primed for moves toward state centralization, and this process is reinforced by the political bargaining among groups within society. I discuss the mechanics of how political centralization is likely to occur when a state's territory is threatened.

I examine the effects of territorial threat on the individual and the state in the second part of the book. Chapter 4 tests the individual-level expectations of the theory by focusing on individual survey responses to questions of tolerance in 36 different countries. Tolerance of outsiders is one way of measuring the strength of majority group cohesion, and, if my theory is correct, territorial threats should lead to individuals who are intolerant of those who do not conform to majority interests. Chapter 5 then examines how territorial threat affects the development of the military and how that development affects the repressive capacity of the state. My final domestic-level chapter, Chapter 6, focuses on the bargaining climate within the state. I expect territorial threats to lead to stymied oppositions and the long-term decline of institutional checks on executive powers. Indeed, we should witness the rise of centralized states in regions with traditionally high levels of territorial conflict.

The final part of the book is split into three chapters. Chapter 7 provides tests of the theory using a data set of contiguous dyads. I expect that many of the arguments associated with a peace between democracies really results from the establishment of peace among neighbors. Territorial conflicts lead to centralization and recurrent conflict, while the removal of these threats is associated with liberalization and democracy. States free from territorial threat should find that any conflicts that do arise will be more easily negotiated and less likely to provoke escalation. I explore this expectation in Chapter 8. The final empirical chapter, Chapter 9, then examines my argument that territorial threats place constraints on state leaders. Leaders involved in territorial conflicts with neighbors should be unlikely to involve their states abroad. Those conflicts that do merit escalation by the leader of a state at territorial peace will be more easily won, though, since the leader is able to select conflicts favorable to the state's conflict-fighting interests and abilities. Together, Chapters 7, 8, and 9 present a consistent theory of international conflict based on territorial peace that also subsumes many established empirical relationships associated with democracies.

PART I

International borders

2

Territorial issues and international conflict

2.1 Introduction

Territorial issues are incredibly conflict-prone. These difficult-to-resolve issues account for more disputes and wars, at a higher rate of escalation, than any other type of issue. This conclusion is well documented, and I describe the empirical basis for the claim very early in this chapter. However, the purpose of this chapter actually rests with developing the ways in which previous studies have treated the domestic political implications of territorial conflict. As I describe, almost all explanations of conflict rely on the salience of territorial issues to generate a domestic political environment that makes international conflict initiation likely. Relying mostly on the strong empirical connection between territory and war, studies search for the factor that makes the land valuable to the conflict-initiating state. An association of ethnic lands, resources, or strategic territory, with territorial conflict, also offers proof of the domestic political argument. There is little development, if any, of how territorial issues actually structure the domestic political bargaining within the state.

There are two exceptions to this pattern. First, the Steps-to-War explanation, offered by Vasquez (1993, 2009), finds the relationship between territorial conflicts and domestic politics to be somewhat recursive. Territorial conflicts affect the composition of the leadership by promoting the ascendance of hard-liners, and these leadership changes make war more likely. A second exception concerns the growing number of studies that examine the ability of democratic institutions to mollify territorial conflict. Granting again the potential salience of these issues for the public at large, the goal of these studies is to determine how exactly democratic institutions influence leaders to avoid direct confrontation over these issues (Huth and Allee 2002; Bueno de Mesquita *et al.* 2003).

I actually believe these three types of studies can be understood as part of a broader argument on the effects of territorial issues. For example, the recursive effects of territorial conflicts are probably much greater than even Vasquez (1993, 2009) imagined. Indeed, state centralization, the size of the electorate, and the rise of authoritarianism are all likely consequences for states targeted by dangerous territorial issues. Of course, if this is the case, if territorial conflict leads to non-democracy, then studies that focus solely on democratic institutions will also only be examining a highly selected sample of dispute cases. Conflicts involving democracies will be easier to resolve and will lack the power to truly challenge domestic institutions. This argument then returns to the original attempts to associate different types of territory with variations in conflict-proneness. Rather than focusing on the attributes of the land, however, I argue that the public will be most concerned with the conflict that has a high probability of directly affecting them. Individuals living in fear of conflict will turn to their leaders for security, allowing the state more and more power in the process, which also encourages more centralized institutions.

I begin this argument in the next section. After establishing first the connection between territorial issues, disputes, and wars, and the theories that have been used to explain these findings, I then outline the Steps-to-War explanation of territorial conflict. I argue that many of the policies associated with this explanation of conflict also provide insight into what makes domestic centralization likely. The next section then describes the studies that select on democracy and how this selection mechanism may hint at more fundamental variations in the types of issues that confront state leaders. Finally, I close with a discussion of the data sets that have been used by all of these studies to identify those states involved in conflict over territorial issues. This last section is important because, from it, I develop an argument for measuring those conflicts that will most affect the lives of individual citizens. These are the salient territorial issues.

2.2 Territorial issues, disputes, and wars

The literature on territorial issues originally began as an outgrowth of the many studies that linked contiguity to conflict. States that border each other are much more likely to fight each other. Bremer (1992) provides some of the most compelling evidence on this, demonstrating that contiguity is the single most important predictor of war-proneness in a dyad; in his analysis, contiguous states were 35 times more likely to experience war than non-contiguous states between the years 1816 and 1965. Though the strength of the relationship is powerful, does this finding really have any substantive import? Contiguity is a constant for neighboring states, and war varies, so contiguity cannot be a cause of war on its own. Contiguity could merely be a proxy for the distance between states, identifying those states more likely to have a large number of interactions and a greater ability to fight each other. Nevertheless, Vasquez (1993) argues that the contiguity findings are instructive because they hint at a more fundamental relationship. Contiguous states are also those states most likely to have disagreements over their borders, and it is these territorial issues and how they are handled that really drives the findings associating contiguity with disputes and wars.

The substantial literature that has developed since Vasquez's first argument provides strong support for the territorial explanation. First, when comparing different types of militarized interstate disputes (MIDs), the disputes over territory are those most often associated with conflicts of greater severity. Territorial issues provoke dispute reciprocation, stalemates, and dispute recurrence at higher rates than the disputes over policy or regime concerns, which are the two other principal types of dispute; territorial disputes are also about three times more likely than other dispute types to escalate to war (Hensel 1996; 59). Fatalities occur at a higher rate in territorial disputes as well. According to Senese (1996), territorial issues increase the chances that a dispute escalates from the threat of force to the display of force and also from the use of force to war. Importantly, this is true even when controlling for contiguity, which suggests that it is really the territorial issue and not proximity or interactions that drives the relationship. Senese (1996) also finds that fatalities are much higher when the conflict involves territorial issues, and, again, this is true even after controlling for the increased number of casualties found in conflicts between contiguous states. Senese's findings for fatalities were confirmed in a separate study by Hensel (2000). The associations between territorial issues and conflict onset, escalation, and conflict resolution have also been confirmed by numerous studies (see, for example, Holsti 1991; Hensel 1994; Kocs 1995; Huth 1998; Vasquez and Gibler 2001; Vasquez and Henehan 2001; Gibler 2007; Vasquez and Valeriano 2010).

The empirical importance of territorial issues has been impervious to research design changes. Studies that use spatial rivalries – those most likely to involve territorial conflict – as a sample produce similar results regarding the conflict-proneness of these issues (Colaresi and Thompson 2005). Changing the dependent variable from disputes to crises also offers no substantive changes in the relationship (Brecher and Wilkenfeld 1997). Territorial crises continue to be more violent and more war-prone than other crisis types (Ben-Yehuda 2004). Finally, controlling for the selection process that generates a dispute or conflict has no effect on the underlying relationship. As both Senese and Vasquez (2003) and Senese (2005) demonstrate, territorial disputes are often found in contiguous states and between those states with territorial claims, but that selection process has little effect on the dynamic of escalation. Territorial conflicts still remain more war-prone than other issue types.

2.2.1 Symbolic land as motivation for conflict

Much attention has been paid to the ethnic and group diversity within disputed lands as a way of explaining why states fight over territory. For example, one explanation asserts that certain territories are symbolic sources of national pride and identity for the population (Saideman 1997, 2001; Ambrosio 2001; Toft 2003; Kornprobst 2008). From this perspective, elites use and frame the symbolic nature of territorial issues to cultivate and harden certain group identities. However, as a result of this manipulation, these identities also sometimes serve as motivation for conflict between other groups or other states on behalf of their ethnic or religious brethren. Thus, identity is viewed as a cause of conflict, and the symbolic nature of the territory is the trigger.

Ethnic ties may also contribute to cross-border conflict when a state begins persecuting a minority group that shares ethnic ties with a larger group in a neighboring state. Russia moving to protect the Serbs from an Austro-Hungarian crackdown in the Balkans at the start of World War I provides a good example, but there have actually been many instances of severe conflict that were linked in some way to ethnicity-based issues. These instances include many aspects of the wars between India and Pakistan, the Arab-Israeli wars, Iran and Iraq, and the conflicts associated with the breakup of Yugoslavia. According to Huth (1998), the presence of ethnicity does predict territorial conflict, with cultural or ethnic similarity increasing the likelihood of border conflict by about 16 percent. Ethnic borders are almost equally split between dispute and non-dispute cases, however, and Huth searched for an explanation of why certain cases never erupted in conflict. The argument he offers is based on the tendency of the non-dispute cases to cluster in Central and South America and in North Africa, well after the establishment of international borders in the respective regions. This may be evidence that strong state definition may mitigate the effects of ethnic groups divided by international borders (Huth 1998, 79–80).

Ethnicity-based theories of territorial conflict share many commonalities with explanations that begin with nationalism as a motivating force for violence, especially in their use of ethnic or group out-bidding as a causal mechanism for conflict. For example, in what began as a criticism of the democratic peace, Mansfield and Snyder (1995) argue that regimes in transition are especially prone to violence as elites battle for domestic political power (see also Mansfield and Snyder 2002, 2005). According to this theory, democratic transitions present a time of opportunity for competing elites because the institutions that normally constrain domestic political bargaining no longer function very well. Elites who wish to gain power take advantage and rally domestic support behind nationalist, often irredentist agendas, bidding higher and higher returns in exchange for constituent support. While these rallies increase the political power of the elites, the resulting rise of nationalism can no longer be contained by the regime because of the weakened institutions. Conflict initiation to please the now-galvanized public then follows. Territorial issues are a likely source of national pride, and, thus, territorial dispute initiations will often occur during political transitions. However, despite strong case evidence linking nationalist and ethnic bidding with external conflict (Mansfield and Snyder 2002, 2005), almost all large-N treatments of the theory have failed to confirm the relationship as it applies to democratic transitions (see, for example, Gleditsch and Ward 1997; Thompson and Tucker 1997; Braumoeller 2004).

The failure to confirm the link between nationalistic out-bidding and demo-cratic transitions does not necessarily overturn the strong case study support for nationalism causing conflict initiation. Instead, it is more likely that nation-alism itself can be dangerous when leaders engage in domestic bidding wars, and this is true regardless of the institutional environment within the state. Roy (1997), for example, found this to be the case in the Russo-Turkish conflict as well as in the conflicts between India and Pakistan. It could also be the case that new states and revolutionary regimes are more likely to engage in out-bidding to garner domestic political support, and it is this process that leads to conflict initiation (Vasquez 1993; 140–141 and 143–144).

Note that all of these examinations of territorial attributes are really just attempts to identify whether the land will be symbolically important to the publics of those states that can control it. Rather than thinking about the conflict process in terms of salience, though, territorial issues may simply be difficult to divide – at least those territories that are conflict-prone. The intractability of the territorial issue then controls whether disputes and wars follow. For example, Goddard (2006) provides evidence that negotiating strategies them-selves could serve to divide actors in such a way that solutions to territorial conflict become intractable. Actors divvy the land among constituencies, and these maneuvers change the type of agreement that is acceptable to each actor. Similarly, Hassner (2010) argues that territorial issues become symbolic as occupying forces engage in a cultural and religious entrenchment within a territory, replacing those elements associated with the competing actor. This process leads to an absorption of the territory by the occupying force.

2.2.2 Strategic territories, resources, and conflict

Traditional international relations theories of course put little stock in these domestic politics explanations of international conflict. For traditional realism, the bifurcation between "high" and "low" politics is assured with the assumption that all leaders, regardless of regime type or personal interest, pursue the national interest whenever possible. Thus, theories of international conflict that attempt to explain territorial issues from a realist perspective tend to focus on the strategic aspects of the land itself, and states are likely to fight over territory when the land itself provides some benefit to the national interest. Improvements to the national interest could come from either advances in war-fighting and power projection gained by territorial acquisition or the resources made available to conquering states. Valueless lands hold little potential for conflict, and so, again, it is not the territory itself that causes war but instead the ability of the territory to add wealth or opportunity to the nation's interests.

The most comprehensive test of the effects of strategic land values on the likelihood of territorial conflict can again be found in Huth (1998). Defining strategic value in terms of proximity to shipping lanes, key military bases, and ports, or as providing advantages when fighting wars, Huth found that the presence of strategic territory had the strongest effect among all predictors of territorial dispute initiation. Conflict occurred in about 81 percent (or 25 out of 31 cases) of the cases in which strategic territory was present. As Huth argues, "the presence of strategic territory was relatively close to being a sufficient condition for a dispute to exist" (1998, 73–75). Nevertheless, the presence of strategic value was not a necessary condition for territorial conflict since only a minority of disputes (25 percent or 767 of 3,039 cases) involved strategic territories. As Huth's data imply, very few tracts of land and very few shipping lanes further the strategic interests of the state. Huth (1998, 75–76) also finds that resource-rich territories are likely sources of conflict. Lands proximate to a border that hold some sort of economic value increase the chances of dyadic conflict by almost 7 percent, which again confirms that leaders may pay more attention to wealth-producing territories.

2.3 Territorial issues and the steps to war

Vasquez (1993, 2009) presents the most comprehensive theory for explaining why territorial issues are more likely to end in war. The Steps-to-War argument turns principally on how territorial issues are handled. If actors contest territorial issues by resorting to power politics, such as alliances, military buildups, and the use of other realpolitik tactics and demonstrations of resolve in crisis bargaining, then the probability of war increases along with the escalation of these practices. Among equals, these coercive acts fail to gain compliance because territorial issues are too salient for the actors involved; nothing short of war can resolve these types of stakes. In spite of the likely dangers, actors who engage in power politics tend to resort to higher and higher levels of coercion. Power politics then becomes a set of proximate causes of war because these practices follow the rise of territorial disputes and are more closely tied to the outbreak of war.

The effects of territorial disputes on pairs of states have important implications both internationally and domestically in Vasquez's theory. For example, the logic of the security dilemma encourages actors to take additional measures to increase their capability; this leads to an upward spiral of increasing insecurity, threat perception, and hostility (Jervis 1978). States then resort more frequently to coercive diplomacy to get the other side to come to an agreement on outstanding issues. Each of these external interactions has the domestic effect of increasing the influence and number of hard-liners within the polity and reducing the number and influence of accommodationists. The increase in hard-liners in turn encourages the adoption of realist practices that fuel hostility and encourage coercive moves that result in the outbreak of international crises. War usually occurs after a series of crises between two states, with the crisis that escalates to war having certain characteristics: (a) initiating a crisis with a physical threat to a territorial stake; (b) an ongoing arms race; (c) escalatory bargaining across crises; (d) a hostile spiral; and (e) hard-liners on at least one side (Vasquez 1993, 1996, 2009; Vasquez and Gibler 2001).

Vasquez was mostly concerned with the international ramifications of these policies and had little time to spend on their domestic effects. Nevertheless, each of these responses to territorial threat is likely to encourage domestic centralization. For example, alliances during times of threat require that the public be galvanized to support the leader and the administration in order to overcome the costs of linking the foreign policy of the state with the foreign policy choices of a potential partner. An even more forceful domestic effect follows military buildups since these policies literally alter the productive capacity of the economy in order to increase the destructive power of the military. In order to carry out these buildups, the leadership must demonize the enemy, which further hardens public opinion, while also increasing the ability of the leadership to wage war. Finally, aggressive crisis bargaining and multiple crises harden both elites and the public, as Vasquez's analysis suggests. The in-group/out-group dynamics of the conflict unify state opinion against the rival and increase the public's trust in the leadership.

In Vasquez's theory there is little differentiation across types of territorial threat. Rather, most territorial issues are likely to be salient so long as the states are equally capable and rival each other. If rivalry can be established in the dyad, then territorial issues predispose leaders and publics toward the realist policies that, unintentionally, increase the risk of war in the dyad. One commonality between this argument and the theories that rely on specific attributes of disputed lands to generate conflict is the domestic political hardening that should follow territorial threat. For Vasquez, the domestic politics of territorial conflict is controlled by the balance of hard-liners among the leadership, which is itself an implicit function of the sensitivity of the state to rivalry and repeated conflict (Vasquez 1993, chapter 6). Thus, like the ethnicity-based arguments or the theories of nationalism and conflict, territorially based conflicts can serve as a means of ossifying the state against a rival while also privileging the state's leadership with greater powers to fight and win a potential war.

2.4 Regime type, dyadic conflict and cooperation, and territorial issues

Several important studies have examined territorial issues in relation to democracy. Selecting a sample of territorial disputes – an established set of the most dangerous conflicts – the question then becomes whether democracy or some form of the democratic peace can ameliorate the conflict-proneness of these cases. This is exactly what Huth and Allee (2002) do. First, using only territorial dispute cases, they separate the conflict process into several stages, from the decision to challenge the status quo by force or claim, through negotiations, to possible escalation. They find that a domestic, political accountability model consistently accounts for decisions to initiate talks at the status quo stage and to offer concessions during negotiations. An international politics model that emphasizes security ties, the strategic value of territory, and the military balance in the dyad, better explains decisions to initiate force and to escalate the dispute. These two models thus provide rather complementary explanations of the conflict process in territorial disputes.

Allee and Huth (2006) build on their earlier study by further examining the incentives placed on leaders during territorial disputes. Since democratic accountability greatly constrains elected officials, appeals to legal settlement and arbitration of territorial issues are often preferred over bilateral negotiation. The international arbiters provide domestic political coverage for potential losses that bilateral negotiation would not. This finding confirms earlier work by Simmons (1999) that found arbitration attempts often follow when international agreements are not ratified at home. Again, the arbitration process provides domestic leaders political coverage for difficult decisions over territory.

These strong constraints even make it likely that democratic leaders will try to avoid territorial conflicts before they even begin. Bueno de Mesquita *et al.* (2003), for example, suggest that the constraints placed on elected leaders make them unlikely to involve their states in territorial conflict. As they argue, democratic leaders have strong political incentives to fight only over goods that can be widely distributed to the public at large. Since democracies often have electoral institutions that favor large winning coalitions, wars of territorial conquest make little political sense because few territories can be distributed in a way that would please enough of the leader's supporters. Instead, these leaders are more likely to fight when attacked and will only initiate wars against dangerous regimes or to change broad policy issues to their favor. The sole territorial conflicts in which democratic leaders are likely to involve themselves are fights over strategic territories that will facilitate the provision of more public goods. According to their argument, "The larger the winning coalition of a warring state, the less likely it is to seek to take territory from the other side" (Bueno de Mesquita *et al.* 2003, 419). Their tests of this argument rely on the observation that democracies do not fight over territory (2003, 426–432).

The facile conclusion made from these studies is that territorial claims are dangerous, but democratic institutions can constrain leaders so that conflict is negotiated or avoided. This type of reasoning is consistent with the empirical evidence that suggests democracies only face certain types of disputes, with territorial disputes least likely to be among them. Mitchell and Prins (1999) are most relevant here, finding that the disputes between democracies involve "fisheries, maritime boundaries, and resources of the sea." Rarely do mature democracies fight over territorial issues that are likely to be salient to the public at large. I build on this relationship between democracy and the lack of territorial conflict throughout the book, offering a competing explanation for these findings that also pays attention to the importance of territorial issues for shaping the domestic politics of the state. That explanation begins with understanding which types of territorial conflicts are likely to be most salient to both publics and leaders.

2.5 When are territorial issues salient?

Though territorial issues are important for predicting international conflict, as most of the above theories attest, not all territorial issues are the same. The development of different explanations for territorial conflict has mostly been an exercise in identifying what types of issues will be salient for the state and its leadership. Here, I depart from the literature's search for attribute-based answers to salience, and I instead focus on (1) the proximity of the conflict and (2) the military environment that serves as the background context for the issue. Disputes that arise over inadvertent border crossings or colonial holdings will not carry the same weight with the public as recurrent threats to territorial homelands, and these two factors capture that fact well. In this section I describe the various methods that have been used to identify the presence (or absence) of dyadic territorial issues in general. These range from data sets of territorial claims and peace treaties to complete data sets of actual conflicts over territory. I then show how these data sets can be used to identify those territorial conflicts that will most likely generate salience within the state. These salient conflicts serve as the starting point for the theory of state centralization and territorial conflict I develop in the rest of the book.

2.5.1 Territorial disputes

The principal data set currently used in most studies of international conflict is the Militarized Interstate Dispute (MID) data set released by the Correlates of War Project (Jones, Bremer and Singer 1996; Ghosn, Palmer and Bremer 2004). This data set identifies every single instance of the threat, display, or use of force by one state against another state since 1816. The data set currently extends to 2001 and includes over 2,300 cases of disputes (MIDs).

The MID data classify issues according to a typology based on the combatants' satisfaction with the status quo immediately prior to the onset of the dispute. The typology is threefold – territory, regime, or policy; issues that cannot be classified are labeled "unclear" (Jones, Bremer and Singer 1996). Territory refers to attempts "by the revisionist state to gain control over a piece of turf that it claims but does not effectively possess." Policy disputes concern attempts to "change the foreign policy behavior of another state." Finally, regime disputes try "to change the government of another state" (Jones, Bremer and Singer 1996, 178).

There are 2,670 dyadic pairs initiating disputes in the current data. Of these, 725 cases have territorial issues as the primary revision type for at least one state in the dyad. Policy disputes are more numerous, with 1,263 dyads having policy as the primary revision type. Regime disputes are least numerous at 143 cases. Eighty-one disputes list unclear revision types for at least one state.

These revisionist categories are not mutually exclusive. The MID coding rules imply that a state can have multiple revisionist issues, and this is true for approximately 4 percent of the dyad pairs (111 cases). Interestingly, all but 23 of these multiple-issue cases have territory as the primary revisionist issue for the state. Each dispute can have multiple revisionists as well, and this occurs about 10 percent of the time (270 cases); again, a large number of these cases also involve territory primarily (191 cases, or over 70 percent).

These data are important for my purposes because the cases of territorial dispute identify, at minimum, threats to territory that have been made by the leader(s) of at least one state. Multiple disputes, if numerous enough, may also imply the start of a rivalry (Goertz and Diehl 1992). Note, however, that the MID data are not an exhaustive list of those instances in which a potential target may find another state threatening. As I describe below, there may be instances in which territorial claims become activated prior to the occurrence of an actual dispute; or, a sense of enmity and rivalry develops prior to actual territorial conflict. Nevertheless, these territorial disputes do represent confirmed cases of threats, displays, or uses of force, and the cases can be limited to those in which territory was the primary issue.

2.5.2 Territorial claims and territorial settlements

Huth (1998) has provided a data set of all instances in which two states have had disagreements over territorial sovereignty. Using only behavioral indicators of disagreement, Huth considers two states to have a dispute when (1) the states disagree over the proper demarcation of an international border, (2) one state occupies territory claimed by the other and refuses to relinquish control, or (3) one state fails to recognize the independence and sovereignty of the other and seeks to annex all or part of its territory. There have been over 300 cases of such disagreements since 1919 (see also Huth and Allee 2002).

Though Huth labels these cases disputes, in this book I generally refer to these data as territorial claims since active threats or fighting are not necessary for inclusion in the data set. Indeed, theoretically, two states can disagree over demarcation without the case ever escalating to the point where even a threat or display of force is used. Of 6,542 observations involving various types of diplomatic or military responses to these disagreements, only 390, or 6 percent, involved an escalation to the threat to use force (Huth and Allee 2002, Table 2.9). Huth's data set is important for understanding the evolution from territorial disagreement, to claim, to military force, but the inclusion of non-threatening disagreements makes the data less useful for my purposes. As I argue throughout this book, salient threats to the state alter domestic political bargaining, but seldom will mere disagreements of border demarcation be sufficient to induce fear in a population affected by the issue.[1]

Several data sets have also recently been used to identify the absence of territorial claims in the dyad. The Kocs (1995) study, for example, used a sample of international borders that had been settled peacefully; Owsiak (2012) has updated this earlier study with a more systematic extension of the data. I have also operationalized peaceful borders in my own previous work in several different ways. I have used the existence of territorial settlements within international alliances to describe those dyads least likely to have border conflicts (Gibler 1996, 1997; Gibler and Wolford 2006). Elsewhere, Jaroslav Tir and I have used peaceful territorial transfers between states to distinguish those states most likely to have settled their territorial claims (Gibler and Tir 2010).

Each of these peaceful-border data sets is of course useful for distinguishing those states least likely to fight, and at least some of these instances are associated with the type of state decentralization that concerns this book (Gibler and Tir 2010). Nevertheless, the settlement of a claim does not necessarily imply that territorial threats no longer target the state. All of these data sets are dyadic, and states often have multiple borders. More importantly, however, the signing of a peace accord or demarcation treaty most often represents mere cheap talk – words that come with little adjustment of attitudes or actions. Indeed, only the extreme cases of territorial exchange followed by demilitarization will provide relief from threats to the state, and this is usually only true in a dyadic context. Territorial peace is the removal of all threats to the state, and in only rare cases will these data provide accurate samples of these cases.[2]

2.5.3 Territorial rivalries

Persistent threats to the state often take the form of rivalry, especially when those conflicts all concern the same basic issue. Goertz and Diehl (1992) have demonstrated the empirical importance of these recurring conflicts at the international level. Basing their definition of rivalry on re-occurrence of MIDs over time in

---

[1] Hensel *et al.* (2008) are also developing a similar data set of claims called the Issue Correlates of War (ICOW). Currently available for the Western Hemisphere and Europe, these data depend critically on "explicit contention by official representatives of two or more nation-states" over an issue for inclusion in the data set (Hensel *et al.*, 2008, 128). Again, however, contention is not synonymous with threat as contentious issues are many times resolved prior to either state contemplating any type of militarized action.

[2] I should also note that these peaceful border data sets would also require the development of a full model of democracy to be useful for most of the analyses in this book. I argue that state centralization occurs when the salient threats target the state. The absence of these threats does not necessarily imply state decentralization, however. Lots of factors, such as wealth, the presence of a middle class, or low-income equality among groups, may be needed before state decentralization and democratization will occur.

a dyad, Goertz and Diehl have successfully demonstrated that there are certain spatial dependencies in much of the conflict data we analyze. Rivalry turns out to be an incredibly good predictor of which states will fight future conflicts.

Realized threats of this sort should also have strong effects on the populations of the states involved. However, identification of a rivalry based on dispute involvement is problematic if I also wish to examine the effects of individual disputes. Thompson (2001) addresses this concern by providing an alternate definition of rivalry based on the qualitative analysis of historical records to determine perceptions of enmity by leaders. There are three basic criteria for identifying these "strategic rivals": both states must view the other as (1) a competitor, (2) a source of actual or latent threats that pose some possibility of becoming militarized, and (3) as an enemy (2001, 560). Conceptually, mutual recognition of competitiveness is central when establishing two states as potential rivals and is used by or suggested as important in several studies (Kuenne 1989; McGinnis and Williams 1989; Vasquez 1993; Thompson 1995). Intuitively, the standard of mutual recognition is also fundamental because, for two states to truly compete, they need to recognize the other as the target of that competition. The emphasis on threat is especially appealing for distinguishing the cases of persistent conflict that are likely to be salient to the public. Finally, Colaresi, Rasler and Thompson (2007, 172) further amend the data and distinguish between spatial and positional rivalries, with the former corresponding roughly to rivalries over territorial issues. These data are most useful for capturing those instances of persistent territorial threat to the state.

2.5.4 Territorial threats

In order to be threatened by an issue, I assume that the population will have to have some expectation that the conflict may affect them directly. The higher the likelihood that the conflict will directly affect an individual, the higher the salience of the issue will be for that person. Leader salience is probably derivative of that linkage, attenuated by the importance of the individual for the leader's ability to remain in power.

These assumptions imply that certain types of territorial conflicts will be more important than others. For example, issues labeled territorial often refer to colonial holdings or conflicts involving far-off lands, but these conflicts over non-homeland territories will most likely be remote from the average individual. Instead, perceptions of threat for an individual will be highest when the issue targets land occupied by or near the individual. The anticipation of conflict and occupation drives the perceptions of fear. This is why territorial threats from neighboring countries will be the threats most likely to be salient to the average individual.

It is easy to distinguish between contiguous and non-contiguous territorial disputes. For example, 548 of the 736 dyadic pairs (74 percent) that fought a militarized dispute over territory since 1816 bordered each other. A large majority of the remaining cases, 124 of 188 dyads, were between non-contiguous states, while the remaining 64 cases were fought by states separated by substantial distances of water.

Similarly, repeated conflicts and rivalries can be distinguished according to contiguity as recurring disputes over colonial holdings are less likely to affect the population than rivalries over adjacent territories. In fact, Colaresi, Rasler and Thompson (2007, 172–173) note this implicitly when developing rules for classifying spatial and positional rivalries. When both territory and status are at stake in a rivalry, spatial issues take precedence when the disputed territories are local. Distant territories more often concern global positioning among the rivals.

The importance of territorial claims is more difficult to identify. While the Issue Correlates of War Project (ICOW) distinguishes between colonial and homeland territories, for example, variations in salience within these categories are usually based on the descriptives of the contested territory – ethnic differences, the presence of resources, etc. Hensel *et al.* (2008). This is similar to the framework used by Huth (1998), who distinguishes among ethnic lands, strategic territories, and resource-based claims. Perhaps different types of disputes will be more difficult to resolve or more likely to escalate, but, again, salience for the individual will be higher as the probability of the conflict affecting the individual increases. For disputes and rivalries, conflict is already present, but that is not the case with claims. Thus, neither the location nor the cause of the claim is enough to establish the salience of the issue for the individual. More information is needed.

Territorial claims can be useful when combined with other behavioral indicators. The difference between an active and a latent claim may simply be the difference between a claim that is militarized and one that is not. Unexplained militarization often carries a certain level of threat on its own, but that militarization takes on new meaning when combined with latent threats to territory. The potential of conflict increases for individuals in claimed territories, and the fear of this conflict makes the claim more salient. Using the Correlates of War Composite Index of National Capabilities (CINC) (Singer, Bremer and Stuckey 1972), salient territorial claims are likely to be those that also have military personnel buildups that can be used to conquer and hold claimed territories.

While all these data sets are useful for identifying the salience of territorial issues, each will be associated with different types of domestic changes – one of the core concerns of this book. Immediate threats to territory, like dispute involvements and militarized territorial claims, are more likely to affect the behavior of individual citizens, and this, in turn, will alter the bargaining among their representatives. However, the main effect of militarized claims and disputes will be the arming of the state. States need troops to fight. As disputes persist and rivalries form, large land armies will develop, and it is then that the institutional structures of the state will begin to change and centralize. This is especially true when the territorial challenges involve neighbors.

2.6 Conclusions

This chapter has outlined a literature replete with demonstrations of the empirical importance of territorial issues. Indeed, disputes over territory are more likely than other issues to be reciprocated, remain unresolved, cause fatalities, escalate to war, and recur. This is true using several different data sets on conflict and multiple research designs that control for different aspects of the selection process that leads to dyadic conflict.

Despite this consensus on the importance of territorial issues, however, no clear answer has been developed that identifies which of the many territorial claims in the world will escalate to disputes and wars. Not all do. There remains a great deal of variation in the level of conflict-proneness among territorial issues, and the literature has responded mostly by trying to connect the attributes of disputed lands with expectations for conflict escalation. This exercise has largely been a search for the factors that make an issue salient to the public and its leaders.

Once salience has been identified, the explanations of territorial conflict actually share many assumptions regarding the likely domestic effects of territorial issues. Almost all the theories describe a leadership that will be constrained by the seriousness of the issue and a public that is concerned with the outcome. Most theories also assume that the public's concern for the issue leads to greater political centralization in the state. Since we know well the policies that are likely to follow salient territorial issues (Vasquez 1993, 2009), the debate really turns on identifying, *ex ante*, which territorial issues will indeed be salient for the state. It is here where my argument begins.

By isolating the territorial disputes that are salient to leaders and publics, I am able to demonstrate that these issues change the nature of domestic political bargaining and the institutions of the state. Equating salience with the proximity and the militarized nature of the territorial threat, I show that militarized territorial disputes between neighbors lead to centralization – of public opinion, of the party system, and of political institutions. This political centralization then controls the development of the state, its regime type, and also how it fights current and future conflicts. That theory is developed in the next chapter.

3

Individual, state, and territorial issues

3.1 Introduction

We know well that territorial issues are linked to an increased rate of disputes and war. Completely underdeveloped, however, are explanations of why territorial issues are so salient to the states that fight these conflicts. Unlike other types of issues, I argue that territorial issues often constitute direct threats to individual lives and livelihoods, and this triggers many of the basic biological and psychological responses to threat that are endemic to humans. Indeed, for an individual in a threatened country, territorial issues may overshadow all other environmental factors that determine such core political attitudes as personal identity and tolerance for others. Of course, wars are organized violence perpetrated by states, and just because individuals are affected by territorial issues does not mean that international conflict follows. This is especially true in states that do not necessarily reflect citizen interests. I therefore develop the link between individual behavior and international conflict in two distinct ways.

First, I argue that individuals in threatened territories are apprehensive, for many reasons, about their land and the risk of war. These citizens seek security from the state. This type of political environment aids the creation of large, standing armies and allows the leader to centralize their own power within the regime.

Second, territorial issues will affect the state for a long time. The creation of large, standing armies alters both the repressive capacity of elites and the distribution of power among groups within a society. Few groups can overcome the domestic capabilities of the military, and this makes control of the military an important political prize. This then implies that compromise among competing groups has few long-term advantages because any group allied with the military can capture the state. States with stable regimes witness greater long-term political and economic inequality while unstable regimes suffer as domestic groups fight for control of the tools of repression.

Both of these processes imply a correlation between territorial threat and non-democracy, but the argument does not suggest that state centralization leads to conflict. Similarly, there will often be a correlation between the absence of territorial threats to the state and democracy; without territorial threats, political decentralization and democratization are easier in the state. This suggests that regime type follows conflict, and the association between democracy and peace may be caused by the absence of territorial issues.

3.2 Territorial issues and the individual

The Correlates of War Project provides a straightforward classification of various issue types – territory, regime, policy, and other issues define separate categories of militarized interstate dispute (Jones, Bremer and Singer 1996). Other classifications follow similar patterns. For example, Holsti (1991) examines the wars since Westphalia (1648) with a 12-part list of issue types, but his typology can easily be aggregated into the basic categories of territory, regime, and policy.[1] This suggests that similar types of issues occur over time; but, also importantly, it provides a consistent basis for comparisons of the effects of issue type on international conflict and the states who fight.

I argue that territorial issues are different from other issues because they trigger multiple biological and psychological responses by individuals in threatened states. First, targeting land also directly targets individuals' lives and livelihoods. Unlike most other types of conflict, territorial conflicts affect humans' strong biological drive for survival. Territorial issues also activate the individual's attachment to their own homeland, which is often made even more important by group attachments to regional territories. Group attachment is complemented in turn by the psychological dimensions of conflict: threats to territory enable the (in/out) group comparisons that are at the heart of many individual political values, including identity choice. Once these in-group and out-group dynamics are established, secondary values such as political tolerance, trust, and other democratic values become more difficult to maintain. Taken as a whole, then, territorial conflicts comprise an issue type that is highly salient for the individual. I discuss these processes in turn.

---

[1] Territorial issues are listed in the two categories labeled strategic territory and, simply, territory. Policy issues include the categories commerce/navigation, protect religious confrères, enforce treaty terms, balance of power, etc. Finally, regime issues include dynastic/succession claims, state/regime survival, and national liberation/state creation.

3.2.1 Land and economic well-being

In early, hunter-gatherer societies, land was the primary source of food, shelter, and other resources necessary for survival (Wilson 1975; Vayda 1976; John 1989), and in many ways that still holds true for individuals in developing countries. Competition for scarce resources means that groups who hold particular pieces of land thrive, while those who do not suffer. The problem of constantly worrying about survival has dwindled for most with modernization, but land ownership still comprises a key economic resource in even the most developed countries. Indeed, it oftentimes represents an individual's most valuable asset. Land still provides shelter, and with a strong legal system, private property can be leveraged into higher-order goods and services or the tools needed for personal wealth creation. Threats to the territories of the state therefore also carry threats to individual property, which translates into threats to individual lives and livelihoods that are only mildly attenuated by the level of economic development within the state.

Territorial conflicts are often doubly dangerous because of their possible indirect effects on individual fortunes. For example, the likelihood of being proximate to active fighting is much higher for individuals in states targeted by territorial issues. This is just the nature of territorial conflict itself. Occupation and control of territory is the goal of the conflict, and, therefore, the targeted territory becomes a battleground itself. These effects will be exacerbated in those conflicts that use primitive supply techniques in which the army literally feeds off the land. Intense conflicts also sap the resources available to the area to manage the public health and relocation issues that follow the end of fighting (Ghobarah, Huth and Russett 2003). Thus, the average individual residing in or near disputed territories has reason to fear the start of conflicts over their land since most status quos are better than the likely outcome of nearby conflicts.

By comparison, it seems difficult to connect an increased individual wariness with threats to foreign policy decisions or to the regime status within the state. Most regime disputes, for example, concern foreign governments that are targeting the leadership of non-democratic, mostly authoritarian states.[2] Under an authoritarian government, most individual citizens would benefit in the long term following some type of regime change; at the very least, most would expect the chance of benefiting through regime change. This is perhaps why targeting countries have sometimes assumed mass support would follow their attempts to impose some type of regime change on their rivals.

---

[2] Only 5 of 103 regime challenges targeted democracies between 1816 and 2001, according to version 3.1 of the Correlates of War Militarized Interstate Dispute (MID) data. Of the remaining cases, 56 targeted states were at or below −5 on the combined Polity IV scale.

Conflicts over policy are identified by Jones, Bremer and Singer (1996) as "effort[s] by the revisionist state to change the foreign policy behavior of another state." Disputes in this catch-all category include conflicts as varied as the seizure of personnel or matériel, disputes over trade policies, banking receipts, postal service, and a host of other, often rather idiosyncratic issues. Indeed, policy issues comprise an incredibly heterogeneous category, but few of these disputes directly increase the likelihood of gains or losses for the individual. For trade disputes, perhaps, there is a general sense of state-level profit and loss, but the chances remain slim for direct, individual effects. The costs and benefits are often so dispersed across all individuals in the country that salience for any particular trade issue remains low for the average individual.[3]

3.2.2 Attachments to land

Territory also holds more than economic value for most individuals. Vasquez (1993, chapter 4; 1995) argues that there is a biological basis for the salience of territorial issues in individuals. According to this argument, humans are "soft-wired" to have certain predilections when exposed to external stimuli such as threat. Constituting neither instinct nor drive, humans are instead *socialized* to treat violence as an appropriate means of resolving disputes over land. This tendency explains the empirical association between threats to property and aggressive behavior in the individual. It is also consistent with a substantial anthropological literature that suggests humans are like other animals who use aggressive displays to hold and gain territories (Wilson 1975; Goodall 2000). Of course, the implication of the socialization argument is that humans can also un-learn these tendencies toward aggressive behavior when territory is threatened.

Aggregated to the society or state level, the human tendency toward aggressive displays when property is threatened is used to explain the strong, positive correlation between territorial issues and war. Individuals, leaders, and societies learn that war is a preferred method of distributing political goods such as territory. Power and war thus determine land ownership, at great cost to those who fight, of course.

The move to conflict or war need not take a precipitous jump from individual to society or state, however, for socialization to explain the salience of territorial issues. Instead, the socialization of territory may be actively encouraged by

---

[3] Of course there are occasions when trade or similar issues impose concentrated benefits or costs for particular individuals in the state. But by their very nature, these disputes remain particular to certain groups, serving as private goods for the individuals in that group, and do not affect issue salience for the average citizen (Lowi 1972).

groups within society, in a top-down approach. At least some research suggests that the definition of group identities relies on the ability of cohesive groups to employ myths and legends, signs and symbols, education, and religion to attach the individual to particular lands associated with the group (Duchacek 1970; Tuan 1991; Paasi 1996). This is why diaspora groups often refer to traditional lands and ancestral homelands; missing an ownership of the soil, the group recalls formative events that are physically attached to particular places (Smith 1981). Numerous studies of civil conflict have also identified the importance of biological and socio-psychological attachments of individuals and groups to their land. In these studies the ethnic nature of the conflict is actually defined as such by the elites within the community. For example, Brass (1997) makes this claim by showing how Indian elites frame violent incidents as "communal" when it serves their interest, thus conditioning publics to favor additional conflict (see also Brubaker and Laitin 1998; Brubaker 2004). Threats to territories, while clearly affecting group identities, also present serious threats to individual identities and are therefore highly salient to those affected by potential conflict.

Quite simply, territorial threats matter more to individuals than policy or regime issues. Who derives their individual identity based upon their leaders' foreign policy choices? Many individuals would have an opinion on the normative rightness of each proposal, perhaps even based on empirical evidence, but again, few would derive their personal identity choice from such policy decisions. Similarly, few would consider themselves intimately linked with their leaders, such that threats to the regimes that rule them also affect their own, individual identities. The rally effects literature, for example, relies on the mechanism of support for the state as a whole, not any particular leader, when threatened by external rivals. Threats to the state lead to nationalism, and a subsidiary effect of that nationalism is the observation of popular support for the leader. This is why rallies are so ephemeral; 90 percent popularity can become less than 40 percent quite quickly.

3.2.3 In-group definition

Vasquez's (1993, 2009) territorial explanation of conflict has clear theoretical roots in the early social psychology literature, specifically the work of Georg Simmel and Lewis Coser. Building on Simmel's (1955) hypothesis that conflict is a socialization mechanism, Coser (1956, 38) extended the socialization hypothesis to argue that "conflict serves to establish and maintain the identity and boundary lines of societies and groups." In this sense, external threat serves to increase the internal cohesion of a group. Thus, territorial threats that target the state increase nationalist responses among ordinary citizens, and these encourage popular rallies in support of the leader. But why would territorial issues and not other conflicts control this socio-psychological response?

Conflicts over regime status may sometimes create the same in-group versus out-group dynamic that results from territorial issues, but one condition must first be met for this to occur on a large scale within the targeted country. The average individual has to have some type of bond with the regime. Absent this, the average individual is presented with conflicting cross-pressures. Threats from outside the state compete with threats from the regime to define group comparisons. If the external threat promises liberation, or at least some sort of positive change in domestic policy, then the dynamics of group definition become quite complicated and inconsistent. If, however, regime status is equated with wholesale political change directed against the entire state, then the average individual would fear conflict, fear change, and thus identify with the threatened nation. Only the few regime conflicts that target the entire state – regime and people – are capable of eliciting the type of in-group versus out-group definitions. These conflicts do not promote the type of consistent group-conflict-based response that follows territorial threats.

Least likely to provoke group definitions consistently are policy disputes. As I describe above, these conflicts are quite heterogeneous. More importantly, these disputes are almost always directed at the foreign policies of the state, not the state itself nor its populace. Few individuals are directly threatened on average, and those who are affected tend to be agents of the leadership and not average citizens. Seizures, postal conflicts, trade disputes, and other policy conflicts do not provide a consistent narrative from which to construct a coherent in-group that fosters centralized political attitudes.

3.2.4 Issue salience and diversionary conflict

These arguments all suggest that territorial issues resonate with individual citizens differently than other types of conflict. Territory affects base survival instincts and also the more developed socio-psychological attachments to land derived from group identities. This issue salience imposes an interesting dynamic upon the domestic politics of the state.

When individual attitudes of security are threatened, leaders and regimes are going to be better positioned politically to institute policies that are consistent with the defense of the state, which is why leaders will often want to manufacture issue salience themselves. But can they? This entire discussion of issue salience has revolved around biological tendencies to react to threat and the socio-psychological attachments individuals develop with their homeland.

If correct, these attachments seem difficult to threaten artificially. To affect survival instincts, external threats have to be real and palpable to the individual. The same must be true for group attachments as well. When an individual's leader targets another state, initiating some type of diversionary conflict to rally popular support in their favor, average citizens are only likely to respond when their lands are somehow targeted. The rival must respond and directly threaten territories. Otherwise, any rally of support is likely to be weak and inconsistent. Put simply, most leaders would find it incredibly difficult to manufacture the types of disputes that encourage the centralization of their political power within the state.

One exception may be conflict initiations during territorial rivalry. Individuals in countries with active rivals are already prone to heightened expectations of conflict. Moreover, and perhaps because of the increased sense of threat in the dyad, any initiation of conflict by one rival leader will most likely be met with a counter response, directed at the territory of the initiating state. Huth (1998) argues that this is one important source of territorial conflict. Politicians pursue domestic political power through a process of ethnic out-bidding, and this then constrains the new leader to a rivalry relationship over territory. Further, as Colaresi (2004) describes, political leaders in targeted countries have strong political incentives to respond aggressively during rivalries. Thus, there are situations in which domestic politics encourages the maintenance of territorial rivalries that are salient to the individuals in both states, and what began as an artificial initiation of conflict for domestic reasons transforms into a conflict with serious implications for both states.

But territorial rivalries are fortunately rare, and seldom are leaders able to play so easily on the tendencies of individuals to respond aggressively to threats to their homelands. Instead, most threats to territory that we observe tend not to be manufactured. I think this explains why the rally effects literature observes strong popular support following several highly salient conflicts (Zaller 1993; Mueller 1994; Parker 1995; Lai and Reiter 2005), but the diversionary conflict literature produces only mixed and inconsistent support for opinion rallies following interventions abroad (Levy 1988; Oneal and Tir 2006). It is very difficult to manufacture issue salience for the average citizen.

3.3 Territorial issues and the state

Thus far I have argued that territorial issues are salient for individuals. Of course, there is a reason for the importance of the issue – the homeland is threatened and needs defense. I argue that the nature of territorial issues implies a defense that is possession-based, requiring troops to defend and hold territory. A large, standing land army also gives elites the resources necessary to repress other segments of society. Together, the salience of the issue to the public and the presence of a standing army impose powerful centralizing forces on the composition of the state.

3.3.1 The creation of standing armies

Territorial conflict, unlike other types of conflict, has the occupation of land as its primary goal. Of course, in order to occupy land, countries that initiate territorial conflicts must construct armies capable of both defeating the enemy and also holding the land once it has been taken. Note the differences across conflict types though, especially with regard to possession of the status quo in the dispute. Prior to challenge, the land is physically held by the targeted states. In most other types of disputes, the status quo is more ephemeral, relating to the stated policy position of the target. This position can be changed much more easily than possession of land, but more importantly for my argument, policy positions can be defended by means other than occupation. Simply increasing the costs of conflict enables better defense of the policy position, providing deterrence, and, if conflict does occur, the combat is not strictly land-based. Territorial issues, conversely, force defense by land possession, and this makes standing, land armies a necessary tool for this type of conflict.

There are two key determinants of domestic military structure: type and location of threats to state interests. Threats to far-flung interests such as trade routes should lead to the construction of navies and air forces for defense since no occupation of land is required, only protection of the policy interests of the state.

This is also true for states with many colonies abroad. Land occupation is technically necessary for colonial disputes but not to the extent that this type of threat would, by itself, affect the military structure of the state. If threats are posed by indigenous forces, the technology advantage of a major state compared to the local population often makes a small land force and navy enough to put down the conflict. If another major state initiates the threat, then the locus of conflict shifts to Europe or wherever the major states are positioned, and the conflict devolves to major state versus major state and forces the use of militaries appropriate to that particular dyadic conflict. Regardless, the very nature of the colonial holding – that it is abroad – suggests that whatever occupying force is necessary in the conflict is physically removed from the state for the duration of the conflict. In most cases, colonial holdings actually *weaken* the repressive power of the elites at home.[4]

Threats from far-flung states may also target locations in or contiguous to the state. This has been especially true recently as many non-democratic regimes have been targeted by major states. In these cases the location of the conflict necessitates the construction of at least some land army force to repel the threat (or maintain order). However, the primary goal for the defender is repelling the threat. Therefore, the threatened leader uses whatever forces are best designed to thwart an invasion or conquering force. Armies have no intrinsic advantage over other types of forces in these cases, unless they provide a cost-effective means of damaging the challenger.

Threats made by contiguous states are usually more serious because of their location, which makes force projection much easier. Contiguity also conditions at least some of the targeted state's defenses, but this varies by type of threat. For policy disputes or for disputes over trade, repelling the intentions of the initiator is paramount, and again, the mix of forces does not necessarily pre-suppose an army-led force. In fact, air forces or other quick-strike forces may be best equipped to provide quick, flexible responses. Since the goal of the threat is not land occupation, and any territorial acquisitions are for the goal of policy change, the incentives for the targeted state are to repel and damage the challenging force.

Territorial threats made by contiguous states are different, however. The added costs of occupying and holding the land make large armies indispensable for these types of threats. The goal of the challenger is to take the land, and in order to do this, the challenger constructs an army for occupation. Conversely, the target seeks to hold the territory against land attack and therefore builds an army capable of maintaining occupation. Possession is the goal for both states.

Issue types are also likely to affect threat duration. According to Vasquez (1993, 2009), states will continue to fight over territorial issues until one side is decisively victorious and can claim the land or a compromise is negotiated that is acceptable to both parties. Remaining are the cases of recurrent conflict, when one state tries to defeat the other but does so only nominally. These cases tend to fester. Short of decisive victory, the losing state has every incentive to maintain its army and attempt a challenge when the conditions best warrant such an attack. The winning state understands this logic and maintains its army's

---

[4] North and Weingast (1989) argue, for example, that the powerful British king had to compromise with his parliament precisely because the bulk of the military force was abroad. The navy could not force increased revenues from the lords. Similarly, Friedberg (1988) argues that a more modern Britain, in trying to maintain its global supremacy, declined rapidly as it tried to service and hold on to its many, far-flung colonial holdings.

presence as well. Thus, territorial conflicts tend to recur (Hensel 1994), and the presence of militarized states across tense borders remains.

Other types of issues are unlikely to affect threat duration in quite the same way. Policy and trade disputes are more likely to be time and place specific, as conflicts end once there has been either a change in or confirmation of the status quo. Those conflicts that do recur – over regime type, perhaps – are still unlikely to engender the same type of military structure as territorial disputes. So, militarized states may tend to be found proximate to recurrent policy or regime disputes, but the land army will probably not be as politically dominant within the state.

3.3.2 Repressive bargaining between elites and poor

The economic nature of large land armies reinforces the trend toward greater concentration of power in the hands of the elite within society. Standing armies require high levels of taxation as well as a broad centralization of authority – to acquire, arm, equip, feed, and otherwise maintain the troops. High taxation and centralization both contribute to a widened gap between the fortunes of the elites and the poor as compared to the status quo. High levels of military spending and frequent conflict also depress domestic consumption and economic growth. This makes the costs of adopting democracy and conceding to the poor's redistributive demands far higher than the costs of using the army to pursue a strategy of exclusion and suppression of competing social groups.

As an example of this logic, consider a society with relatively few domestic groups that represent varying proportions of interests related to land, labor, and capital (Rogowski 1990). In one country, land is less abundant and more valuable relative to both labor and capital, and, therefore, the regime is likely to favor landed elites. If the differences in political power are great enough, the regime becomes authoritarian, dominated by the landed interests, and political change only arrives when international trade affects the relative scarcity of the land factor. In fact, in this society the army is likely to be already allied with the elites. The elites raised the military to protect the state from invasion, and no other interest is capable of possessing enough political power to damage the political alliance. In this society, repressive bargaining practices are only reinforced by the presence of the army, which extracts rents from the other groups for the landed interests.

Contrast that country of landed aristocracy with a society in which interests are equally distributed among the groups representing the various factor endowments. In most cases this country would end up democratic since no single group could maintain political dominance over the other two groups. Compromise would be preferred to continual conflict (Olson 1993). However, if the country had experienced territorial conflict and had militarized in defense of those territories, political bargaining changes. Any group allied with a strong military could enforce its dominance over the other groups because the land army increases the political resources available to repress. If labor achieves dominance, for example, then repression by the military of both land and capital follows. If no group can dominate, conflict and repression are likely to remain because each of the groups now has an incentive to capture the military in order to extract rents from society. The prize of the land army outweighs any incentive to cooperate among the groups. Worse still, each group now operates within a security dilemma – should another group capture the state, exclusion and repression of their own group may follow.

This argument suggests that strong, land-based militaries in politically competitive societies are likely to lead to domestic conflict among groups. At the very least, there should be consistent regime turnovers that oscillate between military-led governments and elite regimes in league with military leaders. In societies that are not politically competitive, standing armies reinforce elite-dominance and make transitions more difficult. In both cases, authoritarian governments are likely; the only difference remains the stability of the regime which is endogenous to the relative power among groups.

3.3.3 The centralization of political power

As I argue above, individuals in threatened territories are likely to seek security. The consequences of this attitude change are such that most leaders – both in and out of power – will turn their attention to security and support the state against the now common foe. The opposition is placed in an incredibly precarious political position. If the opposition opposes the leader, they can easily be labeled as traitors. Further, if the war effort is lost, the opposition can be blamed for undermining the ability of the leadership to fight the rival. The safer position is then to support the leadership in the war effort, but few political rewards follow from this positioning. If the war effort is lost and the opposition backs the leader, the opposition demonstrated itself unable to provide an alternative to the leader's failed policies. Of course, if the war effort is won, the leadership claims credit for the victory.

This type of rally effect can happen in both democracies and non-democracies. While opposition forces in non-democracies often must remain silent until the opportunity for regime change presents itself, the opposition in democracies tends to be quite vocal. Nevertheless, in both types of regimes opposition leaders must be responsive to their own bases of political support. When such an important issue as territorial threat affects the average individual, the opposition must shift or maintain a position of security against the common threat. This quest for security therefore often results in the opposition supporting the leader, who is actively defending the state as well.

Repression only amplifies this effect. Just as elites may use the military structure of the state to extract greater rents from society, so too may leaders turn the military against opposition forces, even when the opposition includes the ranks of the economic or political elite of society. In fact, the mere threat of military repression may be enough to quell opposition unrest in most cases, because the opposition fears both retribution and also the implementation of a repressive police state. This is perhaps why some regimes in territorially unsettled environments can reach a type of autocratic equilibrium with few organized opposition groups.

The final stage of the centralization process occurs as the leader seeks to implement the elite's preferred policies. As opposition forces move to support the leader, the favorable political climate provides the executive in power a unique opportunity to institutionalize their increased domestic political power. Checks against the leader then fade as the regime centralizes authority. Reorganizations to better fight the rival's threat now also include greater powers for the executive. With a pliant opposition, most institutions become prone to restructuring or elimination by the leadership. Few have the political wherewithal to oppose the leader.

3.4 Territorial issues and democracy

Territorial threat should predict state centralization, and the pacification of territorial issues should eventually lead to state decentralization. Thus, because democracy is often dependent upon the establishment of a liberal state, my theory suggests a strong correlation between authoritarianism and territorial threat, democracy and territorial peace. Still, the concepts are distinct. Not all states free from territorial threat will be democracies, and not all democracies will always be free from territorial threat. States with settled borders may still lack the economic or political factors that encourage democratization. Conversely, territorial threat may sometimes force political centralization within established democracies. Each of these possibilities assures that the correlation between settled borders and democracy will remain imperfect.

3.4.1 Decentralization among non-democracies

Over 50 years ago Lipset (1959) demonstrated the role of wealth in predicting states likely to be democratic, and the literature has since consistently affirmed that wealth and democracy are strongly linked.[5] Indeed, this is one of the strongest findings in the comparative literature on democracy. But wealth is not necessarily affected by an absence of territorial threat. Resolved borders do not put raw materials in the ground, educate the workforce, or create strong property rights systems. While states with settled borders are not likely to have politically powerful militaries, standing land armies, and domestic forces that push for centralization of the state, the lack of territorial threat does not immediately translate into greater wealth for society or competitive middle-class interests. The poorest states that have otherwise resolved their borders may therefore still remain non-democratic if other components of democracy are absent. This is the case for many sub-Saharan states that accepted their colonial borders upon independence in the early 1960s but have remained non-democratic since. Mired in civil wars and poverty, few of these states have been able to democratize even while territorial threat remains low across the continent (Lemke 2002, chapter 7).

The removal of territorial issues may be a condition necessary for long-term economic growth. The resources diverted to the military can be better spent on productive assets. Further, the political power of the military will be associated with greater wealth inequality as elites use repression or the threat of repression to extract more from the economy for their own ends. Eliminating the military may therefore encourage the growth of the middle class and more secure property rights. In the long run, these will likely contribute to democratization.

3.4.2 Centralization among democracies

There are still some notable exceptions to the expectation that territorial threats will lead to highly centralized, mostly authoritarian states. Israel, for example, has fought several of its neighbors over territorial issues and remains in an extremely threatening regional environment; in fact, many countries in the

---

[5] This relationship has been repeatedly confirmed, but the cause of the wealth–democracy link remains debated. Przeworski and various coauthors (Przeworski *et al.* 1996; Przeworski and Limongi 1997; Przeworski 2000) contend that wealth does not cause democratization but instead provides the antidote to all types of anti-democratic reversions. According to this argument, democratic transitions occur for myriad reasons that are often unrelated to economic development, but high levels of state wealth (usually measured by GDP) provide strong societal protections against reversions from democracy. Wealth is also generally found when other important domestic determinants of democracy are present. Wealthy states have a strong middle class that makes autocratic repression more difficult (Moore 1966; Rueschemeyer, Stephens and Stephens 2000), and more generally, an increase in the number of powerful actors within society can be found in wealthier states, which makes a competitive, democratic equilibrium more likely (Olson 1993). Ultimately, though the role of wealth in establishing democracy continues to be questioned (Boix 2003; Boix and Stokes 2003; Epstein *et al.* 2006), no one seems to doubt that wealth prevents reversions from democracy.

region overtly seek Israel's demise. Similarly, India has fought wars against Pakistan multiple times, with Jammu and Kashmir providing the backdrop for each conflict and continued tensions in the dyad. Indeed, it is rather incredible that both have maintained effective institutional democracies through some very difficult times.

Nevertheless, there are at least three reasons why democracy may maintain in both states. First, both states have generally been more powerful than their neighbors, and neither has feared total conquest by its neighbors in some time. This is especially true after the development of nuclear weapons by both states. Also aiding democracy is the amount of military aid both countries have received throughout their histories to maintain their strategic advantage. For example, the Correlates of War Composite Index of National Capabilities consistently lists India's power as four to five times the power of Pakistan (Singer, Bremer and Stuckey 1972). Israel also dwarfs the capabilities of most of its neighbors, though the population components of the measure bring the ratio closer to parity.

Second, the nature of the military in Israel and the huge population in India greatly undermine the forces of repression that often result from territorial threat. Israel has maintained a quick strike force, based primarily on air power instead of occupation, and this makes repression of the population difficult. Meanwhile, India's large population makes successful enforcement of a repressive regime nearly impossible.

Third, and finally, both states entered the international system as democracies, and once a democratic equilibrium emerges within a state, breaking it becomes difficult, barring any serious external shocks (Boix 2003). Even in the face of growing or significant external threats, democracies can build large militaries without worrying that they might provide incentives for any social groups to pursue exclusionary policies. Rent seeking and exclusion will likely be punished at the polls before any would-be autocrats can alter institutions through domestic conflict.

Whatever the cause of democracy, these cases provide evidence that settled borders and democracy, though correlated, are distinct concepts. Thus, while Israel and India remain democratic, both tend to have greater centralization of political power within the state as compared to other democracies. Their citizens should also be more cognizant of the territorial issues that affect the state, should identify with their nation against their rival, should be less tolerant of minorities, and should feel greater attachments to their land. The institutional structures of these democracies will also tend to reflect centralization as leaders often run for office, based, at least in part, on fears related to rivalries. Compared to other democracies, then, these regimes are likely to have fewer institutional checks against leaders in power, especially during times of imminent territorial threat or conflict.

3.4.3 Decentralization and military power

Decentralization also depends on the role of the military. When the role of the standing army as guardian of the state is reduced or eliminated, the domestic political bargaining process looks much different. No longer does the army present a force for dominating the state. Hence, the actors within the state have no incentives to try to co-opt the military in order to dominate other groups. Groups within society will instead compete using their own political power, and, with fewer resources available, repression by a dominant group becomes more costly. In this sense, the rise of the middle class within the state may actually be reconsidered as the decline of the political power of the military.

Of course, just as decentralization does not automatically lead to democratization, the elimination of territorial threat also does not imply complete demilitarization within the state. In fact, the strongest military in the world can be found in the United States, a state that has been at peace with its neighbors for some time. Even before the current international system, Great Britain had the world's most powerful armed force and took colonies abroad and ruled a system it labeled *Pax Britannica*, even though this island, too, had no contiguous neighbors to threaten it.

Note, however, the type of military possessed by both the United States and, previously, Great Britain. Technologically sophisticated and designed for quick response to far-flung conflicts, the United States military relies heavily on air and sea power, and, while it still maintains powerful army and marine forces, these units are ill-equipped to repress local populations. Perhaps most importantly, the lack of direct territorial threats to the state has ensured that the political power of the military remains subservient to civilian authority, even though it could be considered a "garrison state" (Friedberg 2000). Similarly, Britain relied on its navy to enforce its will abroad. The lack of threat from neighbors assured there was little need for a strong, land-occupying army, and this further allowed the kings and queens of Britain to pour their monies into forces dedicated to taking and holding territories abroad. Indeed, as I pointed out above, North and Weingast (1989) argue that the strong navy had little repressive power and, hence, little ability to thwart parliamentary attempts to liberalize the state and diminish the power of the crown.

In the end, the actual size of the military will always be an imperfect predictor of its domestic political strength. Militaries that are built to guard the state from threats to homelands will have much more political power than those created by societies to project the interests of the state. Guardian militaries are privileged by public opinion and the lack of incentives for group competition, and the weapons they use for securing the homeland can be turned on both enemies and citizens of the state. Fear of external threat leads to quests for expediency that outweigh concerns over potential threats to domestic institutions. Conversely, militaries built for force projection are created by the dominant interests of the state. One would have to assume a great deal of irrationality to expect a leader or group to create or strengthen a military that could have enough political power to displace its creator domestically, unless there was a greater threat that was more imminent. These types of militaries are more likely to have strong civilian controls on the use of force, and their weapons will be built for force projection outside the confines of the state.

3.5 Territorial issues and international conflict

The process of state development in the shadow of territorial threat influences relations with other states. The favorable domestic political climate created by external threats often arrives at some cost to the leader when bargaining internationally. The heightened threat from a rival forces the leader to actively engage and defend against the threat in order to ease the fears of the public. Negotiating over territorial issues is difficult since the leader must guarantee the removal of threat to the public as a result of any settlement. However, once territorial issues are settled, leaders in states at territorial peace are released from these constraints and may be able to engage rivals abroad, provided the state has the ability to project power the necessary distance.

3.5.1 Domestic politics, difficult negotiations, and recurrent conflict

As I mentioned in the last chapter, there is ample evidence that territorial issues tend to recur (see, for example, Vasquez 1993, 2009; Hensel 1994; Colaresi and Thompson 2005). This makes sense considering how territorial disputes are fought. Unless one army can completely destroy the other army, negotiations must provide some credible guarantee to the population that potential threats to homeland territories no longer exist. However, that is difficult to do when a large, standing army continues to sit across the border. Even genuine peace agreements, arrived at by both leaders with the intention of fostering peace across the border, may not work unless the militaries can be quickly dismantled. However, dismantling an army takes time and can provide an uncertain shock to the country and its economy. More than that, there are strategic reasons to proceed slowly when dismantling the army since demilitarization can create force asymmetries across the border, and unilateral demilitarization can leave the state prone to unanswered attacks by the rival. These dynamics make territorial issues more difficult to resolve among neighbors.

Recurrence is also affected by the domestic politics likely to surround territorial issues. Individuals fear the direct threat to their lives and livelihoods, and their representatives have ceded authority to the executive to defend the state. Thus, the salience of territorial issues ensures that leaders may not easily ignore public calls to pacify the threat from the neighbor. The army that was built to defend the state must be maintained and focused on the territorial threat across the border. To do otherwise would cede domestic authority to fight the conflict to the opposition.

In this transnational environment, the leader becomes domestically powerful because of the salience of the external threat, but the leader is also internationally constrained by the need to engage the threat across the border. The foreign policy of the leader must be directed, in large part, toward removal of the threat to homeland territories. Adventurism abroad becomes untenable because it would remove needed resources for homeland defense, and all other policy decisions are assessed by the calculus of likely effects on the outcome of the border rivalry. Thus, decisions on the pursuit of colonies or trade with other states, or the search for alliance partners, are not likely to be measured by the changes in overall wealth and power that these decisions may bring the state. Rather, the rivalry shapes these decisions as maneuvers to gain strategic advantages against the rival in prosecution of the larger, territorial conflict.

Note that it does not really matter how these contentious issues began for this logic to take hold and constrain the leader for future conflicts. I have described the environment in terms of being targeted by an attack, but suppose one leader, for whatever reason, decides to initiate a territorial conflict with a neighbor. The salience of the territorial issue will force reciprocation of the conflict, as above, and that reciprocation leads the once-initiating state to be joined in conflict and a target of the rival across the border.

Of course, both leaders must have the military resources available for the conflict to be dyadic and provide a source for mutual threat. Absent these resources in the initiating state, the challenge is not credible. A lack of resources in the targeted state would lead to overwhelming victory and resolution of the issue, but these instances are rare. Further, the quick escalation of military power in neighboring states, which may be quests for power asymmetries in the dyad, will most often be enough to serve as the initiation of the territorial conflict and will, therefore, be met with military spending in the now targeted state. Few leaders can surprise their neighbors with a fait accompli of complete military domination on the border without a response by the targeted state; again, this is especially true when the nature of the conflict requires the creation and maintenance of an occupying army. Even in the modern system, armies take time to grow and train.

3.5.2 Peaceful borders and conflict choice

The dynamics of territorial issues – consistent threat, domestic pressure, and strategic incentives to maintain a strong, land-based military – make it unlikely that territorial disputes will be easily negotiated. Instead, conflicts over territory are likely to fester and remain unresolved until some shock changes the nature of the rivalry. This shock may come from an unexpected but overwhelming victory and the continued preponderance of the victor, as Vasquez (1993, 2009) notes. Or, the leaders of both conflicting states may actually overcome the odds and reach a mutually acceptable settlement that lasts.[6]

However resolved, the removal of territorial issues from the agenda of the state substantially changes the international and domestic leverage afforded the leader. Internationally, the leader no longer fears incursions against homeland territories.[7] This lack of direct threat frees the leader to better engage states abroad. Choosing to build a conquering army would be a threat to neighboring states and risk reciprocation by neighbors, invoking the logic of the security dilemma. However, a military built for force projection – navies and air forces – need not always be a challenge to the homelands of neighboring states. And, if these forces actually challenge neighboring states, the logic of contiguous threat would make it likely that the rivalry returns to a logic of competing standing armies to eliminate the threat from the neighbor.

Instead, the real impediment to the construction of militaries built for force projection is likely to be domestic. Without the constant threat posed by a neighbor targeting the homeland, calls to increase or even maintain military readiness become muted. The opposition no longer cedes political authority to the leader and can challenge any redistribution of resources that affect themselves or their constituencies. Further, it becomes more difficult to justify building a military at the expense of the economy. The leader risks disloyalty among supporters and does so for uncertain gains from conflict involvement abroad. Should the

---

[6] As I describe in Chapter 7, these settlements are more likely in cases in which the natural geography reinforces borders that are seemingly fair and defensible by both sides.

[7] I am writing as if the context were dyadic, with only one state across the border. However, some states have many contiguous neighbors, and all conflicts with neighbors would have to be resolved in order for the state to be at territorial peace. Island states are much more likely to be at territorial peace, of course, since they have no contiguous neighbors threatening them.

state already possess the capability to extend its forces, or somehow be able to build those forces while at territorial peace, then the leader has resources to seriously engage other states abroad. Again, however, these cases will likely prove the exception rather than the rule. Militaries that are strengthened without the political context of threats to the state are also likely to be weaker politically than similarly sized militaries in other states. The military owes its strength to other domestic groups and was not created to assuage fearful citizens.[8]

Nevertheless, should the state possess the resources to challenge other states abroad, the decision of whether to intervene now becomes a matter of choice for the leader. Again, territorial issues with neighbors leave little room for considerations of costs, benefits, and probabilities of victory or defeat. The salience of the issue and the domestic environment force reciprocation. For foreign interventions, however, the leader now may weigh the state's ability to prosecute an intervention or conflict to the benefit of the leader and the state. Freed from conflicts with neighbors, the choice of conflicts that will yield victories becomes much easier; therefore, there should be a correlation between states at territorial peace and victories in their conflicts abroad.

3.5.3 Implications for regime-based models of conflict

Explicit in the territorial peace argument is the contention that states must resolve their territorial issues in order to decentralize political and economic power. This often leads to democracy. Of course, by settling these issues, states at territorial peace are also likely to have resolved the most dangerous issue on their agendas. States at territorial peace should therefore experience fewer, less-intense conflicts, especially over territorial issues with their neighbors. Because border legitimacy is prior to and explains both peace and democracy, what we know as the democratic peace can better be explained as a subset of the territorial peace. The democratic peace is therefore spurious to stable borders.

Ample evidence also suggests that democracies, when they do involve themselves in conflict, tend to fight shorter wars, which they are likely to win. The explanation for this has been based on regime type. Democratic leaders fear punishment at the polls, so they tend to carefully select their targets. Once involved in conflict, the leaders use all their resources to fight hard and win since defeat in conflict is likely to bring punishment at the next election.

---

[8] A large part of this logic will also apply to states that developed without ever being threatened. Threats lead to militarization and centralization of the state, but, without those threats, the military will likely remain weak within a decentralized state.

Nevertheless, the observations that democracies fight shorter wars, which they win, need not be explained by regime type. Since territorial conflicts with neighbors have been selected out of the issues facing democratic leaders, the sample of disputes that involve democracies differs fundamentally from those that involve authoritarian leaders. Direct threats to the territorial composition of the state necessarily preoccupy a targeted state and confine its conflicts locally. Once these threats are resolved, however, the decisions for dispute onset or dispute escalation become matters of choice.

The conflicts a state may select itself into typically do not involve border issues. Instead, disputes for states at territorial peace involve less salient issues of imperialist claims and matters of policy and regime preferences around the international system, and when the issues are of minor importance to elites and publics, the need to handle disputes with power politics is reduced. Accordingly, mediation and arbitration for states that enjoy a stable border peace are more likely (Miller and Gibler 2011). Also implied is that any state at territorial peace is advantaged when choosing the disputes they wish to escalate. After all, few leaders, democratic or non-democratic, wish to lose in war.

Finally, theories based on regime type provide conflict expectations divorced from geography. A democracy will have incentives not to challenge another democracy, either across the globe or next door. Thus, all democratic dyads would be expected not to experience conflict. Conversely, states at territorial peace are geographically bound. A state at territorial peace with its neighbors has not necessarily established peaceful relations with other states in the system. Therefore, a state at territorial peace may be just as likely to target another state at peace with its neighbors in another region of the world, provided of course that the initiator has the resources to challenge abroad and that challenge serves some purpose for the leader or the state.

3.6 Conclusions

This chapter presents an explanation for why international territorial issues are highly salient to individuals in targeted states. Different from other types of issues, territorial threats concern citizens and foment insecurity over their lives and livelihoods. Threatened individuals are more likely to support policies that promote security, and this makes the state more likely to aggressively defend against rivals with a strengthened military. Since the threat is territorial, stronger militaries most often take the form of large, standing armies. Group political bargaining is also affected within the state. Opposition parties are more likely to support the leader during times of crisis, and this allows the executive to consolidate power in a centralized government. Faced with a strong army, capable of repression, few groups can withstand these centralizing forces.

Since territorial threats help determine international conflict and state centralization, there will likely be an association between conflict and non-democracy in territorially unstable regions. Removing territorial threats also removes serious impediments to decentralization and democratization, and, therefore, there should be a similar relationship between democracies and peace. With territorial threats removed, peace and democracy follow. This also explains why territorial peace states, including democracies, are more likely to negotiate or win their militarized disputes. Negotiation is easier when conflicts are less salient to the population; leaders are also better able to choose their conflicts when the homeland is secure. Combined, these links between democracy and peace, negotiation, and victory, are commonly referred to as the democratic peace, but, as I demonstrate in the rest of this book, these regularities are also part of a broader, territorial peace.

PART II

State development

4

Territorial threats and political behavior

4.1 Introduction

The first part of the territorial peace argument concerns the salience of territorial issues for the individual. It is probably strange to consider centralization in the context of political behavior – can individuals "centralize" an opinion? But in many respects, that is exactly what happens. As I argued in the last chapter, territory is important for the individual, and threats to land trigger unifying, often nationalistic, responses among targeted groups. The effects of this shift in opinion have several attendant consequences. In this chapter, I explore one such consequence in detail: the level of tolerance individuals have for others in their society.

Political tolerance is of course a central component of democracy. Toleration provides protection for the individual, encourages the individual's freedom, and makes political compromises possible. This is why there has traditionally been an empirical connection between an increased level of political tolerance in society and democratic governance. Nevertheless, toleration of those whom the individual distrusts is much easier when the individual's life and livelihood are not threatened. When serious threats to the state persist, individuals centralize into groups and become intolerant of those in minority groups who are unable or unwilling to unify under the protection of the state. Unified majorities cannot tolerate groups who are somehow different from the rest of the populace when the state is targeted.

This argument is a natural outgrowth of the theories of territorial conflict I discussed in Chapters 2 and 3. For example, both Vasquez (1993, 2009) and Huth (1998) contend that leaders are apt to exaggerate the danger of rivals, either to mobilize the public or to generate strong domestic audience costs, when territorial issues are threatened. Consequently, disputes over territory should then be perceived as more salient external threats to the general public than disputes over non-territorial issues. More importantly for my argument here, though, is that both theories expect their domestic constituencies to harden around a common nationalistic or ethnic theme, which is linked to the territorial issue. That common theme has demonstrably little regard for opinions or groups that cannot be assimilated within the larger group.

World Values Survey data collected from over 30 countries demonstrate the salience of territorial issues at the individual level. Individuals in states targeted by militarized disputes over territory exhibit lower levels of political tolerance toward groups they like the least. Individuals in states targeted by other issues or individuals in states not targeted by any kind of threat exhibit no decreases in basic tolerance levels. In short, external threat matters at the domestic level, but only a certain kind of threat: a threat to territory. After a brief review of the literature on political tolerance in the next section, I describe the results of several multi-level models of political tolerance.

4.2 Territorial threat and political tolerance

4.2.1 In-groups and out-groups

In the last chapter I argued that territorial threat reinforces the dynamic of in-group and out-group definition. Territorial threat creates internal cohesion. Of course, internal cohesion does not necessarily equate with harmony but rather reflects conformity enforced through an intra-group dynamic. As Simmel (1955, 87) notes, "Groups in any sort of war situations are not tolerant. They cannot afford individual deviations from the unity of the coordinating principle beyond a definitely limited degree." Coser (1956, 103) echoes this assessment by adding, "Groups engaged in continued struggle with the outside tend to be intolerant within. They are unlikely to tolerate more than limited departures from the group unity."

This intra-group mechanism of enforced conformity also naturally engenders widespread beliefs about what types of political liberties ought to be extended to unpopular political groups (Gibson 1992b). Thus, as the salience of external threats increases, political tolerance for unpopular groups should decrease. While some social psychology studies show a negative relationship between external threat and social tolerance (Feldman and Stenner 1997; Huddy *et al.* 2005), the type of tolerance that Simmel and Coser describe is more akin to political tolerance. During times of high threat, citizens are likely to prefer more security rather than more political tolerance of unpopular groups (Davis and Silver 2004; Shamir and Sagiv-Schifter 2006), suggesting that there should be lower levels of political tolerance in states facing higher levels of external threat. For territorial explanations of conflict, the highest levels of external threat – those threats most likely to structure conformity responses in the domestic populations – are clearly going to result from those international issues most associated with territory.

Although most previous political tolerance studies have been limited to examinations of micro-level sources of tolerance, comparisons across studies that employ similar survey methodology suggest a decreased likelihood of political tolerance in threatened states, whether that threat is real or perceived (see Shamir 1991; Gibson 2004, 1998; Gibson and Duch 1993; Gibson and Gouws 2003). These studies, as well as the few cross-national tolerance studies (Sullivan *et al.* 1985; Gibson, Duch and Tedin 1992; Sullivan *et al.* 1993; Peffley and Rohrschneider 2003), also observe significant variation in tolerance levels across countries that can only partially be explained by differences in individual-level characteristics.

4.2.2 Tolerance across countries

While the assertion that external threat may be a source of political intolerance is not new (see Sullivan, Piereson and Marcus 1993; Feldman and Stenner 1997), the relationship remains virtually unstudied from a cross-national perspective within the political tolerance literature. The few multi-country studies we do have, however, reveal some patterns consistent with the external threat explanation. For example, Sullivan *et al.* (1993) found that Israeli political elites and citizens tended to be less politically tolerant than those in New Zealand, Australia, and the United States. This makes sense. New Zealand and Australia are islands, suffering few (if any) direct threats to the security of their borders. Similarly, the United States, bordered by friendly countries and vast oceans, is not especially prone to territorial threats from other countries. But Israel has been bordered by numerous, openly hostile countries since its inception; indeed, almost all its neighbors and regional rivals have called for the elimination of Israel as an independent state. This environment of constant threat may make it much more difficult for the Israeli public to tolerate threatening groups, since the high level of external threat to the state reinforces both the national identity of Israelis and the tendency to be intolerant of dissident groups.

This interpretation is consistent with the first empirical link between political tolerance and external threat (broadly defined) demonstrated in the debate over Stouffer's (1955) seminal study on political tolerance. Stouffer observed extremely low levels of political tolerance within the United States during the height of the "Red Scare" era of the 1950s. This study was used by Sullivan,

Piereson and Marcus (1993) and others to highlight the ability of specific groups to engender an intolerant response. In Stouffer's study, respondents were asked whether basic democratic political rights should be extended to communists, socialists, and atheists, who were perceived as dangerous security threats at the time.[1] Sullivan, Piereson and Marcus (1993) argued that subsequent studies, which attributed the increase in American tolerance levels over time to rising education levels (Davis 1975; Nunn, Crockett and Williams 1978), failed to account for the decreasing salience of the threat posed by the groups in Stouffer's original methodology. Using an alternate measure of political tolerance in which the respondents were allowed to choose a group they found objectionable, Sullivan, Piereson and Marcus (1993) corroborated Stouffer's original depiction of a largely intolerant American polity.[2] When considered in tandem with Stouffer's original research, the Sullivan, Piereson and Marcus (1993) study demonstrated the effect of group choice on individual tolerance judgments and suggested that tolerance levels may vary systematically with group choice (see also Gibson 1992a; Mondak and Sanders 2003).

These studies have important implications for the argument that salient external threats decrease overall tolerance levels. If political tolerance levels vary systematically with group choice, as suggested by much of the political tolerance literature (Gibson 1992a; Sullivan, Piereson and Marcus 1993; Mondak and Sanders 2003), then there must be some factor that makes some groups more threatening than others. I believe that the missing factor is the level of association between the group and external threats to the state. At the time of Stouffer's study, "communists" were widely viewed by many Americans to be a serious threat to US security, stemming largely from their connection to the external threat posed by the Soviet Union. This threat was so salient that respondents often believed communists had the ability to undermine state institutions, which suggests that communists during another time period would not seem nearly as threatening.

---

[1] Subsequent studies further reveal the importance of group choice in explaining differences in tolerance judgments (Gibson 1992a; Mondak and Sanders 2003).

[2] Political tolerance is most often measured by asking respondents whether democratic rights should be extended to a particularly unpopular group. The General Social Survey (GSS) studies relying on Stouffer's battery arbitrarily choose the group used as the response stimulus. For Stouffer, respondent choices were confined to "communists," suggesting his research, and others relying on his measure, could best be interpreted as assessments of individual tolerance for left-wing groups rather than political tolerance generally (Mondak and Sanders 2003). Sullivan, Piereson and Marcus (1993) replace the Stouffer method with a "content-controlled" measure in which respondents were asked to select their least-liked group from a list of six choices. Political tolerance is then assessed based on the willingness of the respondents to grant basic rights and freedoms to their chosen least-liked group.

4.2.3 Expectations

As this review of the comparative political tolerance literature suggests, no single study has clearly and consistently demonstrated the dampening effects of salient external threats on political tolerance across a large number of countries. The absence of this empirical evidence is probably due to both a previous lack of cross-national survey data to examine this relationship and a continued focus on all types of external threats rather than the isolation of specific, more salient threats such as militarized disputes over territory. As Davis and Silver (2004) and Gibson (2006) note, threats severe enough to menace the entire domestic system will create conditions that make the promotion of mass intolerance likely. Most international threats do not carry such weight. Rather, direct threats to the territorial integrity of the state are powerful forces in motivating conformity of political opinion at home, an argument entirely consistent with both Vasquez's hard-liner argument (1993, 2009) and Huth's (1998) domestic constituency explanation for the link between territorial issues and dyadic conflict.

To test this territorial threat explanation of cross-country variation in political tolerance, I formulate several hypotheses that are consistent with expectations derived from the territorial conflict and political tolerance literatures. First, the baseline hypothesis is that external threat will lead to domestic intolerance. Specifically,

$H_{4.1}$: *Individuals in states involved in militarized international conflict are less likely to be politically tolerant than individuals in states at peace.*

Of course, this first hypothesis is not a direct test of the proposition that territory matters more than other issues. To accomplish this, I focus on territorial issues in the second hypothesis:

$H_{4.2}$: *Individuals in states involved in militarized international conflict over territorial issues are less likely to be politically tolerant than individuals in other states.*

In the aggregate, political tolerance levels should be lower in those states involved in more disputes over territory. However, both the tolerance literature exploring threat perception and the early social psychology literatures suggest that challengers and defenders in these disputes should also play a significant role in conditioning aggregate tolerance levels. Davis and Silver (2004) state that sociotropic threat perception is the most important factor in an individual's calculus to tolerate groups they oppose, and threat perception is tied tightly to whether those groups threaten the larger group or system (see also Gibson and Gouws 2003). So when outsiders initiate a threat, the group response to enforce conformity becomes stronger (Simmel 1955; Coser 1956; Sherif *et al.* 1961; Tajfel 1981). These theories imply that there should be a stronger effect in aggregate tolerance levels based on whether a state is targeted by an external threat. Additionally, this effect should be strongest when the state is targeted in a territorial dispute as opposed to a non-territorial dispute.

$H_{4.3}$: *Individuals in states that are targeted by militarized international conflict involving territorial issues are less likely to be politically tolerant than individuals in other states.*

The focus on targets also provides an initial test of whether tolerance is driven by elites or the public. Both territorial threat explanations suggest that leaders can manipulate territorial issues, even if the state is not directly targeted in the dispute. Demonization of the enemy is obviously easier if the state is targeted in the dispute, and hence, higher levels of intolerance in targeted states should be expected. Nevertheless, leaders initiating territorial disputes may engage in public manipulation, and political intolerance connected to any territorial dispute involvement would suggest this. Ultimately, confirmation of these hypotheses will help move the territorial conflict literature beyond merely ignoring the domestic effects of these international processes; confirming evidence would also provide an important explanation for systematic variations in political tolerance across states.

4.3 Sample and variable descriptions

The sample used to test the hypotheses developed in the last section comes from the 1995–1997 World Values Survey (WVS). As a single, three-year wave of individual responses in dozens of separate countries, this survey represents the best source of cross-national data measuring within-state tolerance levels.

The survey uses Sullivan, Piereson and Marcus's (1993) "content-controlled" indicators of political tolerance, which first asks respondents to select their least-liked group from a list of unpopular groups and then asks respondents a series of questions regarding whether the respondent thinks the group should be allowed to publicly demonstrate, hold political office, and/or be allowed to teach in schools.[3] Because the first two items (allow the group to demonstrate

---

[3] The respondents are asked to identify the group they like the least from the following list of unpopular groups. Although the standard list includes immigrants, capitalists, communists, extreme right-wing groups, Jews, criminals, and homosexuals, some of the surveys were altered to reflect unpopular groups specific to that state. The use of these groups, rather than

and run for office) better reflect political tolerance, only these two items were used to compile an additive index of political tolerance that ranges from 0 to 2 (positive answers on both questions).[4] The countries surveyed also vary widely in income and political institutions, from the most developed democracies to the least developed authoritarian regimes, and include countries from several regions around the world.

Peffley and Rohrschneider (2003) note that one problem with the political tolerance questions in the WVS is that respondents were allowed to select criminals from the list of unpopular groups. Because in many countries criminals are legally restricted from holding public office and teaching in schools and incarcerated criminals are also, by definition, unable to publicly demonstrate, denying rights to criminals may reflect legal restrictions rather than accurate indicators of political tolerance. Peffley and Rohrschneider therefore eliminated from their sample all respondents selecting criminals as their least-liked group. But since in some countries a sizeable portion of respondents selected criminals, Peffley and Rohrschneider also eliminated from their study any country where either half or more of the respondents chose criminals as their least-liked group or the country sample dropped below 500 respondents. Unfortunately, these standards drastically reduced the number of countries in their study to 17.

The test presented here relaxes these stringent thresholds and instead eliminates countries only if 60 percent or more of the respondents chose criminals as their least-liked group or if the survey sample dropped below 400.[5] There are two reasons for this change. First, relaxing these standards only slightly increases the sampling error for individual countries.[6] Second, the relaxed standards almost double the number of countries used for analysis (from 17 to 33), thus permitting better inferences from the resulting aggregate data.[7] The advantages of the larger sample size, and the focus of the tests on macro-level explanations of tolerance, make the lower threshold more appropriate

ethnic groups particular to each country, probably biases the analyses against finding results linking territorial issues to political intolerance. Intolerance is likely to be strongest toward groups that identify with the source of the threat, but as I argue above, political intolerance also applies to other minority groups during times of threat.

[4] Use of the three-question scale does not alter the results, however.

[5] The following countries drop from the full sample after applying the lowered threshold: Moldavia, China, Ghana, Montenegro, Taiwan, Tambov, Bangladesh, and the Dominican Republic. Also eliminated are Puerto Rico and the four Spanish regions of Basque, Valencia, Galicia, and Andalusia since they are not independent states in the international system. Additionally, Colombia, South Africa, and Poland drop from the sample due to missing data at the individual level.

[6] After relaxing these standards, the sampling error increases from ±4.4 to ±4.8. The benefits gained from an increased sample size more than offset this relatively modest increase in sampling error.

[7] Analyses using the original 17 cases from Peffley and Rohrschneider (2003) do not differ in either direction or statistical significance from the results reported here.

for this study despite the potential for minimal increases in within-country sampling error.

Support for each hypothesis is assessed by jointly estimating two models – a micro model (for individual-level responses) and a macro model (for state-level aggregations of those responses) – using Hierarchical Linear and Nonlinear Model (HLM) estimation. HLM allows correction for two possible biases in estimation. First, by aggregating individual-level responses into a macro-level model, state-level estimates may suffer problems of ecological inference. Second, micro-level-only models ignore the multi-level nature of the data and may seriously underestimate the standard errors of the coefficients for macro-level variables (Byrk and Raudenbush 1996).[8] HLM corrects these biases by estimating separate variance structures on each grouping of nested data (countries in these analyses), and then includes these as estimates in the macro-level model so that standard errors are unbiased. Thus, the macro-level model that estimates variation across countries also includes unexplained variation in country-specific aggregation of individual-level responses.

4.3.1 Dependent variable

Political tolerance is identified using the "allow to demonstrate" and "allow to hold office" responses to the World Values Survey. A "tolerant" individual would allow their "least-liked" group to hold office and to demonstrate. Both of these measures tap what many consider to be fundamental civil liberties (Dahl 1991), and by choosing to restrict these rights for certain groups, the respondent is rejecting core democratic values. Individuals who answer either question affirmatively are coded as 1, while those who answer either question negatively are coded as 0. The two questions are combined into an additive index that ranges from 0 (least tolerant) to 2 (most tolerant).

To demonstrate the wide variation in levels of tolerance, aggregate responses to the "allow to demonstrate" and "allow to hold office" questions, averaged by country, are listed in Table 4.1. The percentages describe the portion of the population sampled who positively responded to both questions and, thus, represents the aggregate tolerance level for each country. These percentages range from a high of 26.6 percent for New Zealand to a low of 1.4 percent for Azerbaijan.

Initial support for my hypotheses can be found in these summary statistics, as many of the least tolerant states have experienced high external levels of

---

[8] Separate models for micro-level responses and the aggregated macro-level data confirm the robustness of the results presented here. These individual models support the findings discussed in the chapter.

Table 4.1 *Aggregate political tolerance levels in 36 countries*

Country	Tolerance	Sample	Country	Tolerance	Sample
Azerbaijan	1.39%	(934)	Lithuania	10.25%	(514)
Macedonia	4.31%	(640)	**Bosnia**	10.37%	(706)
Serbia	4.43%	(766)	**Uruguay**	10.90%	(625)
Peru	4.65%	(1110)	Belarus	10.96%	(984)
Philippines	5.20%	(726)	South Africa	12.32%	(1907)
Spain	5.68%	(1187)	Mexico	12.87%	(904)
Switzerland	6.00%	(1003)	Nigeria	13.79%	(1167)
Estonia	6.56%	(495)	Chile	13.84%	(577)
Croatia	6.90%	(853)	Russia	13.90%	(900)
Ukraine	7.03%	(1344)	Colombia	14.33%	(6025)
Georgia	7.55%	(1575)	**Argentina**	14.55%	(749)
Bulgaria	8.14%	(464)	**Brazil**	16.52%	(628)
Slovenia	8.65%	(666)	Latvia	16.80%	(626)
Venezuela	9.31%	(498)	**Finland**	19.74%	(649)
Armenia	9.57%	(1154)	**Sweden**	20.94%	(938)
Poland	9.82%	(859)	**Australia**	22.40%	(1719)
Germany	9.98%	(1835)	**USA**	26.01%	(967)
India	10.02%	(1061)	New Zealand	26.60%	(828)

Note: This index represents the percentage of respondents who provided a tolerant response to both the "allow to demonstrate" and "allow to hold office" questions. Countries in **bold** are those used in Peffley and Rohrschneider's (2003) sample.

threat. Interestingly, the distribution also reveals that a significant number of the least tolerant states are democracies, suggesting no clear relationship between either political institutions or development in explaining political tolerance. Overall, these results confirm previous findings that most citizens are unwilling to extend basic civil liberties to their least-liked group, even in established democratic states.

4.3.2 Independent variables

Macro-level variables

Individual-level tolerance studies find that perceptions of threat from unpopular groups are powerful determinants of political intolerance. In this chapter, the focus is not on perceived threat but on objective levels of external threat faced by a country involved in various types of international disputes. As the review of the tolerance literature above suggests, countries facing external threats (e.g., Israel) are prone to exhibit much lower levels of tolerance than countries like the US and New Zealand where external threats have been much lower in the post-WWII period. Real external threats may have a larger effect on tolerance levels in a society than perceived or imagined threats from least-liked groups (e.g., communists or neo-Nazis in contemporary US) that pose no real threat to, say, national security. Consistent with a focus on external threat, political tolerance studies find perceptions of sociotropic threats posed to the larger system are one of the more powerful predictors of intolerance (Gibson and Gouws 2003; Davis and Silver 2004; Gibson 2006).[9]

Militarized Interstate Disputes. The Correlates of War Militarized Interstate Disputes (MIDs) data set defines an international dispute as a situation involving the threat, show, or use of force between two states (Ghosn, Palmer and Bremer 2004).[10] I used this data to create a count variable for the total number of MIDs in the year prior to the survey for each country.[11] The one-year dispute count variable ranges from 0 to 4 disputes in the year prior to the survey within the sample.

I argue above that whether these external threats reverberate at the domestic level depends heavily on the type of issue contested and, to a lesser extent, on whether the state is targeted in the dispute. The analyses therefore disaggregate overall threat according to issue and direction.

Territorial Disputes. Disputes between states over territory seem to be the most dangerous, having the highest probability of escalating to war (Holsti 1991; Vasquez 1993, 2009; Senese and Vasquez 2008). Territorial disputes also

---

[9] Although the WVS does not include a measure of perceived threat, its omission should not seriously bias these analyses. In an overview of political tolerance studies conducted over the last 50 years, Gibson (2006) points out that perceived threat is largely uncorrelated with other individual-level predictors of political tolerance and, therefore, can effectively be treated as exogenous without biasing the estimates of other political tolerance predictors (see also Sullivan, Piereson and Marcus 1993; Peffley and Rohrschneider 2003).

[10] Disputes (or MIDs) can vary widely in intensity. At minimum, a MID involves one state threatening to use or displaying force against another state to resolve a contested issue, such as Russia putting their troops on alert following the detainment of two of their generals by Latvia in 1994. Disputes can also be aggregations of multiple militarized incidents that eventually escalate to war, such as the dispute between Ethiopia and Eritrea over territory that eventually led to war in 1998. The results of additional analyses that control for different levels of dispute intensity never altered the substantive results presented here (for more information on these analyses see Hutchison and Gibler 2007).

[11] I also tested the robustness of results using a second count variable that provides the total number of MIDs in the previous five years, lagged to the year of the survey for that specific country. In other words, for this five-year event count, if one country's survey was administered in 1996, disputes from 1991 to 1995 are included; a country with a survey administered in 1995 includes dispute data from 1990 to 1994. This alternate specification allows for lagged effects since a substantial period of time could pass between the manifestation of threat and its diffusion to the domestic level. This is important because some disputes may slowly escalate over time. Nevertheless, the results using the five-year count variables closely mirror the one-year count results, and I therefore include only the one-year results in this chapter.

represent an elevated external threat to a state because of the increased risk that territory may be lost. Using the same one-year and five-year event counts as described above, two additional count variables distinguish the type of issue – territory or other – over which the dispute was contested. The resulting counts of territorial disputes vary from 0 to 2 in the year prior to the survey within the sample of countries.

Non-territorial Disputes. This variable measures external threats not involving territory as the contested issue and is calculated in a similar fashion to the other dispute variables. In fact, summing non-territorial and territorial disputes returns the overall, non-issue-based dispute variable. Non-territorial disputes represent the null model for the tests of territory and external threat. Almost all international conflict theories predict that militarized disputes, regardless of issue type, represent a credible external threat to the state and should, in theory, decrease political tolerance. However, as I argue above, if the territorial explanation of external threat is correct, only disputes over territory should create the type of domestic changes that would drive intolerant responses. Non-territorial dispute counts vary from 0 to 4 in the year prior to the survey within the sample of countries. This variable is once again lagged to the survey year.

Targeted Disputes. The early social psychology literature on group conflict suggests that intolerance is greater in groups targeted by external threats (Simmel 1955; Coser 1956). The MID data set also provides several indicators that help identify initiators and targets. Initiators are defined as those states that attempted to change the status quo from the first day of the dispute using the originator and revisionist codes in the MID data. Targeted states seek to defend the status quo. When all states participated on the first day of the dispute, but no clear guideline suggests which state was revisionist, all dispute participants are coded as initiators. The same one-year event count lagged to the year of the survey generates count variables for both targeted territorial disputes and targeted non-territorial disputes.

Democratic Duration. Peffley and Rohrschneider (2003) use Inglehart's (1997) measure of democratic longevity and find it to be the strongest macro-level predictor of variations in tolerance across states. However, to be more consistent with the comparative politics and international relations literatures, the Polity IV index developed by Marshall and Jaggers (2002) is used to identify democracies. Using the combined democracy/autocracy score, the number of years each state was a continuous democracy prior to the year of the survey measures democratic age, with democracy defined as any state-year scoring 6 or above on the combined democracy/autocracy scale. In this sample of states, democratic duration ranges from 0 to 186 years. This indicator also represents a control for regime type within the models since any positive score indicates the presence of a democratic regime type at the time of the survey. Non-democracies have democratic duration equal to zero.

Economic Development. Several political tolerance studies observe higher levels of political tolerance in advanced, industrialized countries. The level of development in each country is measured using per capita GDP in the macro-level models, measured in 1995 dollars (Heston, Summers and Aten 2002). Within the sample, this continuous variable ranges from a per-capita low of $256.2 to a high of $43,573.9. Consistent with much of the literature, tolerance should be positively correlated with the level of state development.

Ethnic Fractionalization. It is conceivable that a state's level of fractionalization may condition group responses to external threat. Although Donald (1985) suggests that the relationship between diversity and conflict may be curvilinear – conflict is less likely in both extremely homogenous and heterogeneous states – this view is not necessarily consistent with the social psychology literature on group dynamics. Instead, most expect internal fractionalization to be negatively related to tolerance. This empirical question is tested using the degree of the ethnic division in each country based on CIA Factbook assessments of the percentage share of the largest ethnic group within the state population (Fearon and Laitin 2003). Within the sample, the ethnic fractionalization variable ranges from 0.047 to 0.879. Lower values indicate higher degrees of ethnic fractionalization.

Micro-level variables

The hypotheses focus exclusively on explaining cross-country variation at the macro level, and therefore, micro-level indicators of tolerance in the multi-level models function as controls only. These variables include standard micro-level predictors of tolerance, including indices for democratic ideals, free speech priority, conformity, political interest, democratic activism, as well as measures of education, age, gender, and political ideology. These measures tap into an individual's political orientation (democratic ideals, free speech priority, and political ideology), personality attributes (conformity), political behavior (political interest and democratic activism), and socioeconomic characteristics (education, age, and gender).[12]

4.4 Predicting political tolerance

Table 4.2 presents the results of several multi-level political tolerance models. Model 1 includes common individual-level predictors of political tolerance.

---

[12] For a full description of these variables, see Peffley and Rohrschneider (2003) or Hutchison and Gibler (2007).

Table 4.2 *Multi-level models of political tolerance*

Individual-level	(1)	(2)	(3)	(4)
Democratic activism	0.15***	0.15***	0.15***	0.15***
	(0.02)	(0.02)	(0.02)	(0.02)
Political interest	0.07*	0.07*	0.07*	0.07*
	(0.03)	(0.03)	(0.03)	(0.03)
Conformity	−0.22***	−0.22***	−0.22***	−0.22***
	(0.04)	(0.04)	(0.04)	(0.04)
Democratic ideals	0.11***	0.11***	0.11***	0.11***
	(0.03)	(0.03)	(0.03)	(0.03)
Free speech priority	0.26***	0.26***	0.26***	0.26***
	(0.04)	(0.04)	(0.04)	(0.04)
Gender (0 = male)	−0.29***	−0.29***	−0.29***	−0.29***
	(0.06)	(0.06)	(0.06)	(0.06)
Age	−0.01***	−0.01***	−0.01***	−0.01***
	(0.00)	(0.00)	(0.00)	(0.00)
Education	0.11***	0.11***	0.11***	0.11***
	(0.02)	(0.02)	(0.02)	(0.02)
Ideology (high = left)	0.01	0.01	0.01	0.01
	(0.02)	(0.02)	(0.02)	(0.02)
Any MID		−0.003		
		(0.18)		
Territorial MID			−0.53***	
			(0.09)	
Non-territorial MID			0.11	
			(0.10)	
Target of territorial MID				−0.60*
				(0.26)
Target of non-territorial MID				−0.04
				(0.44)
Territorial MID, not target				0.05
				(0.73)
Non-territorial MID, not target				0.14
				(0.25)
Democratic duration		0.005	0.004	0.004
		(0.005)	(0.005)	(0.004)
Log GDP		0.14	0.13	0.12
		(0.18)	(0.14)	(0.13)
Ethnic fractionalization		0.20	0.34	0.39
		(0.99)	(0.88)	(0.74)
Random effect				
Variance component	0.67	0.50	0.43	0.42
χ^2	1635.2***	944.1***	848.9***	814.9***

Source: World Values Survey 1995–1997. Entries are full maximum-likelihood coefficients with robust standard errors estimated using HLM 6.02. Total number of respondents is 17,977. *$p < 0.05$, **$p < 0.01$, ***$p < 0.001$.

After controlling for the multi-level nature of the data structure, and despite the inclusion of states in the sample not extensively studied in the extant literature, all of the individual-level parameter estimates are consistent with previous findings on political tolerance. Indeed, conventional individual-level predictors such as democratic ideals, free speech priority, democratic activism and education are all strongly and positively associated with political tolerance, while conformity and age both tend to decrease tolerant responses. Most importantly for the overall argument, the χ^2 statistic of this model suggests that there is significant unexplained cross-country variation across macro-level units in the model.[13] This variation is modeled in the remaining estimations.

In Models 2, 3, and 4, macro-level components are added to the baseline model in order to estimate the effects of external threat on political tolerance. The variables of interest in these models are the four macro-level measures of external threat. First, Model 2, which includes the generalized threat variable, militarized dispute, finds no relationship with political tolerance and casts doubt on the argument that unspecified external threats will affect domestic tolerance levels.

When Models 3 and 4 include specifications for the type of external threat, however, a clear pattern begins to emerge. For example, in Model 3, the external threat variable is differentiated by issue type. This model finds a strong, negative relationship between disputes over territory and political tolerance ($\beta = -0.53$, $p < 0.05$) and no significant relationship with non-territorial disputes.[14] As hypothesized, territorial and non-territorial disputes have different substantive effects on tolerance levels. This finding is consistent with the claim that territorial disputes are more salient than non-territorial disputes and lends support to the contention that territorial disputes increase the likelihood that elites employ strategies designed to mobilize their respective publics. That salient external threats decrease political tolerance is also consistent with Simmel's (1955) and Coser's (1956) expectation of increased conformity in the face of hostility.

I should emphasize that the tolerance measure only asks respondents to exercise judgments towards a generalized list of unpopular groups in most of the

[13] The χ^2 statistic indicates the amount of unexplained cross-national variation in the model after accounting for the effects of the independent variables. Thus, a smaller χ^2 statistic indicates a reduction in the amount of unexplained cross-national variation which also suggests an improvement in the model's goodness of fit.

[14] The differential effects of territorial and non-territorial disputes on political tolerance levels may explain why the generalized threat variable is not significant in Model 2. Because the generalized threat variable does not distinguish by issue type, it is capturing both a strong negative effect from territorial disputes and the null effect correlated with the non-territorial disputes.

countries in the sample. Thus, there is not a direct measure of the tolerance for groups that are the source of the external threat to each country. Of course, the absence of this direct measure should bias the results *against* finding a correlation between external threat and political tolerance. That a connection between territorial threat and least-liked groups is still observed should underscore the strength of the overall relationship.[15]

One of the key statistics of interest in HLM estimation is the variance component for each model, which indicates the amount of variance left unexplained by the predictors included in the model. Using this statistic, comparisons across models can determine whether changes in the specification of the macro-level variables improve the overall goodness of fit. This technique is particularly helpful for testing the hypotheses regarding the inclusion of the macro-level variables, especially those measuring external threat, and whether macro-level specification is necessary to adequately explain individual responses to questions of tolerance. For example, further specification of the external threat variable not only confirms the relationship between threat and tolerance but also yields a notable increase in the explanatory power of the tolerance model. In comparing Models 2 and 3, there is a significant reduction in the variance component, indicating that further specification of the external threat variable provides a more complete understanding of the relationship between threat and political tolerance. The variance component also provides additional supportive evidence that disputes over territory are qualitatively different than non-territorial disputes in their effects at the domestic level. Domestic publics are clearly less likely to tolerate nonconformist opinion during territorial conflict.

In Model 4, the specification of the external threat variables changes to compare the difference between targets and non-targets of militarized disputes. Critical to the analysis, particularly with regard to hypothesis 4.3, is the number of times each state was targeted by either territorial or non-territorial disputes. As expected, territorial issues once again decrease political tolerance while non-territorial disputes have no effect. However, most importantly, territorial issues

[15] One might think that these results are consistent with the possibility that states which persecute small, ethnic minorities are likely to be the targets of foreign states controlled by that same ethnic group. Ethnic ties thus draw states into conflict over a focused intolerance of certain minority groups. This argument, however, neglects a major weakness of the World Values Survey (WVS) – the panel of minority groups does not include responses consistent with this explanation of international conflict. Put another way, the international system includes no states dominated by homosexuals, gypsies, or other WVS least-liked groups, that are capable of targeting the politically intolerant states. Thus, what serves as an important bias against finding statistically significant results for territorial conflict in the model estimation actually helps address concerns over endogeneity. Nevertheless, I also used the dispute summaries available from the Correlates of War Project (MID 3.0) to conduct a qualitative examination of the MIDs in the sample. Not one of the disputes in my sample constituted a conflict over minority group protection.

only decrease political tolerance if the state is the target. In those cases in which the states are non-targets of territorial disputes, the effect on political tolerance is negligible. Furthermore, territorial disputes now have a stronger substantive impact on aggregate tolerance levels if the state is targeted in the dispute.[16] These results suggest that while territorial disputes are more salient than other issue types, the effect is most pronounced for targeted states, as this variable appears to drive the overall statistical relationship.[17] The results clearly reinforce the contention that domestic publics react more strongly to threats over territory. Compared to Models 1–3, Model 4 represents an improvement in the unexplained variance (0.42). Therefore, of the models estimated, Model 4 seems to represent the best explanation of political tolerance levels for this sample of countries.[18]

While the relationship between external threat and political tolerance is clear in Models 2–4, another interesting finding is that other macro-level variables have almost no effect on political tolerance once external threat is specified. Indeed, the parameter estimates for the other macro-level variables reveal some surprising findings in light of previous examinations of political tolerance. For example, democratic duration is not statistically significant in any models controlling for both external threat and individual-level characteristics. This suggests that the effects of democracy are really derivative of the external threat environment. Democratic governments most often appear in peaceful environments, and peace makes tolerance easier.

There is also no statistically significant relationship between economic development and political tolerance. This challenges some of the propositions found in the modernization and democratization literature linking modernity to democratic values (Verba and Almond 1963; Inglehart 1997) but also supports

---

[16] Separate analyses assessed whether the intensity of conflict affected these results. First, a control for disputes during "strategic rivalry" years demonstrated no statistically significant effects for the added variable and no substantive changes in the variables of interest reported above. A second variable – the use of force during a dispute – actually strengthened the magnitude of the findings reported above. Only territorial disputes that used force predict changes in political tolerance.

[17] Separate analyses using only democracies and non-democracies were estimated to ensure that these results are not simply the product of authoritarian governments' higher propensity to engage in territorial disputes. The results of these models demonstrated the same substantive effects in both the democratic and non-democratic samples.

[18] Many of the states in the sample were recently communist and former members of the Soviet Union. Since these states are relatively new additions to the international state system, they are also quite prone to being targeted by territorial disputes from their neighbors. Therefore, as an additional robustness check, additional models with a dummy variable that controls for former Soviet states were estimated, and indeed, this dummy variable was statistically significant in most models and predicted general political intolerance in the state. However, the inclusion of the dummy variable does not alter any of the findings (in direction or statistical significance) for the other variables of interest.

tolerance studies that find advanced states to be relatively intolerant (Duch and Gibson 1992; Peffley and Rohrschneider 2003).

The macro-level results have important ramifications for international conflict studies. Although the previous literature on territory and conflict provides strong theoretical and anecdotal support for the idea that territory is domestically salient (Vasquez 1993, 2009; Vasquez and Gibler 2001; Senese and Vasquez 2008), the supporting empirical evidence is limited to examining patterns of conflict and inferring issue salience. These results confirm those inferences: as territorial threat levels increase, the state becomes increasingly intolerant of nonconformist domestic groups. External threat theories are also confirmed, but only for issues of territory.

Finally, these findings suggest that future cross-national studies of political tolerance levels must estimate the threat environment prior to the survey to avoid omitted variable bias in either individual- or macro-level explanations. This is most evident when one considers the insignificant results for ethnic fractionalization, democratic duration, and economic development. None of these variables is statistically significant in any multi-level model that controls for both external threats to the state and the individual-level characteristics of the respondents. Thus, future institutional explanations of political tolerance should consider the context in which democratic institutions are formed in addition to naive measures of institutional age; salient external threats may overpower traditional institutional safeguards of liberalism.

In sum, the results fully support the propositions regarding the importance of territorial issues. States experiencing territorial issues, especially those states targeted by such issues, are much more likely to have publics that are less tolerant of nonconformist ideas. The macro-level models support the contention that a strong relationship exists between threat and political tolerance found previously in single-country studies (Gibson and Duch 1993; Gibson and Gouws 2003; Sullivan, Piereson and Marcus 1993; Davis and Silver 2004), but this effect is variegated. Only territorial issues seem to be salient domestically. Further, these results hold even after controlling for common individual-level predictors of tolerance as well as several macro-level predictors of cross-country variation.

4.5 Some caveats, with a note on other political behaviors

This chapter provides strong evidence that is consistent with my explanation of territorial salience for the individual. Nevertheless, problems of data availability for testing this type of tolerance argument prevent full confirmation of the territorial salience argument. First, the theory I outlined in the last chapter is a dynamic theory – territorial threats *change* the level of tolerance in the individual – while the tests in this chapter use static, cross-sectional data. This type of research design was controlled by the availability of political tolerance data for as many countries as possible. The World Values Survey represents the most complete survey data available, but it does not provide an opportunity to identify the tolerance levels for the same individuals before and after conflict. Thus, caution should be used in interpreting my results as fully confirming the dynamic aspects of the territorial threat explanation.

The second data-related problem is also unavoidable. Recall that this study expands the number of countries covered by other studies to include 33 states over a three-year period. This is of course a small fraction of the country-years I will test in the remainder of this book, with tests that usually employ a temporal range of 1816 to 2001. Again, however, data are simply not available for a longer time period, and the World Values Survey represents the best available coverage. This limited temporal coverage also implies caution when interpreting the significance of my findings.

One method of overcoming these data-availability issues is to test the logic of the argument using other indicators of individual salience (or political centralization), and this is what I and others have recently done. For example, the territorial salience argument may also apply directly to individual identity choice. In a separate work I wrote with Marc Hutchison and Steve Miller, we found that territorial threats affect whether individuals, when asked, will self-identify with their nation or their group (Gibler, Hutchison and Miller in press). Our theory builds upon the ethnicity-based territorial conflict literature that argues that leaders may sometimes have strong incentives to cultivate cross-border ethnic tensions, especially when the ethnicity represents an important political group within their own country. However, consistent with the in-group/out-group dynamic tested in this chapter, we find that individuals in states targeted by territorial threats are more likely to unify and self-identify with the nation or state.

We tested the identity argument with what is essentially the first cross-national, multi-level analysis of individual self-identification responses to international conflict. Using Afrobarometer survey data from over 31,000 respondents in 16 separate sub-Saharan countries, we measured the likelihood an individual will identify themselves as a member of a particular group rather than their nation. As expected, international conflict led individuals in targeted countries to identify themselves as citizens of their country, while individuals in countries initiating territorial disputes are more likely to self-identify as members of a particular ethnicity or group.[19] We also found this to be the case when examining identity questions from the World Values Survey, which includes 27 countries from all regions of the globe (an additional 50,000 respondents in all). The estimates across data sets were, in fact, remarkably similar. Our results were also robust when we considered regional and temporal changes in the one country (Nigeria) for which we had multiple surveys and changes in the conflict environment. Our identity model was able to predict the timing, location, and content of changes in individual self-identification choices in Nigeria across surveys. Together, these findings suggest individual identity responses are indeed tied to the location of conflict, the content of the contested issue, and the individual's relationship with the *ex ante* status quo.

These nationalist responses among the majority of targeted populations are consistent with the expectations of public opinion centralization that are described above. The findings again confirm the salience of territory at the individual level and demonstrate that salient external threats may lead to important changes in individual political behavior. We also provide some of the first evidence that individual identities respond to contexts provided by international conflict (Goertz 1994).

Marc Hutchison has also found some interesting individual-level behaviors that are consistent with the territorial salience argument. First, Hutchison (2011a) finds that, while there is a "rally around the flag" effect in public opinion following threats to the state, territorial threats actually decrease the level of trust citizens have for their government. After all, these citizens are not being well protected by their regime. These findings provide at least a partial explanation for why public opinion rallies tend not to last very long. In separate work using Afrobarometer survey data, Hutchison (2011b) notes that territorial threats to the state decrease protests against the state, which is consistent with the argument of conformity I describe above. This does not mean that citizens are unmotivated to participate in politics, however. As Hutchison demonstrates, unconventional participation increases substantially when the state is threatened with territorial issues. Together, these studies demonstrate the strong salience of territorial issues among the public while also describing the search for conformity among populations under territorial threat.

Overall, the territorial salience argument is consistent with many of the explanations motivating "rally around the flag" phenomena. Salient external threats trigger a unifying dynamic at the domestic level, whether that effect is enforced conformity, support for government institutions, or both. Unfortunately, this

---

[19] The effect of civil conflict was inconsistent across models; civil conflict only mattered for individual identity formation when international conflict was fully specified (target/initiator and territorial/non-territorial) in the multi-level model.

literature has been plagued by inconsistent findings thus far, so it would seem that a focus on issue salience may be an important next step for understanding individual behavior. For example, as I show in Chapter 6, the salience of territorial issues is important for conditioning the responses among the political opposition, and this, in turn, affects institutional centralization as well.

4.6 Conclusions

Differences in threat environments shape political tolerance levels across states as citizens are forced to choose between security and egalitarian values and exhibit tendencies to enforce conformity. Although conventional wisdom suggests that any external threat should negatively affect political tolerance levels, this chapter demonstrates that this effect is dependent on the type of issue threatening the state. External threats involving territorial issues have a strong, negative effect on individual tolerance levels in these analyses, especially when the state is targeted by the threat, and these findings are robust against numerous changes to both sample and model specification. Threats based on other issue types have no statistically significant effect on tolerance.

By linking exogenous threat to endogenous domestic processes, these findings fill an important gap in the international conflict literature. The strong empirical evidence showing that territorial issues are generally more salient at the domestic level confirms what was previously an untested assumption made by the territorial conflict literature – that territorial issues are qualitatively different from other types of issues. In providing *ex ante* evidence of the negative domestic-level consequences of territorial issues, these results not only further validate claims made by the territorial conflict theories but also present a framework for future research exploring similar diffusion of international events to other domestic-level processes.

Also noteworthy is the emergence of external threat environment as a key macro-level determinant of aggregate political tolerance levels. Recall that none of the multi-level models demonstrate a significant relationship between any of the other macro-level variables and political tolerance, once controls for the state's external threat environment are included in the estimation. These results are particularly robust to both changes in sample and model specification. Put simply, threat matters more than any other macro-level factor in accounting for the differences in tolerance levels across countries.

5

Territorial threats, standing armies, and state repression

5.1 Introduction

The last chapter confirmed that territorial threats generate strong reactions in the citizens of targeted states: public opinion becomes more unified, more nationalistic, and more distrustful and intolerant. The next step of the argument, then, is to examine the domestic policies that follow these attitudinal shifts. Here, I argue that threats to the state place strong incentives on leaders and citizens alike to increase their military preparedness. For states targeted by territorial threats, this means substantial increases in army personnel to hold and acquire land. In this way, over time, continuous territorial threats can lead to an army that is well prepared to defend its population.

The creation of a large, standing army in the wake of these territorial conflicts will also eventually impose a formidable political force on domestic politics. After threats subside, excess military personnel can be used to provide domestic support for the elites in power. Alone, or in tandem with other domestic groups, a large military can effectively put down the segments of the population that pose challenges to status quo policies. Even the threat of forced repression will likely alter the nature of domestic opposition challenges since few would be willing to provoke an army-led crackdown.

This process creates conflicting incentives for the individual in targeted states. Short-term survival is balanced against a strengthened state that will pose a serious long-term challenge to individual welfare. Few values, however, can withstand immediate threats to an individual's survival, and this is why territorial conflict will be associated with citizens who are less likely to be free, even though the mechanism for repression will often be built with the consent of the populace.

5.2 The quest for preparedness

I outlined the rationale for why large, standing armies are created when the state is targeted by territorial disputes in Chapter 3. Air forces and navies are not well equipped to secure and hold territory; armies are best suited for control of claimed territories. Further, armies take time to demobilize and few leaders are willing to risk unilateral demobilization, even after a peace accord. This makes the army a near-permanent tool for defense of the homeland and assures that states with threatened territories will maintain large, standing armies for their own protection.

In this section I extend the earlier argument by examining the incentives and constraints facing leaders trying to strengthen their militaries. Every leader benefits to some extent from a strengthened state. Most leaders would also prefer to respond to threats abroad with some form of military preparedness. However, militaristic policies are often costly for the leader, both fiscally and politically, and only territorial threats can consistently ease the constraints placed on the leader by their publics. Fearful citizens are more willing to sacrifice when their land is threatened, and this creates an environment in which the leader may strengthen the military without fear of political retribution. The opportunity costs of policies of guns over butter become less important in the short-term context of survival.

5.2.1 Leader incentives

As Wallace (1979) described, the benefits of military preparedness have been extolled for thousands of years. The fourth-century Roman general Vegetius suggested: "Who would desire peace should prepare for war."[1] Vasquez (2009, Chapter 3) develops this point even further, arguing that foreign policy practices associated with realpolitik behavior have a luminous history in political thought and have been advocated by such political thinkers as Thucydides, Machiavelli, Hobbes, Clausewitz, and Morgenthau. Indeed, the ubiquity of this advice led Vasquez to argue that leaders themselves are often socialized into an environment that favors military responses over cooperation in international crises.

While Vasquez (2009, chapter 3) concentrates mostly on the disastrous, unintended consequences of these realpolitik practices, there is significant empirical support for the proposition that leaders have domestic political incentives to choose aggressive responses to foreign threats. Colaresi (2004), for example, examines the 1950 to 1990 time period and finds that leaders in rivalries were

---

[1] The full Latin quote is: "[Qui] desiderat pacem, praeparet bellum – nemo provocare, nemo audet offendere quem intellegit superiorem esse pugnaturum."

much more likely to be turned out of office if they offered unreciprocated cooperation to their rival. This finding held true even after controlling for the number of citizens involved in the leader selection process. In other words, both democratic and authoritarian leaders may suffer when offering appeasement-type policies to their rival. The Chamberlains of the world will quickly be replaced by Churchills.

The failure to respond to threats from abroad risks leader tenure by capture, but many theories suggest that ineffective responses also pose serious risks for leaders. As I describe in Chapter 9, several democratic peace arguments rely on the mechanism of electoral accountability to suggest that democratic leaders will select themselves out of difficult conflicts because international losses in these cases would lead to punishment at the polls (Reiter and Stam 2002). The punishments of ineffectual authoritarian leaders may be even more severe as poor performance in a crisis can lead to death and imprisonment (Desch 2002; Weeks 2008). In either type of system there may indeed be stiff penalties for poor performance in an international crisis, and, when this occurs in an environment that has historically suggested realpolitik practices, the risk-neutral leader is more apt to follow policies that are consistent with past responses. Strengthening the state's military makes even more sense in this context. Unreciprocated cooperation thwarts convention at a time when leaders are closely watched by their publics. Add to this environment that the rival leader is constrained by these same pressures, and cooperation over salient threats to the state becomes quite difficult.

One point requires further emphasis. Implicit in each of these arguments is the salience of the crisis to the public at large. For Colaresi's (2004) model, the sample included only rival states, which suggests that all issues would be of higher salience to the publics involved. Dovish leaders risked turnover because of the failure to address serious threats. Similarly, the accountability models, democratic and authoritarian, both rely on wars to affirm the issue is indeed salient to the public at large (Gibler 2011). Nevertheless, not all issues are salient for the average individual, and, despite realist precepts suggesting otherwise, not all conflicts will allow the leader to engage in realpolitik practices. Strengthening the military costs money and political capital, and, absent wars or rivalries, only territorial disputes will consistently provide leaders relief from the constraints placed on them by the public at large.

5.2.2 The security of the individual

I argued in Chapter 3 that territorial conflict sorts individuals into in-groups and out-groups. Rival states that initiate territorial disputes provide an identity comparison for individuals within the state, and the threatened public coalesces around a majority, potentially nationalistic, group opinion. This centralization of public opinion leads to political intolerance of minority groups by most individuals within the society.

This type of group sorting will also influence the level of support for policies that aggressively respond to threats against the majority group. Remember that the sorting mechanism depends explicitly on perceptions of threat from conflict-initiating groups. Thus, confirmation of majority group cohesion – the high levels of intolerance following territorial disputes – also confirms the salience of the issue and the presence of threatened individuals among that majority group. Threats demand responses from leaders, and individuals in the majority group are likely to support strengthening the military.

There are other reasons to suspect that individuals in threatened states will favor aggressive responses to threats from abroad. Take first the recent arguments over ethnocentrism. According to Kam and Kinder (2007), there is a common tendency among humans to believe that their own group has numerous advantages over other groups. This form of broad prejudice affects an individual's feelings toward other groups, especially when inter-group differences are stark. Kam and Kinder link these beliefs to increased support in the United States for the war on terrorism. Individuals who are predisposed to ethnocentric views are more likely to support increased spending on homeland security, border control, defense, and the war in Iraq, presumably taking at least some of the spending from US foreign aid programs (Kam and Kinder 2007, 328–331).[2]

Kam and Kinder (2007, 333) argue that 9/11 activated individual tendencies toward ethnocentrism for three reasons. First, the conflict was initiated by a group that differed markedly from the majority of Americans; this resonated with those who tend to view the world in ethnocentric terms. Further, elite discourse simplified to an "us" versus "them" mentality, which was reinforced by the third reason: increased perceptions of threat from hostile groups. Combined, these factors made ethnocentric tendencies likely among individuals in the United States.

---

[2] See also Kinder and Kam (2009). Less emphasized in both studies are the findings that perceived threat led individuals to favor the same policies as ethnocentrics. Threat did not translate into leader support, but individual policy responses were more likely to be favored by those who perceived threat following 9/11. This result adds further confirmation to the social conflict theory argument for group sorting. Individuals who coalesce in majority groups because of salient threats will also favor policies that attempt to aggressively ameliorate those threats. Huddy *et al.* (2005) also confirm that salient threats lead to increased support for aggressive state policies. They argue for one important caveat, however. Perceived threats activate anxiety in the individual in some cases, and anxiety correlates with decreased support for aggressiveness in this minority of their sample. Aside from gender and lower levels of education, personal experience with the threat seems to be the most consistent indicator of which individuals will experience anxiety following salient threats. In territorial conflict, these individuals are likely to be among the population that resides in the disputed lands.

These same factors are also present in almost all territorial disputes. Irredentist conflicts are usually waged in order to separate minority groups from majorities that differ from them. The conflict itself emphasizes the differences of the initiator from the targeted country. Similarly, one of Vasquez's key premises is that territorial disputes often foster simplistic decision-making, corresponding to "us" versus "them" (Vasquez 2009, chapter 6), and, as I demonstrate in the last chapter and throughout this work, territorial disputes are more likely than other disputes to be perceived as threatening to individuals. In short, serious territorial disputes have the potential to activate ethnocentric responses among individuals in targeted states, which would naturally translate into support for militarized responses to threat.

Threats may also activate authoritarian tendencies in many individuals, making them more likely to obey authority, to conform to conventional norms of behavior, and to support aggressivity toward out-group members (Altemeyer 1996). Hetherington and Suhay (2011) find, for example, that individuals not normally predisposed toward authoritarian thinking are more likely to have authoritarian leanings when threatened. These individuals join the ranks of those already predisposed to authoritarianism. Again using the backdrop of the War on Terror in the United States, Hetherington and Suhay (2011) demonstrate that support for reductions in civil liberties increased mostly among those not scoring highly on an authoritarian index. These individuals also favored "strength over diplomacy" as responses to threats from abroad. Thus, during peacetime, authoritarian predispositions well predict support for policies that reduce civil liberties; however, during crises, the level of threat overrides these personal predispositions (see also Hetherington and Weiler 2009). This evidence depends upon survey data within one country, but there is reason to believe that territorial threats may be consistently more threatening to individuals since the average risk of mortality for targeted citizens is often much higher. Regardless, the clear implication is that threatened individuals are more likely to obey authority and support policies that aggressively defend the state.

These three sets of theories – social conflict theory, ethnocentrism, and authoritarianism – all suggest increased individual support for aggressive state policies in threatened states. In states targeted by territorial issues, this should translate into greater acceptance of policies that increase the ability of the military to deal with territorial threats. This public support eases the potential domestic fiscal and political constraints associated with strengthening the armed forces. Non-territorial issues are unlikely to activate similar levels of support unless they comprise such transcendental threats as 9/11 or communism, and, hence, leaders will face domestic constraints when responding to most non-territorial issues. Since strengthening the military following territorial disputes is often equivalent to increasing the number of military personnel protecting the state, there should be sharp increases in armed troop levels following the initiation of a territorial dispute by a state's neighbor. Moreover, these policies will generally be favored by the public, even though the strengthened army may constitute a strong, repressive force in future years.

5.3 External threat, standing armies, and repression

The role of the military in domestic repression is well documented. Davenport (1995), for example, found that military influences within the state affect both censorship and government-imposed political restrictions (see also Gurr 1986; Ziegenhagen 1986). International conflict scholars have added to the military-led repression literature by linking international crisis to the need for domestic stability. During crises, both the leadership and the majority of the public prefer safety and order and tolerate the domestic repression of dissent. This is perhaps why Poe, Tate and Keith (1999) found that international wars increased government repression scores by 44 percent over ten-year periods.[3] More recently, Davenport (2007) argues that international crises provide increased political support for the leader, which then leads to fewer restrictions on leaders willing to repress.

Nevertheless, because of the attention paid to crisis stability, much of the conflict literature ignores the effects of recurrent conflict on domestic military strength. This is unfortunate because recurrent conflicts increase the political strength of the military substantially, perhaps playing an even greater role than short, international wars. The emphasis on conflict severity also ignores the importance of conflict type. War involvements – a commonly used predictor of domestic repression – do indicate the presence of a highly salient issue, but that issue can be temporary or even remote from the core interests of the state. A short, foreign war is likely to have a lesser effect than an extended territorial rivalry on the composition and organization of the military. The duration and salience of these conflicts to the public are important. For example, non-territorial wars or wars in far-flung territories are unlikely to substantially increase the repressive capacity of the state since navies and air forces are ill-suited to employ force at home. However, the threat from an extended border rivalry necessitates the construction of a large army to conquer territory, and, domestically, these armies can be sent anywhere within the country, can occupy the territory, and can impose the elites' will upon the population. This is why

---

[3] See also Poe and Tate (1994), for demonstration of an even stronger relationship.

territorial conflicts, of any severity level, should matter more for the state's capacity to repress.

The theoretical focus on actual crises has also caused scholars to miss the point that threat may matter as much as participation in conflict when predicting repression. The literature is nearly uniform in measuring international crisis using conflict involvement, but the mere threat of an international crisis often warrants mobilization of the state and an increase in defensive forces. Many crises fester without ever breaking out into open warfare, and those crises that do break out into open warfare may not be decisive enough to provide an end to the rival's threat. A tense, militarized peace is likely to follow, which further contributes to the need for a strong military within the state.

Finally, missing from most theoretical depictions of international conflict and repression is the timing of elite-led repression at home. Except for perhaps Rasler (1986), who looked at the intentions of the governing elite during crisis and identified whether elites would prefer accommodation or repression during crisis, most analyses have considered only simple relationships between international conflict and incidences of repression. This type of approach, however, obscures the fact that the ability to repress is much different than the observed levels of repression within society. Overt repression is perhaps most likely when the elite is weakest within society. There is little need for repression when opposition forces understand well that the elite is powerful and willing to put down demonstrations and revolts.

5.3.1 Specifying the relationship

Boix (2003) presents a formal model that captures well the relationships between wealthy and poor in a society. In the model the wealthy's decision over whether to maintain an autocratic regime or establish a democracy depends on the distribution and mobility of economic assets within society. When inequality is low, the poor make few redistributive demands on the wealthy, and the costs of transitioning to a power-sharing agreement – a democratic constitution – are low. When capital mobility is high, the high taxation and extraction of an autocratic elite are more tenuous, and assets can flee to less repressive regimes. The costs of repression also figure prominently in the analysis; when the elite can easily suppress redistributive pressures from below, autocratic outcomes are most likely. Democracy becomes a stable equilibrium when no single actor – whether the wealthy in power or the potentially victorious poor – has an incentive to play an exclusionary strategy; that is, relative to the costs of accepting a democratic outcome, the costs of imposing the preferred distributive regime are prohibitively high.

Boix (2003, 26–27, 44–47) argues that elites within non-democracies are likely to repress when three conditions are met: (1) repressive costs are relatively low; (2) elite status is illiquid as asset specificity would make forceable redistribution difficult to counter; and (3) elites are threatened by redistributive revolutionary movements. Boix argues that the first condition turns on organizational asymmetries between elite and poor. The poorer classes face collective action problems when organizing against an elite-led regime, and this increases their costs of revolt. Meanwhile, elites have advantages over the poor due to their smaller numbers and greater access to technological advantages; favorable geography may also help their ability to put down the population (Fearon and Laitin 2003).

Standing land armies affect, directly or indirectly, each of Boix's conditions for repression. First, while not always technologically advanced, a land army almost always increases the resources available to elites considering repression. In addition to their ready availability, land armies raised for defense of the state lower the political costs of repression for elites. After all, it would be difficult for most regimes to raise the necessary personnel to enforce repressive practices without cause. However, elites in territorially threatened states raise these armies to protect the state, not to repress, and thus avoid the difficult process of convincing potential soldiers and families that the state must be protected from its citizens.

Second, land armies may control the mobility of elite status. The dominance of a land army domestically makes elite status possible for any group – religious, ideological, or ethnic – that is able to capture or ally with the military. Absent the alliance, elite status is surrendered, as are all the private goods of political office. This then makes it likely that elites in military-dominated societies will fight especially hard to maintain their military control whenever they are faced with redistributive pressures from the population.

Third, once a land army becomes an important political force within society, its allies are likely to use the soldiers as a means of aiding their own wealth. Or, the army acts on its own and increases the amount of monies it receives. In either case, political redistribution of this sort increases the level of inequality between elites allied with the military and the poor. This, in turn, affects the political and social composition of the state, leading to an entrenchment of elite-led regimes. The elites' interests align toward maintaining their privileged bargaining status so as to extract as much rent from the government and society as possible.

While repression will alter relations between elite and poor within society, the mere ability to repress may have an even stronger effect. Boix (2003) argues that repressive crackdowns are likely when elites are weak relative to the poor, or when the elites have the most to lose. A strong military can ensure that these events never happen. Bargaining in the shadow of a strong military ensures deference to the elites because their capacity to repress is so great. This makes authoritarianism likely.[4] Note also that even an elite that finds a supportive public may also be likely to repress in the hopes of finding greater gains. Redistribution to aid the wealthy is easier when the leadership has the power to easily repress the population.

This analysis suggests a two-part process that will lead to a repressive state. First, territorial disputes, unlike other disputes, will increase the repressive capacity of elites as the military responds to threats with increased troop numbers. Second, as the threat passes, or as elite policies over-staff the military, the larger military reduces the costs of repression for the elite since leaders no longer have to justify personnel increases. The returning boots on the ground provide an ample force for maintaining the status quo preferred by the elites in power. In hypothesis form, I expect:

$H_{5.1}$: *Territorial disputes are more likely than other types of disputes to be associated with large military personnel increases in the state.*

$H_{5.2}$: *Large increases in military personnel increase future levels of repression in the state.*

5.4 The effects of territorial threat on army size

Table 5.1 provides an analysis of my expectations for military size using data from 1816 to 2001. The dependent variable is the change in the number of total military personnel from the previous year in each state. I use the military personnel data from the Correlates of War Composite Index of National Capabilities (CINC) data set to calculate these first differences (Singer, Bremer and Stuckey 1972).[5] Changes in troop levels are measured in thousands, and I estimate the model using state fixed effects.

---

[4] Note that the presence of repression is assumed away in Boix's model. Redistributive forces condition the relations between wealthy and poor, which can ultimately result in democracy. However, that is the end game for the poor, and there remains little use for repression by the elite once democracy is established. Davenport (2007, chapter 5) notes, however, that democratic governments are not immune to repressive practices when targeted by international threats, especially those governments that rely on electoral accountability. Regardless, my theory implies that repressive practices will mostly be restricted to non-democratic governments since few democracies are likely to experience contiguous land disputes that drive the necessary increases in military personnel.

[5] Total military personnel is an imperfect indicator of land army size since navies and air forces are also included in the measure. However, army size is strongly correlated with total military personnel, and the CINC scores provide the best available data on military size over such a large temporal span.

Table 5.1 *Predicting army size with militarized dispute involvement*

Military personnel changes by state-year	β	SE
Conflict predictors		
Contiguous, territorial disputes		
First year of MID	78.51***	(14.68)
Yearly count of MID duration	5.092	(6.084)
Yearly count of MID duration (squared)	−0.571	(0.537)
Last year of MID	36.26*	(16.28)
Contiguous, non-territorial disputes		
First year of MID	44.87***	(10.73)
Yearly count of MID duration	47.98***	(8.391)
Yearly count of MID duration (squared)	−3.461***	(0.746)
Last year of MID	−44.60**	(16.18)
State-level controls		
State is a major power	207.8***	(21.31)
Total state population	0.000***	(0.000)
Δ in military expenditures from previous year	0.000***	(0.000)
Lag of military personnel	−0.199***	(0.006)
Constant	−2.553	(3.635)
Number of observations	10,348	

Sample includes all states, 1816–2001, inclusive; dependent variable is the change in number of military personnel from previous year (in thousands). The model is estimated using fixed effects for each state. $^*p < 0.05$, $^{**}p < 0.01$, $^{***}p < 0.001$.

I use four controls for predicting changes in military size – total population, major power status, the previous year's military personnel total, and changes in military expenditures from the previous year. States can only leverage so many of their public into the military, and I assume that states with larger populations will have a modest advantage if threatened with conflict. The population measure is another component of the CINC score. I include major power status to proxy the states with regional or global reach, many colonies, and other interests in far-flung territories. These states should have more military personnel to maintain their interests abroad. I use the Correlates of War System Membership Data to identify major state status. The one-year lag of military personnel provides an estimation of general military size for each state.

Finally, changes in military expenditures provide a crude indicator of the choices made by leaders to defend their state. The equipment of navies and air forces generally cost much more than army troop pay in most countries, and large increases in military expenditures may indicate the substitution of advanced weapons for personnel. Further, spending levels for the military also control for each state's level of military development. Less-developed militaries may be more likely to use conscript armies for defense, producing larger, but less capable, militaries.

The predictors of military size are all forms of threat posed by land-contiguous states. First, I include two measures that indicate whether a state was initially targeted by a Militarized Interstate Dispute (Ghosn, Palmer and Bremer 2004); these dummy variables identify separately whether the dispute was over territorial or non-territorial issues. Second, I include two separate variables for the termination of territorial and non-territorial disputes. I lag these one year from the termination of the dispute since that is when military personnel levels are most likely to decrease. Finally, I include yearly count variables for territorial and non-territorial disputes, beginning with the second year of the dispute since dispute initiation is a separate variable. As disputes endure, military personnel should increase as well to fight the lingering dispute. I also test for non-linear effects for duration by including the square terms of the count variables in the model.

As Table 5.1 demonstrates, there are indeed differences between the effects of territorial and non-territorial contiguous threats, and this is true for each measure of dispute involvement.[6] States targeted by territorial disputes have an immediate increase of 78,000 troops; this is an increase that is almost 33,000 troops greater than non-territorial dispute targetings. Further, ending a territorial dispute seems to provide no immediate dismantling of troop levels. One year after a territorial dispute ends, the state is still increasing its military by 36,000 troops, which suggests that most territorial dispute settlements are ineffective at reducing the level of threat to the state. This contrasts with the pacifying effects of ending non-territorial disputes. The end of these non-territorial disputes are correlated with a 44,000 reduction in the number of troops guarding the state.[7]

---

[6] As expected, military expenditures, total population, and major state status are all positive, statistically significant predictors of troop levels, though only the presence of major power status has any appreciable effect. Major powers are likely to have 200,000 more troops than other states, on average.

[7] Note that I am not necessarily arguing that troop level increases *cause* dispute onset in these analyses. Rather, these analyses simply demonstrate a correlation between dispute targeting and military personnel increases in the same year. The causal arrow could flow in either direction and still support my point that territorial disputes are associated with a greater number of military personnel in the state.

Table 5.2 *Substantive effects of militarized disputes on army size*

MID duration	Territorial MID	Non-territorial MID
1-year MID	+114,771 soldiers	+270 soldiers
2-year MID	+119,292 soldiers	+44,785 soldiers
3-year MID	+122,670 soldiers	+82,378 soldiers
4-year MID	+124,905 soldiers	+113,049 soldiers
5-year MID	+125,998 soldiers	+136,797 soldiers

Substantive effects are based on the model in Table 5.2; all non-reported variables were held at their mean value.

Table 5.1 also suggests that, though non-territorial disputes do not provide an initial impetus for increased military size, personnel numbers do increase over time as the dispute endures. The effect is indeed non-linear, though, so personnel gains decrease over time, perhaps as available manpower is exhausted. Interestingly, territorial disputes have just minimal effects on personnel size as conflicts persist. Only the shock of being targeted by a territorial dispute – its initiation and its termination – affects troop size. Both of these events are correlated with military personnel increases.

To provide some context for how troop levels change over time in different dispute scenarios, I calculated the substantive effects for territorial and non-territorial disputes of various durations. These are presented in Table 5.2. Holding all other variables from Table 5.1 at their mean, I provide troop-change estimates based on the territorial and non-territorial variables of dispute initiation, duration and its square, and dispute termination.

This type of analysis provides a good example of how territorial disputes provoke immediate changes in military size – 114,771 troops are added to the military for a dispute that lasts one year or less. This compares to negligible increases in troop size during years in which the state is targeted by non-territorial disputes. The duration of the dispute does matter, however. If a non-territorial dispute lasts five or more years, then the resultant troop level increases outpace those associated with territorial disputes of the same duration. This is an important point. Territorial disputes seem to have immediate salience for the state, provoking drastic increases in the number of military personnel. The salience of non-territorial disputes takes time to establish, and only those non-territorial disputes that last a long time are going to have substantively significant effects on the size of the military.

Fortunately, very few non-territorial disputes last a significant amount of time. There were only 12 states in my data set that had contiguous, non-territorial disputes that lasted longer than four years, and, in one-third of these cases, the number of military personnel decreased in the final years of the dispute, from year 5 to dispute termination. Territorial disputes tend to last longer. There were 28 cases of states having territorial disputes of five or more years, and there were military personnel increases in 21 of these cases. Most often, these personnel increases were quite substantial. The differences in the number of disputes in the sample underscore the importance of differentiating across dispute type. The likelihood that a state will increase its military during a non-territorial dispute just as it would during a territorial dispute is quite small. There simply are not that many non-territorial disputes that are of high enough salience for the state.

5.4.1 Military size as a resource for repression

The analyses of personnel increases make intuitive sense – it would be surprising if external threat did not increase the military personnel of targeted states. However, the extent of likely troop buildups and the variegated effects by issue type have never before been assessed, much less quantified. Such troop level increases can alter the domestic politics of the average country substantially, and identifying these average historical changes permits an assessment of their effects with much more detail.

For example, some analyses of stabilizing force ratios – the number of personnel needed to instill order within countries – hint at the real importance of a land army when measuring the resources available to elites in militarized societies. For example, Quinlivan (1995), the seminal work in this area, estimates that force requirements to provide basic law and order for a generally peaceful society range from 1 to 4 troops per thousand of population. The United States rests in this range with 2.3 police officers per thousand people, and this matches other advanced democracies. That ratio also matches the intervention in West Germany following World War II and was "entirely adequate to its limited objectives of enforcing public order, controlling black market transactions, and related police functions" (1995, 62). The largest stability operations, such as the British pre-peace settlement presence in Northern Ireland or the British intervention in Malaysia, in 1952, have a larger footprint of roughly 20 personnel per thousand, which correlates with more difficult operations and populations that are less compliant.

Stability operations are naturally different from the actual repression of a population, and, if the population is rebellious, then the number of troops necessary to instill a repressive order may be high. However, a few illustrative cases suggest that repressive force ratios are not too different from those observed by Quinlivan (1995). Argentina, for example, during the Dirty War of 1976–1983, had a population of just over 28 million and total armed forces of

80,000 (45,000 in the army) (CIA 2009; *World Development Indicators* 2009). This suggests a 3-troops-per-thousand force ratio to prosecute mass killing, disappearances, and other egregious acts over a prolonged period of time. Higher force ratios were present in Cambodia during the "killing field" years. In 1977, Cambodia had approximately 110,000 troops, almost all of whom were army regulars (CIA 2009; *World Development Indicators* 2009). This force was responsible for maintaining a repressive regime that killed, actively or through disease and starvation, between 1.4 and 2.2 million of the 7 million total population. This included the summary execution of 200,000 people. The regime committed these horrible crimes while also initiating a prolonged territorial war against its rival, Vietnam (Chandler 1999). Even including the troops involved in the conflict, the force ratio in Cambodia was approximately 15 troops per thousand of population.[8]

Given the analysis of territorial issues and military strength above, a state which experiences just a one-year territorial dispute with its neighbor generates more than 114,000 additional troops. That type of increase could reasonably enable a regime to repress an additional population the size of 1970s Cambodia. These troops constitute increases to existing troops that are already present in the country. This point also ignores the tendency of territorial disputes to recur over time. A territorial rivalry, with multiple disputes over contiguous land, would seriously alter the repressive forces available to the leader, in a way that is probably less politically costly for the leader than other means. Indeed, states in extended territorial disputes will have strong land armies that could comprise an incredibly strong force in the domestic politics of the state.

5.5 Predicting state repression

The analyses presented thus far have made a compelling case that territorial disputes lead to larger militaries in targeted states. In fact, the personnel increases are large enough in size to be equivalent to the armed forces used by several historically brutal regimes. Equivalence, however, does not imply actual repression. Other factors may still determine whether the armed forces are turned against the citizens of the state.

---

[8] Also note the connection between these particular cases and territorial conflict. Argentina and Chile had a long-standing rivalry over issues related to their long border, specifically land in Patagonia, the Andes, and the Beagle Channel Islands. Cambodia's eventual war opponent was Vietnam, a long-standing territorial rival resulting from border issues dating to the French colonial period. Both rivalries contributed mightily to the increased role of the military within domestic society.

While most examinations of repression confirm a link between strong militaries and higher levels of state repression, that link is most often proxied using direct war involvement or outright military control of the government. My argument suggests a more nuanced mechanism for repression though. Rather than war involvement or military control of the government, military personnel increases over time should better account for the repressive capacity of elites. Elites need armed personnel in order to repress, and prior territorial disputes are the types of conflicts most likely to lead to increases in military personnel within the state. In times of peace, or even in times of reduced threat, the military that was used to guard the state then becomes an important domestic political force.

To identify changes in elite repressive capacity, I begin with a basic model of state repression based on the work of Poe and Tate (1994).[9] Their original model controls for the level of democracy, the population of the state, the condition of the economy, whether the government is leftist, and any past British colonial history. The effects of prior conflicts are measured using dummy variables for the (lagged) presence of international or civil conflict for the state as well as whether the state is currently under military control.[10] While I keep the latter two dummy variables, I replace the international war variable with several different indicators of military personnel.

I use multiple indicators of military personnel for two reasons. First, I assume that international conflicts require troops to fight the rival, and those battlegrounds may be abroad or in isolated parts of the state. By taking these troops away from the rest of the population, elite repressive capacity within a state is reduced substantially. Of course, some states have more than enough troops to both protect against rivals and repress the citzenry at home. The key, then, is to estimate the number of troops constrained to engage in conflict separately from those available to maintain some level of repression. Second, past threats and past conflicts affect current troop levels; so, too, do historical decisions on how to deal with these previous threat environments. Some leaders may overstaff a military, others may try to guard against a rival with fewer-than-normal personnel levels, while still others may prove the average true. Again, then, the number of troops available to repress becomes a function of currently available forces, moderated by the state's ability to meet current threats from rivals.

Given the importance that current threats to the state play in constraining the number of troops available to elites, I rely heavily on estimates of military personnel that are likely needed to guard the state in various threat environments.

---

[9] See Poe, Tate and Keith (1999) and Melander (2005) for similar work.
[10] I use Melander's (2005) replication data for these analyses, which are consistent with the original Poe and Tate (1994) specifications.

For example, to estimate the relative changes in the repressive strength of the military, I first calculate the average troop increase for a given state, using the model in Table 5.1 as a best estimate of what is a likely personnel increase for the state in a given year. This estimated value represents the average force response, over time, by states facing similar threats. I then difference the actual number of military personnel increases from the estimated value, creating a residual value of troop availability. Since I substract personnel from the estimate, high residual values correspond to lower than normal levels of troop increases. With lower than normal troop levels, elites should have difficulties repressing their citizens. Conversely, negative residuals suggest excessive troop capacity, and these are likely to be associated with higher levels of repression.

These personnel changes of course occur in context, so I apply a similar procedure to analyze existing troop levels in the state. First, I use a static version of the model in Table 5.1 to estimate the existing level of military personnel in each state-year given the threat environment.[11] I then once again differentiate between actual military personnel size and the estimate of troop levels to calculate a residual of troop capacity. As with the personnel changes model, high residual values imply lower than normal troop levels and less capacity for repression, while lower residual values will correlate with greater repressive capacity.

With four predictors of domestic military personnel strength – actual military changes and the residual as well as actual troop size and its residual – I can estimate the effects of troop increases on changes in the level of state repression. To do this, I use the Poe and Tate (1994) model but estimate a slightly different specification of the dependent variable. While Poe and Tate (1994) used the actual Political Terror Score for each state and included the lagged dependent variable as an estimator, I instead estimate the *change* in the level of repression. Thus, I use the first difference of the repression score and provide an estimation using state-level fixed effects. I also vary the lag effect of my military personnel indicators, estimating three models based on lag effects that are one, two, or three years prior to the state-year examined. The results are in Table 5.3.

Only two state-level controls are able to predict changes in repression in the three models. First, military governments tend to repress more, which is consistent with almost all previous studies. Second, the lagged dependent variable – the prior year's political terror score – is also statistically significant in each model. States with higher rates of repression are more likely to repress

[11] Technically, the only change in this model from Table 5.1 is the change in the specification of the dependent variable. Yearly military personnel numbers for each state-year is the dependent variable. I drop the lagged measure of the dependent variable but estimate the model using Prais–Winsten corrections for the standard errors.

Table 5.3 *Predicting repression with army size changes*

	3-year lag of military	2-year lag of military	1-year lag of military
Military change variables			
Δ Military personnel	0.0004	0.0005	0.0011*
	(0.0005)	(0.0004)	(0.0005)
Residual (predicted Δ	0.0009*	−0.0004	0.0009*
− actual personnel Δ)	(0.0004)	(0.0004)	(0.0004)
Military personnel	−0.0000	0.0003*	−0.0000
	(0.0002)	(0.0002)	(0.0001)
Residual (predicted personnel	−0.0006	0.0011**	−0.0011**
− actual personnel)	(0.0004)	(0.0004)	(0.0004)
Control variables			
(Lag) political	0.6198***	0.6238***	0.6222***
terror score	(0.0164)	(0.0163)	(0.0163)
GDP per capita	0.0000	0.0000	0.0000*
	(0.0000)	(0.0000)	(0.0000)
Total population	−0.0000	−0.0000*	−0.0000
	(0.0000)	(0.0000)	(0.0000)
Polity score	−0.0049	−0.0030	−0.0028
	(0.0034)	(0.0034)	(0.0034)
Leftist government	0.0263	0.0199	0.0251
	(0.0543)	(0.0537)	(0.0535)
Former British colony	−0.1212	−0.1336	−0.1102
	(0.0708)	(0.0705)	(0.0706)
Civil war	0.0046	0.0093	0.0222
	(0.0568)	(0.0563)	(0.0565)
Military control	0.1162**	0.1131**	0.1132**
of government	(0.0409)	(0.0406)	(0.0407)
Constant	−0.0756	−0.1200*	−0.1085
	(0.0611)	(0.0595)	(0.0588)
Number of observations	2,429	2,447	2,459

Sample includes all states, 1816–2001, inclusive; dependent variable is the human rights record of the state using Political Terror Scores. Military personnel variables include the number of military personnel and changes in military personnel as well as differences between actual and estimated values. The model is estimated using fixed effects for each state. $^*p < 0.05$, $^{**}p < 0.01$, $^{***}p < 0.001$.

even more in the future. The lack of statistical significance for the remaining state-level variables is understandable since I am using fixed effects and the dependent variable represents yearly change.

As for the variables of interest, an interesting pattern emerges among the military personnel indicators. First, three-year-old changes in the residual value of military personnel – the difference between expected and actual military personnel changes – correlate with increased repression in the current state-year. This suggests that repression is more likely among militaries that had lower than predicted changes in personnel in the past. The actual number of personnel three years prior does not matter. However, when the lag shifts to two years prior, the actual number of personnel and the residual value both predict increased repression. Substantively, this implies that larger militaries are likely to increase repressive capacity, and the state is more likely to repress when the size of the military was below average two years ago. Personnel changes again matter most in the model with one-year lags. Both the actual personnel changes and the residual predict higher levels of repression. Actual troop levels have no statistically significant effect, but, consistent with my assumption that conflict lowers the repressive capacity of the state, the residual of military strength confirms that armies under-staffed in the previous year are less likely to repress.

The use of actual values and residuals might make it difficult to gather an intuitive sense for the implications of these results, so I also provide comparisons of the substantive effects following different types of disputes. Holding all other variables at their mean, I chart the predicted value of repression following the likely personnel changes associated with two separate one-year disputes – one in which the dispute concerns territory and one which is fought over other issues. Recall from Table 5.2 that a one-year territorial dispute usually results in an approximate troop increase of 114,000 while non-territorial disputes predict an increase of 270 troops. These troop increases constitute the likely change in the number of military personnel following conflict, and I vary their substantive effects according to three separate scenarios of state policy. For example, leaders may choose to respond as other states do after being targeted by a dispute; leaders may also under- or over-staff their military as well. Each of the three policies will have different substantive effects on state repression, and I present these in Table 5.4.

The predicted probabilities of repression suggest that, if leaders choose to staff their militaries as predicted, territorial disputes are associated with a decline in repression levels in the year following the dispute. Two years after the dispute, however, the repression rate increases by 21.4 percent, before returning to a more modest increase in year three. Non-territorial disputes have only

Table 5.4 *Substantive effects of army size changes on repression*

% increase, state repression score, year	$t+1$	$t+2$	$t+3$
Military increases 50% less than predicted			
Territorial dispute, year t	−11.6%	24.7%	3.7%
Non-territorial dispute, year t	0.0%	3.7%	0.0%
Military increases as predicted by conflict model			
Territorial dispute, year t	−6.3%	21.4%	0.1%
Non-territorial dispute, year t	0.0%	3.7%	0.1%
Military increases 50% greater than predicted			
Territorial dispute, year t	−4.3%	36.0%	11.0%
Non-territorial dispute, year t	0.0%	3.7%	0.1%

Substantive effects are based on the model in Table 5.3. Troop increases are based on dispute duration of one year or less, while all non-reported variables were held at their mean value.

limited effects in these staffing cases – the repression level remains unchanged in years one and three and changes only modestly in the second year.

Leaders who under-staff their militaries by 50 percent are much less likely to repress in the year following a territorial dispute. The troops may be too busy protecting the state. When the troops return, by year two after the dispute, the level of repression is almost 25 percent higher. Perhaps this is because leaders are putting down the unrest that stemmed from the conflict, or because the repressive capacity was formerly spread too thin. Once the capacity of the state to repress returns, the rate jumps, and modest increases remain in year three. Again, non-territorial disputes have little or no substantive effects on repression.

Repression is also likely when the military is staffed by personnel at higher-than-normal rates. There is a first year decrease again, but the level of repression increases by 36 percent in the second year following territorial disputes. The rate remains 11 percent higher in year three. The added military personnel seem to increase the repressive capacity of the elites substantially. Since few increases are associated with non-territorial disputes, however, the results again remain limited to disputes over territory.

These substantive effects confirm several expectations. Increased military personnel is associated with higher levels of repression. This is true in all contexts. The effect is lagged by at least one year, however, because those personnel must be available to fight potential and real rivals. Once the conflict has passed, the level of repression increases. Over-staffing of the military is also associated with higher levels of repression, but so is under-staffing. The causal processes are probably different – over-staffing leads to greater capacity while under-staffing leads to greater elite need for repression – but the effects are the same. Finally, territorial conflict is likely to have a more substantial effect on repression than other types of conflict. Very few non-territorial conflicts, really only those lasting five or more years, are going to provide the same size personnel increases associated with even limited-duration territorial disputes. Over time, as a state has more and more territorial disputes, elite capacity to repress can become substantial.

5.6 Conclusions

Territorial threats are unlike other types of threats in conditioning the domestic politics of the state. Unlike most other forms of conflict, territorial disputes are more likely to witness sharp increases in the number of military personnel within the state. Only through extended duration, of five or more years, can non-territorial conflicts provoke the same military personnel increases as the shortest territorial disputes.

These military personnel increases are important because they increase the repressive capacity available to elites within the state. My analyses suggest that both existing military personnel and military personnel increases affect the level of repression within the state. This is true whether leaders choose policies of over- or under-staffing the military. Interestingly, both policies lead to increased repression and possibly point to different dynamics causing leaders to repress. Under-staffing a response to foreign threats weakens the power of elites domestically; following the conflict, the elite must use the military to re-establish their repressive order. The path from over-staffing to repression is more straightforward. As with all my analyses, additional troops are consistently correlated with increased repression in future years.

These results confirm the salience of territorial issues and begin to demonstrate the changes in domestic institutional structures that follow state involvements in territorial conflict. Creating a strong, land-based army is essential for thwarting would-be conquerors. However, that same military affects domestic bargaining substantially. As I discuss in the next chapter, a willing populace and a strong military provide an environment that makes institutional centralization likely.

6

Territorial threats and domestic institutions

6.1 Introduction

A common assumption in the recent literature on conflict is that leaders want
to remain in office and will try to extend their domestic political power while
ruling (see, for example, Bueno de Mesquita *et al.* 2003). However, these same
leaders are constantly confronted with an opposition that is also trying to gain
and maintain domestic power within the political process, and strategic bargaining between these groups is greatly affected by changes in the level of threat
confronting the state. This inter-group bargaining is an essential element in the
political centralization of the state.

In this chapter I demonstrate that external threat can dramatically alter the
bargaining dynamic between leaders and oppositions. External threats, especially threats over territory, change the domestic resources available to each
group. With public opinion unified against the threat, seeking security from
the state, and intolerant of diversity from their opinion, any opposition will
likely be stymied by the broad support for the executive. Meanwhile, leaders are gaining domestic political power as they control an arming state,
which can also suppress dissent if needed. These short-term advantages for
the leader translate into a very favorable political environment, and, over time,
an opposition consistently muted by external strife creates the political conditions necessary for domestic institutional change. Without opposition, the
leader can move to institutionalize greater executive powers. Thus, states with
centralized institutional political authority will be found in environments that
suffer from extended external threats to the state that are salient to the public
at large.

This argument explains why the development of centralized political institutions – mostly among non-democracies – often occurs in regions of intense

threat and conflict while democracies tend to stabilize in peaceful international environments (Gleditsch 2002). Direct threats to the territory of the state provoke calls for the centralization of authority for the sake of security, and this reinforces the strategic goals of leaders seeking more power. Even in democracies, threats to homeland territory cause centralizing tendencies that are difficult to avert, as a public that wants protection is more likely to permit increases in executive power. In peaceful regions, however, decentralization and eventual democratization become easier as arguments for centralized power are not buttressed by calls for increased domestic security.

The key to this argument is identifying, *ex ante*, the types of threats that are likely to be perceived as salient threats to the state. To do this, I rely once again on theories of territorial conflict. As I described in Chapter 2, the domestic salience of these types of issues is not well understood, but it seems reasonable to conclude that publics are more likely to allow leaders greater political authority when the state's control of homeland territory is directly challenged. If this argument is empirically true, then political centralization also provides more evidence that territorial issues are indeed different from other types of issues.

I begin the argument in the next section by briefly describing the literatures on rally effects and diversionary theories of conflict. I then argue that evidence that supports these theories may be found more readily in the behavior of opposition parties. The third section brings the first two sections together with a comprehensive theory of institutional centralization, and the remainder of this chapter develops and tests propositions from this theory.

6.2 External conflict and the domestic opposition

Much attention has been paid to the effects of international conflict on the popularity of elected leaders. The theoretical argument is quite clear – external conflict encourages domestic cohesion and amplifies support for the executive. However, unlike the territorial issues literature, empirical studies examining rally effects and diversionary behavior have been somewhat inconclusive, and most studies demonstrate that only the severest conflicts provide just temporary electoral gains for the leader. In this section I argue that a better place to search for the domestic rally may be in the behavior of opposition party leaders. Strategically, opposition parties have strong incentives to provide initial support for their country's leader during times of crisis, especially when the crisis is likely to be salient with the public at large. These strategies should be similar in both democratic and non-democratic regimes.

6.2.1 Rally effects and leader popularity in democracies

Established first within the social-psychology literature, following such works as Simmel (1955) and Coser (1956), the theory of rally behavior among voters argues that conflict increases internal cohesion within the state. During times of salient external threats to the state, individuals seek safety and tend to value conformity and deference to the leadership rather than tolerance and minority rights. This psychological reaction also affects voting preferences as individuals express their need for safety with electoral support for those in power (Berrebi and Klor 2008).

That leaders may sometimes take advantage of the public's willingness to rally provides the basis for the diversionary theory of conflict. During tough economic or political times, leaders can provoke low-level conflicts in order to distract the public from the leader's failures. Successful involvement in foreign conflicts then creates a rally effect that salvages their electoral future, and this dynamic may be more pronounced in the American context since the president has greater political autonomy in foreign affairs.

Debate persists on the empirical connection between international conflict and domestic public opinion. For example, while some studies find support for the diversionary use of force by leaders (Ostrom and Job 1986; Gelpi 1997; Meernik 2000), especially when decisions to use force are modeled simultaneously with public approval (DeRouen 1995, 2000), recent work suggests few linkages between domestic crises and conflict initiation (Oneal and Tir 2006). In the rally effects literature, the results are also mixed (James 1987; Lian and Oneal 1993; James and Rioux 1998; Baker and Oneal 2001; Erikson, MacKuen and Stimson 2002), but some evidence supports public rallies immediately following the outbreak of war – for example, the American public following the Persian Gulf War (Zaller 1993; Mueller 1994; Parker 1995) or in response to direct threats to the national interest (e.g., Lai and Reiter's [2005] time series analysis of British public opinion).

6.2.2 Opposition strategies

One missing element in the literature on rallies and diversion is the strategic nature of domestic political systems under external threat. Indeed, what should elites out of power do when the state is targeted or the leader uses force? I argue that, during salient threats to the state, mainstream opposition parties will be less likely to challenge their leader's decisions.[1] The same rally dynamic

---

[1] I include the qualifier mainstream here because radical parties are probably more inclined to prefer leader embarrassment during international conflicts, or even regime collapse. These

that expects public cohesion within the state would also require parties to shift their position toward support of their country's leader in anticipation of similar movement in public opinion. While division during times of threat can easily be cast as providing sympathy to the enemy, there are also strategic advantages associated with decreasing the opposition's polarization from the party in power.

Opposition parties are often put in precarious political positions during times of crisis. Not knowing the long-term public reaction to each individual international crisis, opposition leaders are likely to choose a conservative position and defer to their leader (Waltz 1967, 275; Brody and Shapiro 1989; Zaller 1993). This provides the opposition with political coverage no matter the outcome of the crisis. The policies of the party in power and its unsuccessful leader are blamed for defeats, while a unified front among all parties takes credit for victories. Over time, as the likely outcome of the crisis becomes clearer, the opposition party may shift its position according to the revealed preferences of the public. Initial conflict involvements are often shrouded in secrecy, the likelihood of success in conflict is never fully known, and perhaps most importantly, party leaders never know how strongly each crisis will resonate with the public at large. Therefore, party leaders are likely to take a conservative position of supporting their leader on policies they believe their supporters will care about most and will then adjust their position as more information about the threat is revealed.

Defining how salient the public will view a crisis has always been difficult for the rally literature. Almost all studies focus on the severity of conflict, but this can never be known *ex ante*, which is problematic for an argument based on the strategic behavior of party leaders at the start of the crisis. Instead, party leaders are likely to take cues from the composition of the crisis as to whether the conflict will resonate with their supporters. If there is uncertainty on how salient the issue will be for the public, opposition party leaders are likely to remain conservative and defer to the leadership in the state.

6.2.3 Rallying behind an unelected leader

Opposition parties in non-democracies are of course often non-existent or impotent, but opposition to the leader usually exists nonetheless. General opposition can be found among the populace who rest outside the private goods network that supports the elite of the country. Lacking any rents derived from the regime,

parties gain little from the current regime, and external threat could provide long-term bargaining advantages for them.

these individuals would prefer regime collapse under almost any circumstances, save for direct conflict on or near the land where they reside. Salient threats to the state may still provoke the same in-group/out-group reactions among these publics at large,[2] but regime collapse is probably preferred if it guarantees a new distribution of goods within society.

Opposition forces in authoritarian societies usually do not openly oppose the leader, often because they still derive economic benefits from the regime in place. Indeed, non-democratic elites benefit greatly from the private goods networks enforced by the leader (see, for example, Bueno de Mesquita *et al.* 2003), and outside threats to these private goods networks are likely to be resisted at all costs. This makes issue salience correlate highly with threats to the economic interests of the elites. External threats to the state can force an imposed leader on the elites, lead to occupation of the country and the overthrow of their elite status, or cause chaos in the country after a defeat. In each case, external threats bring uncertainty over private goods provisions. Thus, faced with the alternative of a new regime, elites will tend to allow their leader even greater access to resources in order to guarantee the maintenance of the private goods network (which is not always equivalent to victory in conflict). Elites facing external threats will also fight hard and support their current leader because they are unlikely to trust any new or foreign imposed leader; every challenger suffers a lack of credibility when compared to the incumbent leader (Bueno de Mesquita *et al.* 2003, 59–60). Of course, granting additional access to the leader to ward off threat also creates a situation that greatly advantages the leader domestically, should that leader survive the threat. More powerful domestically thanks to the external threat, the surviving leader will be less willing to return to the antebellum distribution of private goods once the threat to the regime passes.

Unfortunately, the argument on elite behavior in non-democracies is difficult to test empirically. There is simply no way of systematically gauging the level of elite support across non-democracies. In most of these countries there are few public polls, and elites are not likely to publicize their support for the leader since few would want the value of their private goods revealed. Similarly, open

---

[2] For example, immediately prior to the Iranian national elections in June of 2005, President Bush gave a public speech against the hard-line policies of the conservative candidate, Mahmoud Ahmadinejad. This speech followed a bombing campaign across the country that killed ten civilians. Iranian authorities blamed the Mujahedeen el-Khalq (MEK), or People's Mujahedeen, which represents an Iraqi-based opposition group comprised mostly of remnants of Iraq's intelligence service and Baath party loyalists under Saddam Hussein. The group denied the attack, but the timing of the events – the bombing campaign and the hard-line rhetoric of President Bush – is thought to have contributed to swaying a close election between moderates and conservatives into a clear victory for Ahmadinejad.

Table 6.1 *Non-democracies, party polarization, and territorial threat*

	Party polarization score			
Territorial dispute target?	Unified	Mixed	Polarized	Total
No	2,015	15	34	2,064
Yes	80	2	0	82
Total	2,095	17	34	2,146

Sample includes all states with Polity IV 21-point scale scores of −10 to 6, 1975–2000.

opposition to the leader comes at some cost, even for elites, and is therefore not likely to be advertised.

Cross-national data on party positions in non-democracies is scarce, but some simple summaries of the data do tend to support the argument outlined above. For example, the data listed in Table 6.1 show a cross-tabulation for all non-democracies that includes the presence of a territorial dispute targeting the state in the previous year and the polarization of parties within that state for the years 1975 to 2000.[3] The data on party polarization are taken from the Database of Political Institutions, which captures the ideological distance between the chief executive and the four major parties of the legislature using a three-part scale. In countries with no competitive elections, the polarization score is zero. Polarization is also zero for all countries with legislatures in which the chief executive's party has an absolute majority. Otherwise, polarization is the maximum difference between the chief executive's party and the values of the three largest government parties and the largest opposition party. This variable includes scores for minimum distance (0), intermediate distance (1), and maximum distance (2) (Keefer and Stasavage 2003).

As the cross-tabulation demonstrates, there is little variation in party polarization for non-democracies. Including only states that score between −10 (authoritarian) and 6 (near democracy) on the Polity IV combined scale of autocracy/democracy, there are 51 cases of state-years (of 2,146 total state-years) with either intermediate or maximum party polarization, and 36 of these polarized state-years occur in states that score 5 or 6 on the Polity IV scale. Nevertheless, in none of the state-year cases was there party polarization in a non-democratic state-year experiencing a territorial dispute, and in only two

[3] Disputes are identified using the Correlates of War Militarized Interstate Dispute data set (Ghosn, Palmer and Bremer 2004). A state is considered to be the target of a territorial dispute if the challenging state is listed as revisionist and the first issue code is territorial.

cases was there intermediate polarization. Eighty-two territorial disputes targeted these non-democracies between 1975 and 2000, and all but two of these disputes were followed by state-years with no noticeable opposition.

While these data are suggestive, the relatively small numbers and the structured incentives for elites not to divulge their policy positions make it difficult to draw firm conclusions from the data. Instead, it is perhaps more instructive to examine other, measureable events that are going to be correlated with swings in opposition support in non-democracies. For example, if there are elite rallies in non-democracies, and elites in autocratic states fight hard to protect their private goods, then leaders of autocracies should benefit from increased domestic power following disputes dangerous enough to threaten the private goods networks of the elites. Thus, purges of previously untouchable opposition groups will often follow international conflicts that do not replace the autocratic leader. Similarly, and more consistent with the argument I give in the next section, the long-term effects of decreased opposition in non-democracies will likely be found in institutional changes that solidify the leader's hold on the state. Long-term institutional changes are also easier to measure than opposition party preferences.

6.3 Centralizing political power

Thus far, I have argued that mainstream, organized opposition parties are likely to support their country's leader during times of salient threat to the state. Leaders are likely to take advantage of this muted opposition, and those who are provided enough political leverage during the crisis will use the new domestic political environment to centralize and institutionalize their authority. This effectively combines the research on territorial issues and domestic responses to threat in a cohesive theory of state centralization.

A large literature argues that leaders want to remain in office and otherwise maximize their domestic power (see, for example, Bueno de Mesquita *et al.* (2003), recently, but also Mayhew's, 1974, discussion of the United States Congress). Of course, centralizing power in the leader need not only be for personal reasons since benevolent leaders may want increased political powers to more easily enact their agendas. Regardless of their intentions, however, leaders almost universally prefer more political power to less and will move to increase their political power whenever possible.

Given leader incentives for increased power, the political environment created by a muted opposition strongly favors the centralization of political power in the leader. Often the strongest check against incumbent power is the opposition, and without that voice, the leader is much less constrained. In this environment it makes sense that leaders will press their advantage and try to eliminate future checks against their power. Thus, when the voices of the opposition return to the domestic debate, their access to institutional checks against the executive will be severely constrained as the leader centralizes political power in the state.

Note again that my argument on incentives for the opposition applies to checks against executive power in both democracies and non-democracies. In each case the opposition has strong incentives to back state leadership during times of crisis, and thus, in both types of regimes, this movement of the opposition gives the executive a freer hand. Therefore, since regime type does not significantly alter opposition incentives in the above argument, the centralization effect should occur in both democracies and non-democracies.

The theory outlined above provides expectations for both behavioral and institutional domestic changes following salient threats to the state. Stated as hypotheses, these expectations are:

$H_{6.1}$: *Opposition parties are more likely to support the leadership in states threatened by challenges to homeland territories.*

$H_{6.2}$: *Leaders in states threatened by challenges to homeland territories are more likely to centralize their political power by removing institutional checks on their authority.*

Salience in both phases of this process – from opposition support of the leadership to the leader's centralization of power – is identified using direct threats to homeland territories. Unlike other types of conflict, threats to homeland territory are likely to be the only issue that will provoke public concern on a consistent basis. At least opposition parties expect that to be the case in democracies, and, in non-democracies, the threats to territory are likely to directly affect party elites. I test each of these expectations in the remainder of this chapter.

6.4 Identifying opposition party effects

To test party placement following territorial threats, I again use the party polarization variable from the Database of Political Institutions, which captures the ideological distance between the chief executive and the major parties in each legislature. Recall that this variable includes scores for minimum distance (0), intermediate distance (1), and maximum distance (2) (Keefer and Stasavage 2003). Party polarization data is available for the years 1975 to 2004, but data availability for several independent variables limits the upper end of the temporal range to 2000.

I include seven measures of external threat in each analysis. While the variables are primarily divided between territorial and non-territorial threat, I also differentiate based on the length of threat exposure to the state. Overall, my assumption is that long-term threats will have a greater effect on institutional change, while short-term threats will provoke behavioral changes, such as party polarization. I describe my assumptions regarding time in the threat variable descriptions below.

6.4.1 Territorial threat

I measure immediate territorial threat with a variable that indicates the presence of a territorial Militarized Interstate Dispute (MID) initiated by any neighboring country that targets the state in the previous year. Targeted states are those states fighting on the first day of the dispute to protect the status quo. I include only contiguous neighbors because the theory suggests these types of conflicts are the ones most likely to increase militarization and centralization processes. In this model, I measure the extent of prolonged territorial threat indirectly with a yearly count of the age of the border. As I show elsewhere (Gibler 2007), older borders are more likely to be settled and, hence, less conflict-prone.

6.4.2 General threat and other controls

I assess the effects of generalized threats to the state using two basic measures. First, I use a dummy variable for the presence of a non-territorial MID targeting the state in the previous year; only MIDs initiated by neighboring states are included to better match the results for the territorial MIDs variable. Second, I include the natural logarithm of the highest level of militarization among neighboring states, defined as the neighboring state's military personnel over the number of personnel in the potentially threatened country.

Much of my theory depends upon the role of the military within society. Leaders exaggerate threats to bargain internationally; domestically, strong militaries tend to reinforce the power of these leaders. Controlling for the strength of the military is also important in this model because threats from neighboring states occur in context. A strong domestic military makes militarized states on the border less threatening. Thus, to control for the effects of domestic military strength, I also include a measure of state militarization defined as the number of military personnel divided by the entire population of the state.

Since I have already demonstrated that the party polarization data may be moderated by the strength of democratic institutions within the state, I include a measure of regime score in this analysis that is based on the combined Polity IV democracy–autocracy 21-point scale (Marshall and Jaggers 2002). I also use a variable that approximates the number of political constraints facing the executive in each state-year (Henisz 2002). I argue above that parties are strategic, and thus, it could be the case that opposition parties will only oppose the leader when absolutely necessary or when easy, regardless of the type of regime in which the party operates. I include a control for the wealth of the country, which is operationalized as the logged GDP from the previous year (Heston, Summers and Aten 2002). Wealthier countries tend to have interests that are more disbursed, and economic growth is a relatively standard control variable in the rally effects literature.

Finally, I include two variables that capture the international context of the dispute. First, the presence of the Cold War is indicated by a dummy variable that is positive if the observation year is between 1946 and 1989, inclusive. Second, nuclear states may not fear territorial threats as much as non-nuclear states, and therefore, I include a dummy for the presence of nuclear weapons by the potential target.[4]

6.4.3 Results

The ordered logistic regression results for the trichotomous party polarization variable are listed in Table 6.2. Since the model is non-linear, I also provide estimates of predicted probabilities for the effects of the independent variables on each possible outcome to ease interpretation. The predicted probabilities are calculated by changing each variable from its mean value to its maximum value while holding all other variables at their respective means. These additional estimates are listed in the columns on the right-hand side of the table.

The effects of immediate territorial threat are confirmed with this model. Parties are less polarized in states with territories targeted by their neighbors in a dispute, and the relationship is actually quite strong once one considers the likelihood of the various changes described on the right-hand side of Table 6.2. Recall that the dispute measure is dichotomous: the presence/absence of a territorial dispute. Disputes can and do occur with some frequency during the years in the sample, but seldom do neighboring states increase their level of

---

[4] Since all tests have a lower temporal bound of 1975 and an upper bound of 2000, nuclear weapon states include the United States, the Soviet Union, the United Kingdom, France, China (1975–), Israel (1975–), India (1975–), and Pakistan (1998–). The results are not sensitive to alternate codings of Israeli nuclear power.

Table 6.2 *Party polarization in the state, 1975–2000*

	(1)	Change in polarization		
	(1)	Unified	Mixed	Polarized
Ln per capita GDP	0.380*** (0.111)	−6.68%	2.55%	4.13%
Polity IV score (21-point)	0.262*** (0.024)	−32.48%	10.22%	22.26%
Number of veto players	1.651*** (0.402)	−6.26%	2.38%	3.88%
Ln minimum age of border	0.076 (0.062)			
Ln max neighbor militariz.	−.206* (0.125)	2.95%	−1.15%	−1.80%
Ln state militarization	0.591*** (0.124)	−14.12%	5.14%	8.98%
Cold War year	−.656*** (0.146)	2.12%	−0.83%	−1.29%
State has nuclear weapons	−.241 (0.228)			
Target of territorial MID	−1.166** (0.445)	2.09%	−0.83%	−1.26%
Target of non-territorial MID	0.123 (0.289)			
Number of observations	2,658			
X^2	1320.36			
Pseudo-R^2	0.435			

Entries are ordered logit estimates of party polarization in the state, 1975–2000. Percentage change in polarization calculated by altering the values of each independent variable from its mean to its maximum while holding all other variables at their mean. $*p < 0.05$, $**p < 0.01$, $***p < 0.001$.

militarization to the observed maximum or increase the Polity IV score from its sample mean to its maximum.[5]

---

[5] The mean Polity IV score is 0 in the sample. A 10-point or greater yearly change in Polity IV score occurs only 39 times in the sample, and these changes are almost always isolated events for each state. The likelihood of being targeted by a territorial dispute in a given year is almost four times greater and is likely to recur in subsequent state-years.

The salience of territorial threat is further confirmed with the observation that non-territorial disputes have virtually no effect on party polarization. Indeed, even if the estimate were significant at a conventionally accepted level, the relationship is positive, suggesting that non-territorial disputes *increase* polarization. That dispute type has such an important effect may explain why previous studies linking all external threats to domestic changes have rarely produced consistently strong findings. Inclusion of the non-territorial disputes dampens the effect of the territorial disputes, which are salient to the public.[6]

Continuing with the results described in Table 6.2, wealthier countries and countries with a greater number of political constraints are, as expected, more likely to have polarized parties. Indeed, a change from the average Polity IV score (0) to its maximum (10) increases the likelihood of a polarized party system by almost 21 percent. That same mean-to-max change in Polity IV score makes finding a non-polarized party system over 30 percent less likely though, again, the likelihood of a 10-point or greater change in Polity IV score is quite small in this sample. The number of veto players within the state demonstrates similar effects to the variable for level of democracy. Substantively, however, veto player changes are less powerful and are approximately the same as changes brought by increased wealth. Finally, the Cold War years have a dampening effect on party polarization within the state. This could result from the relatively young nature of most democracies during that era, or the Cold War struggle itself may have led to more rigid party lines within the various political party systems.

These findings obviously confirm my theoretical expectations regarding the role that territorial issues play in centralizing political opinion within the state. But these results may also provide two important clues for the nature of domestic rally effects. The first clue is related to identifying the proper audience for an

An analysis of likely changes across variables tells a similar story. For this comparison, consider first the average probability of a state in the sample possessing a fully polarized party system, which is 0.135. The average change in Polity IV score from year to year is less than 1 on the 21-point combined scale, and this implies a change in the probability of full polarization of approximately 3 percent. A 1-point change is also the modal year-to-year change for the Polity IV variable, occurring 115 times in the sample; so the most likely effect of regime type on full polarization is again approximately 3 percent.

The presence of a territorial dispute is of course a dichotomous variable; thus, the modal change is the onset of targeting against the state. This occurs 160 times in the sample analyzed, and each change accounts for a decrease in polarization of 1.5 percent. Combining this with the average state militarization response used to fend off these challenges, the probability of full polarization decreases by a little more than 3 percent. In other words, the effects of external threats to the state are roughly equivalent to the effects of increasing levels of democracy in this sample; threats and militarized responses also occur more often (160 cases versus 115). These individual substantive changes are quite small in any given year, but consistent threats to the state are likely to debilitate both the party system and political competition within the state.

[6] I also estimated the same model on a sample that included only democratic states (identified as those states with combined Polity IV scores of 6 or more). None of the coefficients for the constrained sample change in strength or significance from the results reported in Table 6.2.

effect. While many studies concentrate on the public at large but find little or no change in public opinion following the use of force (see, for example, Lian and Oneal 1993; James and Rioux 1998; Baker and Oneal 2001), the results of this model suggest the reaction to conflict does take place among elite audiences, which may mean that there is an anticipatory effect in which elite audiences try to divine future public opinion regarding the threat. Second, issue type could potentially be useful in defining the salience of a conflict, as the rallying effect may not be limited to formative events like wars. Regardless of these implications, territorial threats decrease polarization, even when controlling for the effects of democracy and other political constraints, but non-territorial disputes have no effect on party behavior.

6.5 Identifying institutional changes

The findings in the last section suggest that salient external territorial threats create favorable domestic political environments for the leaders of the threatened states. Leaders often take advantage of muted domestic oppositions in order to institutionalize their increased political power. To analyze this portion of the theory, I use the number of veto players as a proxy for the domestic political power of the executive. Leaders generally prefer fewer domestic political constraints against their policies. Further, when benefiting from a compliant domestic opposition, most leaders will often try to institutionalize their newfound domestic political strength and remove the potential vetoes for their future policies.

6.5.1 Measuring institutional centralization

The number of political veto points is a good way of approximating the feasibility of policy change from the status quo (Tsebelis 2002). As veto players increase, the chief executive is less and less likely to have the political authority to substantially alter the status quo. My theory suggests chief executives will both want and be given more authority during times of severe external threat, and thus, changes in the number of veto points should correlate strongly (and negatively) with the level of external threat against the state. This is especially true for prolonged threats against state territory.

Henisz (2002) provides a measure of the number of checks on the chief executive that is well suited to documenting the effects of external threat since it also theoretically incorporates party polarization. The *polcon* indicator counts the number of governmental actors able to check the initiatives of the executive, but each additional veto point is conditioned by a fractionalization term that considers the relative ideological distance from the chief executive and weights highly different actors as greater checks. Thus, additional parties provide diminishing marginal increases in the number of checks against the executive, unless the parties differ markedly from the ideological stances of the executive.

Two measures of *polcon* are available – one measure, *polconv*, includes checks for independent judiciaries and sub-federal institutions while the other measure, *polconiii*, ignores these possible checks. In practice, the *polconv* indicator has higher scores and greater variation for countries in which the judiciary is independent and states or provinces have substantial fiscal powers, such as the United States, Switzerland, and Germany. The *polcon* measures have a theoretical range of 0 (no political constraints) to 1 (totally constrained chief executive) but actually range from 0 to 0.73 and 0 to 0.89 for *polconiii* and *polconv*, respectively. In fact, the measures are highly correlated, and because the overall results are so similar across the two measures, I only present the findings using one of the measures (*polconv*). Data are available for the same years and countries as the Database of Political Institutions variables (1816 to 2004), but the temporal range is again limited by data availability for some of the control variables.

6.5.2 Results

Table 6.3 presents the Prais–Winsten estimates for the number of veto points in a given state-year. I use this generalized least-squares model since there is substantial autocorrelation in the veto player measure (original Durbin–Watson statistic of 0.401). The Prais–Winsten model is well suited for identifying trends in the dependent variable, which is consistent with my original expectations for institutional change following exposure to territorial threat.

For these analyses I estimate the same model as in Table 6.2, but now party polarization is included since it serves as an intervening variable in the overall argument. Since the dependent variable is institutional change, I demonstrate the effects of territorial issues with an indicator of sustained threat to the institutions of the state – the presence of a territorial rivalry. I define territorial rivalries using Thompson's (2001) rivalry data and distinguish between territorial and non-territorial rivalries based on the frequency of territorial disputes in the rivalry. Rivalries in which a majority of disputes are territorial are coded as territorial rivalries. All other rivalries are considered non-territorial.

The veto player model is linear, which obviously permits an easier translation of marginal effects. However, a comparative analysis of variable strength is actually difficult given the differences in scale across each of the variables. I therefore include in Table 6.3 a percentage change indicator that measures the

Table 6.3 *The number of veto players in the state, 1975–2000*

	(1)	(2)	% Change
Polarization of major parties	0.031***	0.031***	6.11%
	(0.006)	(0.006)	
Ln per capita GDP	0.112***	0.111***	69.33%
	(0.014)	(0.014)	
Polity IV score (21-point)	0.007***	0.007***	13.98%
	(0.001)	(0.001)	
Ln minimum age of border	0.019**	0.019**	9.74%
	(0.009)	(0.009)	
Ln max neighbor militarization	−0.014	−0.015	
	(0.010)	(0.010)	
Ln state militarization	−0.011	−0.011	
	(0.009)	(0.009)	
Cold War year	−0.021**	−0.021**	−2.10%
	(0.010)	(0.010)	
State has nuclear weapons	0.099	0.102*	10.18%
	(0.062)	(0.062)	
Territorial rivalry (Thompson)	−0.050**	−0.052**	−5.15%
	(0.024)	(0.024)	
Territorial rivalry × polity		−0.001	
		(0.002)	
Non-territorial rivalry (Thompson)	−0.025	−0.030	
	(0.023)	(0.024)	
Non-territorial rivalry × polity		−0.003	
		(0.003)	
Constant	0.017	0.016	
	(0.073)	(0.073)	
Number of observations	2,658	2,658	
R^2	0.101	0.101	
DW statistic transformed	1.928	1.930	

Entries are Prais–Winsten estimates of the number of veto players in the state, 1975–2000. Percentage change in veto players calculated by altering the values of each independent variable from its mean to its maximum while holding all other variables at their mean. $^*p < 0.05$, $^{**}p < 0.01$, $^{***}p < 0.001$.

effect on the dependent variable of changing each independent variable from its mean value to its maximum value in the sample, holding all other variables at their mean.

The results in Table 6.3 suggest that, as expected, long-term territorial threats affect the number of veto players within the state. Territorial rivalries significantly decrease institutional constraints, while states with older borders are more likely to have a greater number of veto players. Substantively, the effects are strong. Increasing either of these variables from the mean to the maximum score produces a change of over 10 percent in the number of veto players. This is a level of change approximately equal to the change in veto players created by polarized parties or about half the change associated with a full democratic revolution. Further, given that party polarization is likely to be, in part, a function of territorial threat, the overall effect of territorial conflict on domestic institutions is even larger than these estimates suggest.

The differences in threat type are again apparent in this model. Non-territorial conflict has very little effect in the model predicting domestic changes. The variable is not statistically significant at any conventional level, though the sign is negative in this model. Similarly, the generalized threat that comes with increased militarization on the border does not alter domestic institutions. These results also confirm the argument that territorial conflict has greater salience within the state.

To determine whether the results in column one were determined wholly by variation in veto players among democracies, I also estimated the model listed in column two, which includes interactions for the presence of rivalry with Polity IV score. In neither case was the interaction statistically significant at any conventional level. Further, the results for both constituent terms remain statistically significant and in the same direction as the results in Table 6.2. Given this, it seems safe to argue that the effects of threat apply to political centralization in both democratic and non-democratic political systems.[7]

---

[7] As an additional robustness check, I also estimated the model using the veto players measure from the Database of Political Institutions (Keefer and Stasavage 2003). The *checks* measure ranges from 1 to 18 and provides an absolute count of possible veto points within the government. For countries with no legislative check on the executive, no matter how small, the count stays at 1. Competitive elections for the chief executive, the presence of an elected legislature, opposition party control of the legislature, and the presence of each additional party within the legislature are all examples of the types of factors that increase the number of checks on the chief executive. Data is available for the years 1816 to 2004, for most countries in the Correlates of War interstate system, but for the robustness check, I limited the analyses to 1975 to 2000 to coincide with the sample of states included in the estimates presented above.

  Analyses using the *checks* measure demonstrated no statistically significant effect for any of the external threat measures using the same model as described in Table 6.3. Since the principal difference between the *checks* measure and the *polcon* measure is the fractionalization of additional checks by the polarization of political position in each additional veto player, the

Among the remaining control variables, the log of economic growth is strongly correlated with a greater number of domestic constraints in the state. Substantively, a state would double the number of domestic veto players if wealth increased from the sample mean to the maximum in any given year. Wealth often translates to political power, and increasing wealth also tends to increase the number of politically powerful groups within society. Though wealth is often correlated with democracy, it remains unclear whether rising wealth leads to democratization. Rather, as Przeworski (2000) contends, democratic transitions may occur randomly, and high per capita GDP protects from backsliding those states that do democratize. Epstein *et al.* (2006) disagree, finding that the connection between wealth and democracy in modernization theory holds if democracy measures also include an intermediate category of partial democracy. The results here confirm that increases in wealth are associated with domestic political constraints. Even if democratization is a random tipping point for domestic processes, the number of veto players varies consistently and predictably with increases in GDP. This seems to support the contentions of modernization theory if one believes that democracy is more likely when the number of constraints against the executive increase.

The results for wealth also reinforce the importance of threat for domestic institutions and democracy. Recall my argument that states under territorial threat will often divert economic production to create large land armies to defend the state. This diversion will of course affect long-term GDP growth since government military spending seldom increases the wealth of a country. Thus, threats to territory decrease the level of wealth of a society, and by doing so, also affect the number of veto players that can check executive power. With fewer constraints on the executive, democracy becomes less likely.

Finally, the Cold War variable again dampens the number of veto players, though the substantive effect is rather small. The presence of nuclear weapons also has an effect in both models and is statistically significant (at $p < 0.10$) in the fully specified model of column two. States with nuclear weapons tend to have 10 percent more veto players in their domestic political system, even after

additional analyses confirm the importance of political environment in affecting political centralization. It would seem that additional institutions mean little if they remain unable to check the executive. This finding is of course not limited to inter-party bargaining, since party polarization is included in both analyses.

The territorial threat measures do affect centralization when using the *checks* measure, if the threats are consistent over a number of years. States that have territorial rivalries for ten or more years have fewer veto players than other types of state; this is true in absolute terms, without regard to polarization across domestic institutions. Together, these additional analyses reinforce the contention that salient external threats create a favorable political environment for the leader, both in relation to the opposition and within government itself. Over time, leaders are able to use this favorable environment to shed institutional constraints on their power.

controlling for the effects of democracy and income. Thus, it would seem that the ability to stave off severe threats to homeland territory through nuclear deterrence matters for the maintenance of a decentralized domestic political system.

As a whole, the external threat variables confirm the contention that, among international influences on the state, territorial threat leads to domestic institutional changes and shifts in the behavior of political elites. Some of the changes are subtle and indirect, but, over time and in aggregate, these annual domestic responses lead to a polity that hardens against external territorial threats, regardless of regime type. For states that experience territorial threats in most years, centralized decision-making authority is nearly guaranteed.

6.6 A note on the role of judiciaries

The analyses described in this chapter have provided strong evidence that states under territorial threat are likely to centralize their political institutions. This explains why autocracies (highly centralized regimes) and democracies (with decentralized power structures) tend to cluster in time and space. However, there are exceptions. Democracies do not always revert when facing severe territorial threats; many states are somehow able to inhibit centralization pressures that lead to regime reversals.

In a separate work, I examined the ability of independent judiciaries to block executive power grabs during international conflicts (Gibler and Randazzo 2011). Independent judiciaries are unique because, if viewed as legitimate within the state, these institutions protect the regime. As an institution, most are isolated from the domestic power changes that can result when state territories are threatened.

The model of centralization outlined here relies on changes in the domestic bargaining power of various actors as a mechanism for regime centralization. International conflict advantages the executive vis-à-vis other domestic actors, and eventually, power is concentrated in the executive as democratic principles are eroded. The causal mechanism relies on the opportunity given the executive by international crisis, as this threat, when coupled with popular backing, allows the executive to supersede the constitution in favor of expediency.

An independent judiciary can affect this process in two ways. First, established judiciaries are likely to deter executives from using the crisis as an opportunity to gain power. An executive facing an international crisis will likely not risk additional political decisions that may cause the questioning of their authority. This weak form of judicial independence creates few judicial annulments, but the court does buttress the political power of other societal and governmental interests against executive incursions. A stronger form of judicial independence manifests when the executive is overtly checked with annulments as the court favors minority rights and participatory democracy. In either case the executive is constrained by the court, and democracy maintains. Established judiciaries are probably one of the best institutional guarantees for providing a bulwark against executive-led political centralization.

The empirics support the stabilizing nature of judiciaries. Using 41 years of data (1960–2000) identifying judicial constraints across 163 different countries, we found that the presence of an independent judiciary is consistently associated with regime stability.[8] Specifically, our analyses suggested that established judiciaries help prevent all types of regime changes toward authoritarianism for samples that included all regime types. When the sample was limited to democracies only, independent judiciaries still predicted fewer negative regime changes, but large-scale changes remained unaffected by the courts.[9]

In the end, independent judiciaries did stop political centralization caused by territorial threats. However, judiciaries were incapable of halting centralization during intense, long-term threats, such as those resulting from territorial rivalries. I think future research may want to disentangle the bargaining power of the court – especially those courts with judges appointed for life – as a way of stabilizing new regimes. Few other institutions are so well designed to challenge executives emboldened by domestic rallies and weak oppositions.

6.7 Conclusions

This chapter demonstrates that certain types of external threat affect domestic political institutions. Specifically, territorial threats increase the political authority of chief executives within their governments. Immediate threats lead to behavioral changes within the government in the form of decreased party polarization. Prolonged territorial threats take advantage of the muted opposition and lead to institutional changes, measured as a reduction in the number of political constraints that could oppose the leader's policies. These centralizing effects occur even after state-level controls for regime type, wealth, and ethnic and religious fractionalization.

---

[8] It is important to note that our analyses also confirmed that these results were not spurious to traditional correlates of democracy such as wealth and development history. Nor is our measure of independent judiciaries endogenous to polity changes.

[9] Newly established independent judiciaries were associated with large-scale reversions (magnitude of 4 or more on the Polity IV scale) in both democracies and non-democracies. Our examination of the data suggested this last finding resulted mostly from placement of the courts in difficult political environments, adding additional support to the argument that the power of the court grows over time.

The empirical regularity that territorial issues are more dangerous than other issues has led to the assumption that fights over territory are more salient than other issues to both publics and leaders. Yet, little evidence exists to support this contention *ex ante*, and no consistent story linking territorial issues with domestic escalation currently exists. The findings in this chapter present an important way to resolve this issue, as they largely confirm the territorial explanations of conflict developed in Vasquez (1993, 2009), Huth (1998), and Senese and Vasquez (2008). However, instead of hard-liners rising within governments to formulate aggressive international policies, it would seem that all leaders benefit politically from the centralizing effects of direct threats to the state.

These results also imply an association between regime type and the content of issues facing the state. Since centralization is a common reaction to territorial issues that harry the state, it would seem that states with polarized parties and a greater number of veto players are more likely to be found in regions that are absent territorial threats. This would explain why democracies tend to cluster together in time and space (Gleditsch 2002). As territorial peace develops in a region, liberalization of the affected regimes follows (Thompson 2001; Gibler 2007).[10]

Finally, these findings are obviously consistent with the long tradition of predation theories of state formation that connect war-making and state-making (Hintze 1975; Tilly 1985; Rasler and Thompson 1989; Desch 1996; Thompson 1996; Thies 2005). However, the findings reported here are some of the first to confirm those same state-making dynamics at a stage of political development far removed from state formation (see also Rasler and Thompson 2004). These results also provide a level of institutional detail that other studies have not tried to explicate. Indeed, the paucity of consistent findings and the few theories describing micro-level effects implies that there is much we do not know about domestic reactions to the system. This is true even almost 30 years after Gourevitch's (1978) initial call for second-image-reversed theories. In the remainder of this book, I describe why understanding these processes is so important: once we control for the effects of territorial conflict on state development, our most basic "law" of international relations may in fact be spurious.

---

[10] I have focused here on territorial issues in order to highlight the centralizing tendencies of the state following threat. Issue type is rather easily defined, and its salience is not dependent on casualties or leader and public reactions. Nevertheless, non-territorial issues can sometimes still be highly salient to domestic audiences, in all types of regimes. Following the 2001 terrorist attacks in New York City and Washington, DC, for example, the United States implemented the Patriot Act and the largest restructuring of its government since World War II. However, the difficulty with empirically identifying the effects of these issues remains: defining salience prior to public reaction is difficult and arguments connecting salience to centralization often become tautological. Thus, moving forward, more attention should be paid to understanding the content of issues that most resonate with leaders and publics alike.

PART III

The territorial peace

7

Territorial peace among neighbors

7.1 Introduction

The connection between territorial threats and state centralization may also alter our understanding of international conflict. States with territorial issues are more likely to have recurrent conflicts with their neighbors since these disputes are difficult to resolve. Centralization further encourages these states to remain or become non-democratic. Absent territorial issues, peace and democracy follow, which is why we commonly associate peace with democracy. However, this does not necessarily imply that states at territorial peace with their neighbors are always peaceful in their relations with other states. When freed from engagement in territorial conflict, leaders of states at territorial peace may more easily choose conflict involvements based on terms favorable to their interests. Since territorial issues with neighbors have been resolved, these conflicts are likely to be among non-contiguous states. Those states still involved in territorial conflict with neighbors have little ability to choose their conflicts. Their foreign policy choices are much more constrained; hence, states involved in territorial conflicts have few war-fighting advantages.

In the sections that follow, I outline the first part of the argument by first briefly reviewing the democratic peace literature and then recasting these findings as products of a broader, territorial peace. I then test this application of the theory against a model of conflict that controls for the effects of border relationships and find that joint democracy does not exercise a pacifying effect on dispute initiation among contiguous states. Instead, states that face few threats to homeland territories – the territorial peace states – better explain the relationship between peace and regime type.

7.2 The democratic peace and territorial issues

The democratic peace literature centers on the finding that no two democracies
have gone to war with one another in the modern era (Levy 1988), and a sizeable
body of literature has emerged that verifies the pacifying effects of democracy,
especially in dyads (Bremer 1992, 1993; Chan 1984; Weede 1984; Levy 1988;
Russett and Oneal 2001). For all its empirical strength, however, consensus on
the causes of the democratic peace remains elusive. While monadic arguments
about the general peacefulness of democracies have performed poorly in tests
(Maoz and Russett 1993, 624), the dyadic nature of the democratic peace has
enjoyed far greater support and has been the subject of a great deal of inductive
theory-building. In this section, I examine the democratic peace in terms of its
dominant theoretical models and the many important findings that have emerged
from both proponents and critics. I then offer a way to re-conceptualize these
findings and lay the groundwork for an alternative theory of dyadic peace.

7.2.1 Theoretical models

Two basic models dominate the democratic peace literature: explanations based
on norms of behavior and explanations based on structural incentives for leaders
of democracies. Each model views domestic regime type as the independent
variable responsible for peace, though they disagree over the theory necessary
to explain it and the specific expectations about state behavior that should
constitute the peace.

Norms
Following Immanuel Kant's assertion that states with republican constitutions
should transcend the anarchy and relative gains considerations of the international system and achieve a kind of cooperative peace, the normative model
assumes that states externalize the methods of conflict resolution that define
their regime types (Kant 1796). These democratic norms are externalized when
doing so is not a threat to basic security, such as when dealing with fellow
democracies or substantially weaker states (Maoz and Russett 1993; Dixon
1994; Doyle 1986; Russett and Oneal 2001). Democracies are more likely to
negotiate difficult international issues (Dixon 1994) and generally experience
more cooperative relationships with regimes of similar type.

This normative perspective constitutes the theoretical backdrop for the empirical support linking democratic dyads and peaceful dispute settlements, such as

arbitration, mediation, and mutual compromises. It also explains why democracies may be conflict-prone but not against other democracies. Shared trust and shared norms of dispute resolution, as found between democratic leaders, enable alternatives to conflict escalation.

Domestic structures

The structural model focuses on the difficulties democracies face in mobilizing for war (Rummel 1983; Lake 1992; Fearon 1994; Bueno de Mesquita and Lalman 1994). The need in democratic systems to generate broad public support and to win legitimacy from a variety of decentralized sources of authority represents structural constraints that make the process of mobilizing for war more difficult than in autocratic regimes. Only in rare cases, such as clear security emergencies, can democracies win the support of enough competing domestic interests to go to war. The process is slow and transparent, and, in cases of disputes between democracies, diplomatic solutions can usually be found before either state wins enough domestic support for a war. Less-constrained autocratic regimes should be able to mobilize for war much faster, presenting the kind of immediate threat against which democratic polities are more likely to win support for violent action. Democracies are thus unlikely to fight one another, although they are more likely to aggressively engage less democratic states.

According to Bueno de Mesquita *et al.* (2003), democratic leaders must distribute public goods such as prosperity and security in order to stay in power, while autocratic leaders are loyal to a smaller winning coalition who can be more easily placated with private goods, such as the spoils of conquest. Autocrats, able to divert the costs of war to a populace to whom they are not accountable, are thus more likely to resort to war but, because defeat is less a threat to regime survival, do not try hard to win. Democracies, in contrast, fight only those wars they can win, and, when committed, they fight hard.

Findings

Several important findings emerge from the democratic peace literature beyond the simple dyadic peace, but as yet they have not been subsumed under a single theory. As noted above, the absence of war between democratic states forms the core of the democratic peace. However, democracies are no less war-prone in general than other states; they simply do not fight each other (Maoz and Abdolali 1989; Russett 1993). Second, democracies are more likely than other states to submit their disputes to negotiation and arbitration instead of resorting to force (Dixon 1994; Raymond 1994; Brecher and Wilkenfeld 1997; Mousseau 1998; Huth and Allee 2002).

Both findings suggest that, given the opportunity, democracies will act peacefully and will not resort to unprovoked attack. Studies also suggest that democracies are uniquely able to refrain from escalating territorial disputes to war (Bueno de Mesquita *et al.* 1999; Mitchell and Prins 1999; Huth and Allee 2002). Gleditsch (2002), suggesting the democratic peace is also a regional phenomenon, notes two other critical regularities: democracies rarely if ever fight wars on or near their home territory, and democracies tend to cluster together in space and time, creating regional zones of peace.

7.2.2 Recasting the democratic peace

Each of the above findings is consistent with the assertion that democracies have avoided war with one another because of a lack of territorial issues. First, if neighboring states do not have territorial issues, they should be highly unlikely to fight a priori. To the extent that states with stable borders fight wars at all, they are unlikely to do so on or near their home territory. Should these states enter into disputes with distant states, they are less likely to involve threats to their territorial integrity; as such, they should be less likely to follow the power politics and bargaining processes usually identified with conflict (Vasquez 1993, 2009) and more likely to seek peaceful negotiation and arbitration. To the extent that democracies experience territorial disputes, they are likely to be distant.[1]

Second, if states are more likely to become democratic in the absence of territorial issues, as I have outlined in Part II of this book, then democracies should cluster around stable interstate borders. As a result of settling their borders, neighbors should experience greater chances of both having a peaceful relationship and becoming democratic. In short, if democracies do not fight each other, it is because the borders between them had to be settled before democracy

---

[1] This holds true even for disputes over distant territory. For example, Huth and Allee's (2002) compilations of disputes by region include great powers – often democracies like the United States, Great Britain, and France – from outside the region, whose interests in dispute resolution should be far different from disputes with contiguous neighbors. The 1919 British and French dispute over territory along the border between French Equatorial Africa and Sudan is an important case in point, as the dispute was settled peacefully by negotiation (Huth and Allee 2002: 379). The defense of far-flung lands raised few alarms about the territorial integrity of the British and French homelands. The same kind of non-contiguous disputes that do not threaten home territory can be found in Mitchell and Prins's data as well (1999, Table 2).

could take root. Precisely because democracies share stable borders, peace between them is likely.

This argument also makes sense in light of several important challenges to the democratic peace, notably in Reed's (2000) finding that joint democracy exerts a pacifying effect only on dispute onset and not on escalation to war. Joint democracies are simply less likely to experience disputes than other dyads; if these joint democracies tend to interact across shared stable borders, then this result is clearly expected.[2]

Especially among newly independent states, which are likely to experience territorial disputes (Vasquez 1993, 1995, 2009), new democratic institutions might actually increase the likelihood of disputes escalating to war (Mansfield and Snyder 1995; Snyder 2000; Thompson and Tucker 1997). Territorial issues might then represent clear obstacles to democratic consolidation in transitioning states. While democratic peace scholars generally account for this by holding that the pacific benefits of democracy work chiefly in "mature" democracies (Maoz and Russett 1993), it is probably more plausible that the incidence of territorial issues, which are most likely during and after transition periods, might be the cause.

The confluence of these findings suggests that, if stable borders have something to do not only with peace but also with prospects for democracy, there is reason to believe that the relationship between democracy and peace is spurious. The next step in this argument, then, is to establish the connection between stable borders and the development of democracy.

7.2.3 Expectations

I argued in Chapter 3 that the stabilization of borders in a region should contribute to democratization in that region, establishing what Thompson (1996) and Gleditsch (2002) label as zones or clusters of peaceful democratic states. As neighbors experience fewer and fewer territorial issues, they are more likely to, first, have a peaceful relationship and, second, become more democratic. The democratic peace among neighboring states, as we know it, is simply the outgrowth of a peace across borders. In a purely international context, then,

---

[2] It may also make sense that states at territorial peace, which are more likely to have decentralized power structures, are also more likely to be capitalistic and supportive of property rights and contracts. Both conditions may also affect the relationship between regime type and peace (see Gartzke [2007] and Mousseau [2000], but also see Dafoe [2011] for a rejoinder to Gartzke).

democracy is what can happen when neighbors no longer fear for the safety of their homeland territories.

If democracies cluster spatially because their emergence requires the settling of territorial issues, democratic neighbors should be significantly less likely to enter into disputes than any other dyads. By extension, stable borders between autocracies, to the extent they exist, should also be peaceful. However, since territorial issues place constraints on the leaders involved in the conflict – dealing with an enemy on the border is the first priority of foreign policy – the removal of these issues also frees the hand of the leaders. Adventurism and other types of involvement abroad can be prosecuted more easily and more carefully by leaders at peace with neighbors. Leaders freed from these territorial rivalries may choose which conflicts to enter, and they are likely to base these selections on the overall likelihood of victory. Nevertheless, few issues with states abroad will carry the same domestic salience of the territorial issues with neighbors, and, therefore, these issues are much more likely to end in successful negotiations rather than militarized disputes and wars.

Thus, the predictions that follow from the territorial peace argument are of two basic kinds. First, territorial issues will control the agenda of contiguous states. Unresolved territorial issues will lead to centralization of the state and constrain the leaders from conflict involvements abroad. Resolving these issues affects relations between non-contiguous states, making future peace more likely. In hypothesis form, I expect the following two relationships:

$H_{7.1}$: *The establishment of stable borders leads to state decentralization and encourages democratization.*

$H_{7.2}$: *The establishment of stable borders increases the likelihood of peace in the dyad.*

Political decentralization was of course tested in Part II of the book, by examining the relationship between external territorial threats and political tolerance, militarization, and institutional centralization. Therefore, in this chapter, I restrict the tests of the hypothesis to democracy in the dyad, which is necessary to demonstrate a spurious relationship between democracy and peace.

One additional note: the second hypothesis is left general in its prediction of the dependent variable – other conflict issues should also be affected. Implicit in my argument is that territorial conflict underlies the larger rival relationship, and, therefore, resolving territorial conflict should also resolve, or at least greatly reduce, other issues of contention.[3] Conversely, territorial threats will

---

[3] Hensel (2011) finds preliminary evidence that this is indeed the case (see also Gibler and Tir 2010).

exacerbate other issues of contention as they become fused with claims over territory. In either case, the prediction of variation in conflict levels following dispute resolution deviates from traditional, realist assumptions that issue evolution is of little consequence.

7.3 Operationalizing border stability

Borders are stable when both states accept the demarcation of territory between them. Mutual acceptance is difficult to identify *ex ante*. However, as Vasquez (1995, 288) argues, "natural frontiers that have clear salients – like rivers, mountains, deserts, lakes and oceans – are more likely to lead to a mutually acceptable demarcation of boundaries, especially if people are not living in these areas." These geographic salients reduce the costs of coordination. Geographic landmarks are observable to all parties, are stationary, and are thus less prone to misperception and error. Geographic landmarks therefore provide some of the easiest tools for making agreements that require coordination among two or more actors.

Border acceptance is also likely to be influenced by previous international agreements. Treaties signed without coercion confirm demarcation negotiations that can ease future coordination problems (Carter and Goemans 2011; Owsiak 2012). Territorial transfers provide similar functions while also re-arranging the distribution of territory in ways that are less likely to provoke future conflicts (Gibler and Tir 2010). In both cases, the agreements are likely to reinforce any natural landmarks or other geographic salients. Absent favorable geography, the agreements will then serve as initial salients themselves, as any possible future revisions must take into account the previous, mutually acceptable demarcation.

7.3.1 Geography and borders

Schelling (1960, 54–58) describes the logic of geography and border salients with three examples. First is the somewhat daunting hypothetical of meeting someone in another city without agreeing ahead of time on either the time or place for this meeting or even being able to coordinate with them through any type of communication. Where is the best place to meet? Were you to arrive in New York City, you might go to the Empire State building, at sunset or midnight, expecting the other person to be more likely to coordinate on this particular landmark at this particular time. Or for Schelling's (1960, 56) colleagues at Yale University, coordination was probably easiest at Grand Central Station at noon, since most would be familiar with the train line coming into town from nearby New Haven. Of course, in either case, few would expect their coordinating counterparts to meet them on some nondescript street at some unremarkable time – there would be no focal points upon which both parties could coordinate.

Territorial maps are often replete with focal points for coordination. Imagine parachuting from a plane and needing to coordinate with another jumper already on the ground. Bridges, buildings, rivers, and road intersections – any prominent landmarks – would provide the best possibilities for coordination, as only a dogged search finds the person who sits waiting in an empty field. Further, even if one jumper had a strong personal preference to meet in the middle of the open field, the lay of the map would have prevented such an unrealistic outcome, just as the person in New York City would likely eat alone at their favorite local restaurant. Though strong interests might be attached to the restaurant or the open field, both places would lose as potential meeting places because both lack inherent clarity as focal points for coordination (Schelling 1960, 67–74).

The logic of focal points for coordination on international borders follows. Open plains, featureless desert, and even consistently rugged, mountain terrain all lack the geographically defining features upon which the leaders of two bordering states could easily coordinate. Conversely, if a river divides two states across a border, absent other defining characteristics, that geographic feature would so completely define negotiations over boundaries that any border agreement not based on the river would be inferior, even if the river substantially decreased the land available to one of the states.

Consider a hypothetical division of territory between two countries, one to the north and one to the south. In this hypothetical, a river divides the two countries and competes with a border line proposed by the southern country. The proposed border demarcation is a more equitable division of territory than the river boundary as each country would control roughly 50 percent of the total land occupied by both countries while the river divides the land so that the northern country controls 70 percent of the territory. Nevertheless, if Schelling's analysis of coordination is correct, the river, though inequitable, would dominate debate on the international border because it provides a clear focal point. The demarcation line proposed by the southern country is equivalent to the parachutist waiting in the open field because the river provides the more tangible focal point for coordination.

Of course, there are no guarantees that geography will always determine the focal points for international border coordination. Relative dyadic capabilities also tend to be critically important. Returning again to the hypothetical outlined above, imagine the same divisions of territory, but this time the southern country is clearly more powerful than the northern country. If this were the case, the southern country could press its claim and dictate the boundary line. Absent clear preponderance, though, the southern country would have to militarize the region north of the river, and possibly its homeland, in order to defend the claimed territory.

Military strategy often reinforces coordination on focal points as many types of geography carry strategic advantage as an international border. Rivers themselves, for example, are more easily defensible than the flat lands found in river basins. To defend an entire basin, the supply lines of a defender would have to stretch across a river, and the personnel defending the basin would be open to unimpeded attack. Alternately, a defender that uses a river as a border can dramatically increase the costs of attack by requiring an amphibious crossing; the supply lines that cross the river then become a disadvantage for the attacker.

France provides one of the best examples of the effects of natural frontiers on the history of international boundary lines and state development, as contemporary France traces its borders to the Atlantic, the Pyrenees, the Alps, and the Rhine – an overall border that Cardinal Richelieu claimed to be "marked out by nature" (Sahlins 1989). Indeed, according to Sahlins (1989, 1424), "the idea of natural frontiers sometimes provided the justification, sometimes the organizing principle, of French foreign policy," as a "bounded, delimited territory" competed with a common language and history as constitutive elements defining the French people (see also Goemans 2006). France's border also exemplifies how relative dyadic capabilities can often trump geographic focal points like the river Rhine, as the sovereignty of Alsace and Lorraine shifted with the military capabilities of Germany.

Of course, natural landmarks and power differentials are not the only determinants of coordination on boundaries; border history, border age, and many other factors all may play a part in border definition. For example, and again returning to the hypothetical discussed above, if previous border lines had included the region north of the river – an earlier, colonial border, for example – the claims of the southern country, evinced by the proposed border line, would be more easily made. The colonial border provides an alternate focal point for coordination, and the negotiation strategy of the southern country would thus center on making that alternate focal point, rather than geography, the determinant of demarcation.

Predictors of focal points

To determine when focal points are likely to define an international border, I first identify differences in types of colonial heritage. I assume that land-contiguous dyads that shared the same colonial masters are also likely to have poorly defined borders. Since imperial states had little need to differentiate among their colonial holdings, contiguous states gaining their independence from the same country often suffer from poor border definition. For example, French West Africa eventually became the independent states of Benin, Guinea, Mali, Cote d'Ivoire, Mauritania, Niger, Senegal, and Burkina Faso, but only after comprising administrative units within the French federation of West African states. Benin and Niger also shared a border with Nigeria, a former British colony, and the need to demarcate territories between France and Britain probably necessitated clearer border definition between these states than between the former French colonies.[4]

To operationalize this predictor of border salients, I use *CIA Factbook* data to identify the colonial heritage of each country, 1816 to 2000. Dyads of contiguous states that share the same colonial heritage are coded as 1 and 0 otherwise.

Unfortunately for my purposes, many of the geographic indicators of border salients have little chance to vary substantially over time, absent a major reorganization of the dyadic boundary. Borders are often flexible though, and their perceived stability or legitimacy can change substantially over time. I therefore include several, behavioral indicators of conditions likely to affect the legitimacy of previously drawn borders.

First, I control for the capability ratio within the dyad. The power parity literature (Kugler and Lemke 1996; Geller 2000) has demonstrated that conflict is likely when dyads are at or near parity, and I agree with Wayman (1996) and Vasquez (1995) that territorial renegotiations are a likely mechanism connecting power differentials and conflict. Large differences in power would suggest that a border is unlikely to undergo renegotiation regardless of how the border was previously defined. When a dyad approaches parity, latent territorial claims can be forwarded, upsetting the stability of the dyadic border; this makes transitions in power dangerous when they become linked to ill-defined borders.

---

[4] Unfortunately, this measure may be overwhelmed by the strong correlation between former colonial status and poverty – a strong predictor of non-democracy. I therefore ran separate analyses that controlled for the effects of wealth in the analyses by also adding the natural logarithm of the smaller per capita gross domestic product (GDP) in the dyad. The results I present here remain substantively the same in each analysis.

I therefore include in the analyses the capability ratio of the weaker state to the stronger state, using the latest version of the Composite Index of National Capabilities from the Correlates of War Project (Singer, Bremer and Stuckey 1972).

Second, I also control for the number of years since the last dispute as well as the age of the border. While I should include spells of peace to properly estimate coefficients in binary, cross-sectional time-series studies like this one (Beck, Katz and Tucker 1998; Carter and Signorino 2010), I also believe that the length of peace constitutes a theoretically interesting variable. Traditional, realist theories often assume a constant rate of conflict over time, but it is probably more reasonable to expect that peaceful past relations are likely to condition future relations. This is especially true for borders since revisionism of past territorial distributions is a major cause of dispute recurrence.[5] Stable borders are also a function of age generally: old states whose borders have long been settled and whose neighbors accept the legitimacy of their borders should also perceive a lower territorial threat. Old states should also be less aggressive in desiring the capture of territory as well, as their border relations are an accepted norm. I define the age of the border using a count variable for the number of years since the last system entry date in the dyad (Stinnett *et al.* 2002), and I define the spell of peace as the time since the last Militarized Interstate Dispute (Ghosn, Palmer and Bremer 2004). I control for temporal dependence in the analyses by including the square and cube terms of the peace spell (Carter and Signorino 2010).

Third, as I argue above, political events in neighboring states often put in question the legitimacy of international borders (Vasquez 1995). The outbreak of civil war may lead regional leaders to fear that violence will spread or that victorious regimes might wish to redraw previous territorial divisions. I use the onset of an intra-state war as an indicator of states likely to experience border instability, using Correlates of War definitions (Sarkees and Wayman 2010) and lag the variable one year prior to the year examined.

Fourth, there have been over eight hundred instances in which two states have actually transferred territories between them since 1816 (Tir *et al.* 1998). Jaroslav Tir and I have demonstrated that peaceful territorial transfers signif-icantly reduce the level of threat and militarization in the dyad (Gibler and

---

[5] Measuring time since last territorial dispute best captures this argument. However, I measure time since last dispute (of any kind) in order to correct for temporal dependence in estimating the dependent variable of any dispute onset.

Tir 2010). I therefore include a dichotomous variable for the presence of a peaceful transfer in the dyad during the five years prior to the dyad-year examined. I also include a similar variable for violent transfers during the previous five years. Violent transfers should increase the level of threat for both states, assuming the losing state is capable of launching a viable counter to the transfer.[6]

Fifth, territorial disputes of course represent threats to the states involved. I therefore code for the presence of *any* territorial dispute that targets either state in the dyad during the five years prior to the year examined. I use Maoz's (2005) dyadic dispute data to identify territorial disputes among neighbors, with contiguity again based on Correlates of War definitions (Stinnett *et al.* 2002). I also use Huth and Allee's (2002) data as a robustness check for samples that include only twentieth-century cases.

My sixth threat variable identifies the highest level of militarization among neighboring states. High levels of militarization often signify threats or the potential for threats to the homeland territories. I use the Composite Index of National Capabilities from the Correlates of War Project (Singer, Bremer and Stuckey 1972) to identify the number of military personnel in the state and divide that number by the total population listed in the data set. The highest level of militarization among neighbors is then lagged by one year prior to the year examined.

Finally, I include two alliance-based measures as controls. Forming an alliance demonstrates at least a modicum of cooperation between the two states, and it is possible that, in some cases, that cooperation is strong enough to reduce the level of threat that may emanate from an alliance partner. I define allied dyads using the Correlates of War Formal Interstate Alliance data set (Gibler and Sarkees 2004) and create a dummy variable for the presence of an alliance. I also control for the presence of an active defense pact with all neighbors since I have demonstrated that such regional pacts can reduce external threats and the level of militarization within the state (Gibler and Wolford 2006).

A focus on geographic salients and the behaviors that legitimize them adds two important benefits for conclusions regarding tests of my overall argument. First, using these indicators will effectively insulate several of my variables from questions of reverse causality. This is important because many studies

---

[6] The caveat in this sentence is important. Vasquez (1993, 2009), for example, argues that overwhelming victories often promote future peace and reduced territorial threat in the dyad. Operationally, I use five-year lags for all the threat variables, but the results remain quite similar if I employ ten-year lags instead.

link joint democracy with peaceful dispute settlement generally (Dixon 1994) and territorial dispute settlement in particular. Bueno de Mesquita *et al.* (2003), for example, argue that democratic leaders would find little political leverage in the private goods of territorial claims and will therefore quickly resolve these issues, especially with other democracies. By focusing on geographic conditions, then, I am able to empirically assess whether democracy leads to peaceful dispute settlement or territorial peace leads to democracy. After all, few would contend that democracies can alter history or otherwise alter the physical shape of their geographic borders.

Also importantly, by focusing on geographic conditions and indicators of their legitimacy, the tests that follow are removed from possible strategic biases inherent in claims over territory. For example, the Issues Correlates of War (ICoW) Project identifies all international territorial claims, largely independent of the occurrence of armed conflict (Hensel *et al.* 2008). But, unfortunately for my purposes, juridical claims may be most likely between states that have resolved not to go to war with each other and that instead use international institutions or other supranational legal authority for the redress of these issues. This acceptance, then, selects the dyad out of the sample likely to experience territorial threat, and given the strategic nature of juridical claims, a data set based on speeches, treaties, demonstrations, and the like would all be inappropriate indicators of peaceful territorial environments, at least for my purposes here.

7.3.2 Dependent variables

The dependent variable in the first set of analyses is joint democracy; I code dyads as jointly democratic if both states have combined Polity IV scores (autocracy–democracy) equal to or greater than 6 (Marshall and Jaggers 2002). The dependent variable in the second set of analyses is the presence of a fatal Militarized Interstate Dispute, again using Correlates of War definitions of disputes experiencing at least one military fatality (Ghosn, Palmer and Bremer 2004). I include any dyadic dispute, but only for its first year, and I exclude dyads that join an ongoing MID.

My general expectations for these variables are summarized in Figure 7.1. Consistent with the argument outlined above, I believe that stable borders should increase the likelihood of joint democracy while also decreasing the likelihood of conflict. Moreover, failing to include controls for the likelihood of territorial issues will introduce bias into estimates of the effects of joint

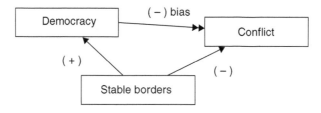

Figure 7.1 Omitted variable bias in the democratic peace

democracy on conflict, possibly resulting in the observation of a spurious relationship.

7.3.3 Sample selection

My sample includes all contiguous dyads from 1816 to 2000. By including observations as recent as 2000, I can compare the effects of the Cold War to other periods; this is important since Farber and Gowa (1997), among others, have argued that the democratic peace may be a function of inter-est similarity during that period of intense bipolarity. More important for purposes of testing the argument I sketched above is the inclusion of the nine post-Cold War years when the norms of self-determination biased states toward entering the international system as democracies. Indeed, as Gleditsch (2002) demonstrates, a higher percentage of states entered the system as democracies during this period than during any other decade. The 1990s also witnessed the relaxation of norms against self-determination and changes in the territorial status quos that were previously guaranteed by superpowers (Germany and the former Soviet Republics), each of which I equate with border instability.

I focus on contiguous dyads because my argument is about borders. Those states that have a high level of territorial threat directed against their homeland are likely to be centralized and, of course, conflict-prone. Removing that threat from their agenda makes the states more likely to be democratic and peace-ful *with their neighbors*. The removal of territorial threat does not necessarily imply peace with non-contiguous states, however. States may have settled their borders but still have the ability and desire to project their power across the globe, as the United States has done since the Cold War. Further, a state at territorial peace may even find an interest in targeting another state at terri-torial peace, in a different part of the world. In the next chapter I discuss in greater detail the implications of territorial peace with neighbors on conflict selection.

7.4 International borders and joint democracy

I begin the analyses by using the stable border proxies to predict the observance of joint democracy in a dyad.[7] Since the dependent variable is dichotomous – jointly democratic or not – I employ logistic regression with robust standard errors. I also split the sample into two time periods based on data availablility – 1816 to 2000 and 1919 to 1995. The results for both time periods are presented in Table 7.1.[8]

Among the basic dyadic controls, the capability ratio within the dyad is consistently related to the observance of joint democracy. Dyads in which one state is preponderant (a low capability ratio of weak state divided by strong state) have a greater chance of experiencing joint democracy, and I argue that this results from either a settled border that favors the claims of the stronger state or the inability of the weaker state to seek redress (or both). Parity adds territorial threat to the dyad because revisionist states at parity with their rivals are more likely to press their latent territorial claims militarily (see Wayman 1996).

Interestingly, the presence of an alliance, which should reduce threat, actually decreases the likelihood of democracy in both specifications. This is mostly due to the inclusion of the variable that marks the presence of defense pacts with all neighboring states. Absent the defense pact variable, the coefficient is positive but not statistically significant at any conventional level.

The temporal controls provide similar results in each model. The length of peace provides a proxy for the overall legitimacy of the border since, after controlling for capability differences, territorial disputes increase the likelihood of conflict. The negative coefficient for this indicator suggests longer peace spells are associated with joint democracy. The behavior of the border age variable provides unexpected results, however. I use the natural log of the variable to control for several outliers, but the sign remains negative and statistically significant in both models. This suggests that democracies are more likely to be found on either side of younger borders, which may be strange given that many of the oldest borders can be found in democratic Europe. Nevertheless, the

---

[7] In previous work (Gibler 2007), I established that many of these variables served as good proxies for the likelihood of territorial threats. In this chapter I therefore restrict the analyses to estimations of democracy and conflict.

[8] Note that these models exclude any domestic-level predictors of democracy in either state. Wealth probably has the most consistent effect on the likelihood of democracy, but little per capita wealth data exist over such a long time period. However, I did estimate these models with GDP data for the post-World War II time period, but none of the results described below changed in either substantive effect or statistical significance. These analyses confirm what I found previously regarding wealth, democracy, and territorial threat (Gibler 2007, Table 2).

Table 7.1 *Predicting joint democracy with territorial threat*

	(1) 1816–2000	(2) 1919–1995
Capability ratio	−0.433*** (0.103)	−0.791*** (0.117)
Allied	−0.585*** (0.060)	−0.349*** (0.065)
Peace years	0.018*** (0.001)	0.019*** (0.001)
Natural log of dyad duration	−0.339*** (0.026)	−0.360*** (0.031)
Intra-state war in either state	−0.763*** (0.082)	−0.951*** (0.097)
Same colonial master	−0.737*** (0.068)	−1.134*** (0.077)
Peaceful territorial transfer	0.721*** (0.077)	0.555*** (0.079)
Violent territorial transfer	0.361*** (0.101)	0.146 (0.107)
Defense pact with all neighbors	0.895*** (0.098)	0.566*** (0.101)
Highest neighbor militarization	−5.654** (1.850)	−12.339*** (2.477)
Either targeted in territorial MID	−0.541*** (0.066)	
Huth and Allee (2002) dispute		−0.764*** (0.059)
Constant	−0.748*** (0.084)	0.041 (0.101)
N	18,449	13,205

Dependent variable is the observation of joint democracy in the dyad. Analyses includes all contiguous dyads, estimated using logistic regression with robust standard errors. Coefficients listed with standard errors in parentheses. $*p < 0.05$, $**p < 0.01$, $***p < 0.001$.

established democracies in the world may be significantly outnumbered by all the new states that have entered the system as democracies since the Cold War.

The civil war onset variable also predicts (negatively) the observation of joint democracy in both models. I believe that civils wars often upset the status quo of the international border by calling into question previous divisions of territory in the dyad. These results are consistent with that interpretation.

Poor border specification may also matter for observation of democracy in the dyad since the same colonial master variable is negative and statistically significant in both models. Countries that have the same colonial master are less likely to have a heritage of strong border definition. There was less of a need for the colonial owner to accurately and consistently demarcate across its own lands, it would seem.

Interestingly, *both* territorial transfer variables – violent and peaceful – are positively related to joint democracy. The rationale for peaceful transfers and democracy is straightforward: peaceful transfers lead to border legitimacy, which leads to demilitarization, decentralization, and, eventually, democratization (Gibler and Tir 2010). But, this argument provides little reason for why violent transfers are related to democracy. It could be the case that violent transfers often represent overwhelming victories, and this then leads to eventual pacification of the border area. That the variable is only statistically significant at any reasonable level in the full model suggests this interpretation may be correct, since many of the violent transfers of the nineteenth century were followed by the preponderance of the victorious side.

Consistent with my earlier work with Scott Wolford, having a defense pact signed with all neighboring states is positively related to joint democracy in the dyad for both models. As we demonstrate (Gibler and Wolford 2006), defense pacts reduce threat, and this leads to demilitarization in both states, and democratization follows. Further confirming that the effects of militarization are indeed counter-productive for democracy, a high level of militarization among at least one neighbor of either state in the dyad contributes strongly to the observance of non-democracy in both models. Again, consistent with the earlier argument and other threat variables, militarization among neighbors leads to centralization in targeted states.

Finally, the presence of a territorial threat, defined as either a MID over territory or one of Huth and Allee's (2002) territorial disputes, discourages joint democracy in the dyad. As with militarization, territorial threat consistently affects regime type as centralization of the targeted state follows these issues.

An implicit result of these analyses is the fact that democracies do tend to cluster together across borders. Were this not so, joint democracy as a dependent variable would be difficult to predict. The analyses include only contiguous states, and almost all the stable border proxies do well at predicting joint democracy in the dyad. Of course, the next step is to determine whether these predictors also account for the effects of democracy on international conflict.

7.5 International borders, joint democracy, and international conflict

I estimate the effects of joint democracy and border stability on conflict using six separate logit models, covering the years 1816 to 2000 and 1919 to 1995, with the shorter sample using Huth and Allee (2002) definitions of territorial disputes. In all cases, the dependent variable is fatal MID onset, and the independent variables include democracy, several common controls for conflict, and the proxies for border stability.

I measure democracy using both a weak link specification based on the lowest Polity IV score in the dyad (Dixon 1994; Russett and Oneal 2001) and a dummy variable for joint democracy, in which the lowest Polity IV score in the dyad is 7 or above. I use both specifications because the results in the last section demonstrate well that the border variables accurately predict the observance of joint democracy in the dyad; therefore, the inclusion of the border variables in the same model with joint democracy as an independent variable may introduce multicollinearity into the models. While not a large problem given the sample sizes in the analyses, the multicollinearity is unnecessary since my theory predicts only that joint democracy is likely, not the level of democracy in each state of the dyad. In other words, strong borders constitute a near necessary condition for the observance of joint democracy in the dyad, but variations in border strength do not predict variations in regime type. Thus, while the border variables are highly correlated with joint democracy, the weak link specification has a more modest relationship with geography.[9]

An even better reason for also using the weak link specification is that recent research suggests it is superior to the dichotomous, joint democracy indicator for measuring the conflict effects of dyadic democracy. Developed by Dixon (1994), and used interchangeably with joint democracy by Russett and Oneal (2001), among others, Dixon and Goertz (2005) demonstrate through a series of empirical tests that, "dyadic relations depend primarily on the behavioral constraints of the less democratic state no matter how tightly constrained its more democratic partner." In any case, as is clear from the results in Table 7.2, the results are robust to each specification of democracy.

The first model again provides a baseline for the lowest democracy score specification and demonstrates that democracy reduces the likelihood of conflict, even after controlling for parity, alliances, and temporal dependence.

---

[9] Joint democracy and the weak link specification are highly correlated but empirically distinct measures of democracy in my data set. For example, joint democracy is correlated with the weak link specification at 0.767 in the sample that includes all years, 1816 to 2000, and 0.778 in the sample that includes 1919 through 1995.

Table 7.2 *International borders and fatal militarized disputes*

	(1) 1816–2000	(2) 1816–2000	(3) 1919–1995	(4) 1816–2000	(5) 1816–2000	(6) 1919–1995
Low democracy score	-0.014*	-0.011	-0.009		-0.060	-0.097
	(0.007)	(0.008)	(0.009)		(0.166)	(0.173)
Joint democracy dummy				-0.311†		
				(0.163)		
Capability ratio	0.777***	0.756***	0.764***	0.778***	0.770***	0.779***
	(0.134)	(0.148)	(0.164)	(0.134)	(0.148)	(0.164)
Allied	-0.649***	-0.588***	-0.802***	-0.632***	-0.575***	-0.790***
	(0.104)	(0.118)	(0.136)	(0.104)	(0.118)	(0.135)
Peace years	-0.456***	-0.409***	-0.443***	-0.454***	-0.409***	-0.443***
	(0.039)	(0.035)	(0.049)	(0.039)	(0.035)	(0.049)
Peace years^2	0.013***	0.012***	0.013***	0.013***	0.012***	0.013***
	(0.002)	(0.002)	(0.003)	(0.002)	(0.002)	(0.003)
Peace years^3	-0.000***	-0.000***	-0.000**	-0.000***	-0.000***	-0.000**
	(0.000)	(0.000)	(0.000)	(0.000)	(0.000)	(0.000)
Natural log of dyad duration		0.223***	0.221***		0.226***	0.225***
		(0.031)	(0.037)		(0.032)	(0.036)
Intra-state war in either state		0.191†	0.230*		0.193†	0.233*
		(0.100)	(0.111)		(0.100)	(0.110)
Same colonial master		0.241*	0.393**		0.228*	0.391**
		(0.107)	(0.123)		(0.107)	(0.124)

Table 7.2 (cont.)

	(1) 1816–2000	(2) 1816–2000	(3) 1919–1995	(4) 1816–2000	(5) 1816–2000	(6) 1919–1995
Peaceful territorial transfer		−0.464*	−0.540**		−0.475**	−0.546**
		(0.181)	(0.197)		(0.181)	(0.197)
Violent territorial transfer		0.467***	0.457***		0.451***	0.447***
		(0.123)	(0.131)		(0.122)	(0.131)
Defense pact with all neighbors		−0.495†	−0.381		−0.533*	−0.414
		(0.270)	(0.286)		(0.267)	(0.279)
Highest neighbor militarization		13.507***	12.078***		13.385***	12.240***
		(1.615)	(2.643)		(1.612)	(2.638)
Either targeted in territorial MID		0.386***			0.386***	
		(0.095)			(0.095)	
Territorial MID × militarization		3.382			3.426	
		(3.350)			(3.368)	
Huth and Allee (2002) dispute			0.014			0.020
			(0.119)			(0.119)
Huth and Allee dispute × militarization			18.070***			17.919***
			(4.084)			(4.077)
Constant	−1.839***	−3.203***	−3.066***	−1.754***	−3.153***	−3.038***
	(0.092)	(0.135)	(0.168)	(0.081)	(0.133)	(0.176)
N	19,026	19,026	13,702	19,026	19,026	13,702

Dependent variable is the initiation of a fatal MID in the dyad. Analyses includes all contiguous dyads, estimated using logistic regression with robust standard errors. Coefficients listed with standard errors in parentheses. $^{†}p < 0.10$, $^{*}p < 0.05$, $^{**}p < 0.01$, $^{***}p < 0.001$.

Each variable is statistically significant, and the results suggest that parity increases conflict while the presence of an alliance decreases conflict. Models 2 and 3 add the border control variables to the basic specification. The control variables remain substantively unchanged in these two models, but the low democracy score in the dyad is no longer statistically significant at any conventional level. Together with the results from the last section predicting joint democracy, this change in effect of democracy suggests the proxies for stable borders are (1) strongly correlated with democracy in the dyad and (2) account for democracy's peace-inducing effects.

The border variables themselves are also again consistent with my theoretical expectations. Civil wars and the presence of two colonies with the same colonial master both predict fatal conflict in each model. Territorial transfers are also related to conflict as peaceful transfers are more likely to be followed by peaceful relations while violent transfers seem to breed additional violence. A defense pact with all neighbors reduces conflict in the full, 1816–2000 model, but not the post-World War I model that uses the Huth and Allee (2002) data. Surprisingly, older borders are associated with more fatal MIDs than younger borders.

Among the territorial threat variables, the highest level of militarization among neighbors predicts fatal conflict well. In models not reported here, the inclusion only of a territorial dispute variable, or a claim identified by Huth and Allee (2002), suggests that territorial threats are indeed conflict-prone at a statistically significant rate. However, that may be due to the conflation of claims and low-level disputes with highly militarized conflicts. As the above models demonstrate, the inclusion of an interaction term identifies the dangerous claims. Disputes or claims are not enough, it would seem, to constitute serious threats to homeland territories. This finding is consistent with the argument that conflicting claims do not always imply salient threats to the states involved.[10]

Models 4–6 repeat the prior models using the joint democracy dummy variable. For each model the results are quite similar to the lowest democracy specification. In fact, there are only minor changes in comparison to Models 1–3, as once again joint democracy is statistically significant ($p < 0.10$) in the baseline model but disappears once controls are added for stable borders. (In Models 5 and 6 the coefficient is actually smaller than the standard error.) These results again provide rather convincing evidence that, at least among contiguous states, the peaceful effects of democracy are spurious to stable borders.

---

[10] See, again, my arguments in Chapter 2 regarding differences in how others have identified territorial threats to the state.

7.6 A note on alternate specifications

Of course these findings are provocative since they challenge a large body of literature with a substantial number of findings supporting the democratic peace. I have therefore tested the argument using multiple specifications of both territorial peace and territorially unstable borders.

First, in a piece I wrote with Jaroslav Tir, we used border specifications based on peaceful transfers of territory (Gibler and Tir 2010). As I have argued throughout this book, not all international borders are the same. In this chapter I argue that stable borders correlate well with the existence of geographic salients. In the work with Tir, we identify peaceful borders using the existence of prior territorial transfers that were mutually agreed upon by the states involved. By focusing the analysis on international borders that have been altered by mutual consent, we identify a set of border cases that are likely to have a greater degree of legitimacy since the neighboring states have demonstrated positive motivation, trust, and credible commitment toward territorial dispute resolution. Borders settled through peaceful transfers therefore provide a critical set of "positive peace" cases for testing the peace-to-democracy thesis found throughout this book.

Our results provide strong support for the argument that settled international boundaries decrease the level of threat to the territorial integrity of states. We demonstrated that peaceful transfers are prominent among the factors increasing the rate of transitions to democracy.[11] We also find that there is empirical support for the expected processes that lead to democratization. First, peaceful transfers reduce the chances that a state will be targeted in the future by military force over its border; this confirms that peacefully adjusted borders are indeed more settled. Second, when examining the effects of peaceful transfers, we confirmed a link to substantially lower levels of militarization within the country during future years. These findings reinforce the contention that settled borders are associated with political decentralization and liberalization within the state.

A second alternate specification leverages the tendency for conflicts to recur spatially and temporally to test the territorial peace theory. In work with Alex Braithwaite (Gibler and Braithwaite N.d.), we find that territorial "hot spots" occur frequently, indicating geographic dependence in the data on conflict (see also Braithwaite 2005). Moreover, these hot spots provide a good, behavioral indicator of territorial threat in the region and eliminate a reliance on geographic salients. Substituting the behavioral, hot spot indicator of territorial

---

[11] Importantly, we also demonstrated that our analyses are not by-products of the argument that democracy leads to peaceful transfers; our analyses clearly affirm that democratic regime type has no appreciable influence on the likelihood of peaceful transfers in the dyad.

threat in models predicting fatal MID onset, we find that the presence of a territorial hot spot eliminates any statistically significant relationship between joint democracy and fatal MIDs. Only an interaction of hot spot indicator and democracy restores the influence of joint democracy in the model, but this indicator implies that peace based on regime type only matters in the context of territorially peaceful regions.

The research in this chapter has been confirmed in three separate studies with alternate codings of the key explanatory variable(s). I have operationalized border stability using geographic salients (Gibler 2007), territorial transfers (Gibler and Tir 2010), and regional territorial "hot spots" (Gibler and Braithwaite N.d.), and the results have been consistent across each specification. This suggests that territorial peace theory is a robust predictor of peace and conflict in the dyad.

7.7 Conclusions

By endogenizing the emergence of jointly democratic dyads to a series of factors that affect democracy and conflict behavior, my results suggest that what scholars know as the democratic peace may be, in fact, a stable border peace. This is the first step toward looking at international conflict a little bit differently.

A stable border peace implies that democratic states are more peaceful with their neighbors, but this is not due to any quality inherent in democratic government; rather, the development path necessary for democratization selects democracies into a group of states that have settled borders, few territorial issues, and, thus, little reason for war against neighbors. With only minor, nonterritorial issues remaining for these states, mediation and arbitration become both easier and more likely for democracies, while the need for defensive alliances, military buildups, and aggressive crisis bargaining also decreases.

Because borders are international institutions (Simmons 2006), they affect the development paths of both states in the dyad, and stabilized borders that decrease the need for militarization and centralization in one state also tend to demilitarize and decentralize the neighboring state. "Zones of peace" can thus be understood as the contagion effect of stabilized borders, as democracies cluster in time and space following the removal of territorial issues. This clustering of peaceful states, a neighborhood effect (Maoz 2010), should also affect the economic development of the states involved. With less money needed for guns, spending for butter increases, and trade across settled borders poses less of a risk.

While this chapter has focused on relations among neighboring, contiguous states, the next piece of the territorial peace puzzle involves explaining how peaceful relations with neighbors affects foreign policy decisions abroad. States that are free from neighbors' threats are uniquely privileged. Freed from constant homeland defense, their leaders face few serious threats to state and interests, and the disputes that do escalate to conflict abroad are much more likely to be matters of choice. I explain the implications of these incentives in the next two chapters.

8

Territorial peace and negotiated compromises

8.1 Introduction

In the last chapter I demonstrated that stable borders greatly affect relations between contiguous states. Settled borders encourage both peace and democratization. I also argued that these states at peace face different types of issues than most other states. With territorial issues removed from their agendas, the conflicts that do confront these states are likely to be of lesser consequence and more easily managed. Thus, states at territorial peace should be more likely to negotiate compromises of their disputes. I test that expectation in this chapter.[1]

The baseline for tests in this chapter is once again a strong empirical regularity demonstrating variation in negotiation according to regime type. The logic of this argument follows from the domestic political norms to which democratic leaders are accustomed: since democratic leaders are normatively bounded not to use violence and coercion in dealing with domestic rivals, they are acculturated to treat potential international rivals in the same way. When two democracies have an international dispute, each trusts that the other is bounded by the same norm and cultured in the same non-violent approach. In short, democracies trust each other enough to peacefully negotiate settlements to their dispute. However, when the dyad includes at least one non-democratic state, this level of trust breaks down (Russett and Oneal 2001, 64–66).

If my argument is correct, norms of behavior are of little consequence in predicting negotiated settlements. Instead, most democracies are likely to be members of a group of states that have settled their border issues with neighbors. The resolution of territorial issues prior to democratization assures that democratic leaders will have few dangerous territorial issues to resolve, and this

---

[1] Chapters 8 and 9 present much revised versions of earlier research that was originally coauthored with Steve Miller (Miller and Gibler 2011; Gibler and Miller 2012).

leads naturally to the empirical regularity associating democracy with peaceful dispute resolution.

My argument of course broadens the class of states likely to settle disputes peacefully, through negotiation. Rather than focusing only on democracy, all territorial peace states are unlikely to face threats to homeland territories. Thus, the issues that are on the agenda will be of low salience to the public, easier to resolve, and constitute little direct threat to the state.

I develop the argument in the following sections. First, I briefly review the democratic peace theory literature that establishes the link between democracy and peaceful dispute settlement. I then discuss the importance of issue selection in understanding the negotiation studies. If, as I suspect, territorial issues are selected out of the sample of issues confronting democratic leaders, then controlling for issue type and settled borders will temper the idea that the incentives democratic leaders face matter in this context.

8.2 Democracies and peaceful dispute settlement

The connection between jointly democratic dyads and the presence of negotiated settlements is an important relationship that developed in the 1990s from the democratic peace research project. Democratic peace theorists were trying to resolve a puzzle: if democracies do not drastically differ from non-democracies in their ability to be involved in international conflict (Vincent 1987) and initiate wars (Small and Singer 1976; Chan 1984; Weede 1984), then why does the presence of joint democracy in a dyad drive the probability of war in a dyad to near zero (Babst 1964, 1972; Rummel 1983; Maoz and Abdolali 1989; Bremer 1992; Maoz and Russett 1992; Russett 1993)?

Initial scholarship that sought to address this anomaly did so by focusing on the unique institutional and decisional constraints of democracies (Merritt and Zinnes 1991; Morgan and Campbell 1991; Lake 1992). However, this initial presentation of an institutional perspective to democratic peace theory suffered from several limitations. The early institutional perspectives struggled with observable rally effects in democracies (Mueller 1973) and generally assumed a monadic perspective of the democratic peace, which does not coincide with the empirical confirmation that democracies are still conflict-prone, just not with each other (see also Bueno de Mesquita *et al.* [2003, chapter 6] for this point).

The competing perspective within the democratic peace theory tradition places most explanatory power on democratic norms, not institutions. Starting with the assumption that there are fundamental normative differences between democracies and autocracies (Russett 1993), it becomes clear that autocrats have few, if any, normative bounds on their behavior. They may capture the state through use of lethal force and violence. They may also keep their hold on power through the same means, suppressing any dissent. Autocratic foreign policy behavior thus reflects the autocrat's preferences. The autocrat does not need or respect the preferences of his subjects within his state and thus behaves the same way towards others outside the state. Democracies, by contrast, rest on fundamental norms of equal competition, minority rights, and consent to be governed. Use of force and repression to govern would be deemed "illegitimate" by both the majority and minority, which enacts normative restraints on violent behavior and is eventually codified in law. Just as autocrats externalize this domestic norm in their foreign policy, so do the democratic leaders externalize their internal norms in foreign policy. International politics then essentially becomes an extension of domestic politics.

Dixon's (1994) "norm of bounded competition" is the clearest articulation of this theory that is able to explain both aspects of the democratic peace research. While democracies vary in some social and cultural norms as well as institutional mechanisms, the norm of bounded competition is common to all democracies. Rivals in democracies openly compete for scarce resources and policy outcomes, but they do so with rules and restraints that normatively restrict political actors not to use coercion or violence. A "contingent consent" follows from this universal democratic norm (Schmitter and Karl 1991). Aware that unregulated competition creates intolerable risks and uncertainty for all, political elites trust each other not to use force or violence during the electoral contest or any time after it. Since leaders, democratic leaders especially (Joffe 1990), view international politics as an extension of democratic politics, this norm of bounded competition surfaces in international disputes. When two democracies are locked in the early phases of an interstate conflict, the leader of each democracy is secure in their knowledge that the leader of the other state is bounded by the same norm. When a democratic leader is confronted by an autocrat, the democrat does not believe that the autocrat is bounded by any norm, and nothing remains to restrain escalation. This normative perspective generates a unique answer to the paradoxes of the democratic peace. Democratic leaders do not trust autocracies but trust each other to the point where they peacefully negotiate settlements to their disputes before war is an option.

This normative explanation of democratic difference applies to other mechanisms as well, and, while the institutional perspective also predicts dyadic peace, the normative perspective constitutes the theoretical backdrop for much of the empirical support linking democratic dyads and peaceful dispute settlements, such as arbitration, mediated settlements, and mutual compromises. For example, Dixon (1993) is the first to identify the absence of conflict management research that links governing arrangements and peaceful dispute settlement. His analysis shows that the presence of joint democracy in a conflict increases the probability that conflict will result in some form of conflict management, as defined by Skjelsbaek (1986). In his later article, Dixon (1994) found that the democracy-settlement hypothesis is robust, even when controlling for past hostilities. Dixon and Senese (2002) reaffirm the positive relationship between democracy and negotiated settlements, which is robust even when the temporal domain of 1816 to 1992 is disaggregated.[2]

The research on norms and negotiation demonstrates persuasively that democracies are more likely to be associated with peaceful dispute settlement. But do these settlements last? Raymond (1996) provides evidence that the duration of democratic settlements differs little from settlements made by other leaders. Operationalizing durability as the absence of a militarized dispute in a five-year window after an arbitration decision, jointly democratic dyads and mixed/non-democratic dyads do not differ in their arbitration outcomes, even when controls for socio-cultural homogeneity and power distribution are introduced. The difference in research design is important here. Raymond (1996) controls for the salience of the dispute when analyzing the arbitration outcome, defining salience, at least in part, based on the presence of a territorial issue in the dispute.[3] This suggests an important connection between territorial issues and the relationship between democracy and peace.

The Raymond (1996) study hints at the territory-based critique of the literature on democracy and peaceful dispute settlement. Simply put, much of the seminal work linking democratic dyads and peaceful conflict management has not taken the issues at stake into consideration. In this case, specification of the issues driving the dispute alters our understanding of the link between democracy and negotiation and demonstrates that certain types of issues are more difficult to resolve than others. Issues like territory are more difficult to manage, and their presence (or absence) in a sample will likely skew most estimates.

---

[2] Raymond (1994) suggests that norms also influence the use of third-party intermediaries. If the democracy-settlement hypothesis and the normative perspective are correct, then democracies should be more likely to employ binding forms of third-party arbitration, which is exactly what Raymond finds.

[3] Partially following Coplin and Rochester (1972), Raymond (1996) incorporates issues of contractual obligations (1), treatment of persons (2), property damages from military operations (3), and territorial issues and seizures (4) into his four-part scale of the "intensity dimension" of the dispute. Where issues of territory are the biggest determinant of salience of an arbitration outcome in this coding, it may not be surprising that jointly democratic dyads do not differ from other dyad types in meaningful arbitration outcomes.

8.3 Territorial issues and negotiation

In Chapter 3, I argued that territorial issues are difficult to resolve for several reasons. First, territorial issues between contiguous states necessitate large, standing, land armies, and these are difficult to dismantle to an extent that will eliminate fear among targeted citizens. These armies are also not easily dismantled without severe consequences to the state, the economy, and the strategic balance of capabilities in the dyad. Territorial conflicts create an international context that makes dispute resolution difficult and recurrence likely.

Territorial peace will also affect the composition of the military. Absent the need for defending homeland territories, the role of the military shifts in order to project power over distances, either through the air or at sea. Neither the air force nor the navy is a useful tool for repression, but both enable the state's leaders to involve the state in distant conflicts. Thus, where territorial disputes do emerge for states with stable borders, the issues are likely to involve colonial holdings or otherwise distant territories. While these issues may mire elites in crisis bargaining, disputes in far-flung stretches of the globe are less salient and unlikely to arouse publics to the same degree as direct threats to the territorial integrity of the state.

Since territorial conflicts with neighbors have been selected out of the issues facing leaders of states at territorial peace, the sample of disputes that do involve these states differs fundamentally from those that involve authoritarian leaders. Direct threats to the territorial composition of the state necessarily preoccupy a targeted state and confine its conflicts locally. Once these threats are resolved, however, the decisions for dispute onset or dispute escalation become matters of choice. The conflicts a state may select itself into typically do not involve border issues. Instead, disputes for states at territorial peace involve less salient issues of imperialist claims, matters of policy, and regime preferences around the international system, and when the issues are of minor importance to elites and publics, the need to handle disputes with power politics is reduced. Accordingly, mediation and arbitration for states that enjoy a stable border peace are more likely.

One way of demonstrating that the basis for negotiation is indeed determined by issue is to actually examine the issues under contention, as Mitchell and Prins (1999) have done. According to Mitchell and Prins, of the 23 disputes between fully democratic states in the international system from 1946 to 1992, only 2 involved issues of territory. By contrast, territorial disputes between states with a Polity III score less than 10 account for 31 of 74 disputes during the same time period. More telling are the types of disputes that do involve fully democratic dyads. Commercial interests are principally at stake in these disputes, but the substance of these commercial interests commonly involves maritime boundaries and fishing rights. Fishing disputes in particular constitute 25 percent of the democratic dyadic disputes from 1946 to 1992. Further, these disputes are reciprocated by the target less than 20 percent of the time, and, actually, more than half of these disputes are only one-day affairs. This sample provides important preliminary evidence that the issues confronting democracies are substantially different in kind from the issues involving most authoritarian states.

This argument has important implications for any search for predictors of negotiation in disputes. For example, I argue that territorial peace is a concept that includes most democracies as a subset. Also included, however, are those non-democracies without the requisite predictors of democracy – wealth, income equality, a middle class, etc. Those studies that focus on regime type only are likely to find the association between democracy and dispute negotiation but miss the larger relationship. Non-territorial issues are, in general, easier to negotiate through compromise, and the empirical relationship is determined by issue, not regime type.

The theoretical consistency across democratic peace scholarship on this empirical problem allows a straightforward comparative test with territorial peace theory. Democratic peace theory provides a regime-type explanation of international relations – democracies are supposed to be fundamentally different from autocracies with respect to norms of governance and this affects their propensity to negotiate compromises of international disputes. However, if my argument is correct, the association between democracy and negotiated compromises should be the result of the different issues that are likely to confront democratic leaders. With territorial issues removed from the agenda, the remaining disputes should be easier to settle peacefully.

Thus, in hypothesis form, I expect first a simple relationship between the presence of a territorial issue and the likelihood of disputants finding a negotiated compromise to the issue:

$H_{8.1}$: *Territorial disputes between contiguous states are the disputes least likely to end with negotiated compromises.*

Of course, $H_{8.1}$ implies, by extension, that any state in which territorial issues have been removed from the agenda will also be more likely to settle their disputes through negotiation. Without territorial threats confronting the homeland, the average salience of all issues decreases. State agendas shift toward cooperation, and any issues that do arise are likely to be less consequential than the zero-sum politics of territorial gain. Thus, I also expect that:

H$_{8.2}$: *States at territorial peace are more likely to settle their disputes with negotiated compromises.*

Finally, if democratic peace theories are correct, the internal norms of democracy should affect their international behavior as well. In hypothesis form:

H$_{8.3}$: *Democratic leaders are more likely than autocratic leaders to settle their disputes with negotiated compromises.*

8.4 Modeling choices and variable definition

I again test my argument using data from the Correlates of War Militarized Interstate Dispute (MID) data set. However, I restrict my sample to those dyad-years in which a dispute was initiated; thus, the sample includes 2,485 directed, dispute-dyad-onset years. I use directed dyads in disputes to capture the regime type and the level of threat facing the initiating state. Using disputes as the unit of analysis has at least two important advantages. First, previous works in the conflict selection literature gave greater emphasis to the onset of wars. In doing so, these previous works ignored the disputes that were peacefully negotiated short of war. I avoid this selection bias by including all disputes. Second, the MID data provide an important robustness check on the earlier research that relied on a cross-section of data from such sources as Darby (1904), Ralston (1929), Levine (1971), Stuyt (1972), Butterworth and Scranton (1976), and Alker and Sherman (1986), and mimics the sampling procedures of Mousseau (1998) and Dixon and Senese (2002). In short, this presents a test of dispute negotiation on the most comprehensive temporal domain available.

8.4.1 Dependent variable

The MID data set has two important variables capturing how a dispute was terminated: "outcome" and "settlement." I am specifically interested in settlements that were negotiated and outcomes that were the result of compromise. Negotiation as a conflict resolution process exists when the effort by disputants to confer, bargain, or discuss an issue of contention among the disputants is successfully executed en route to a mutually acceptable settlement. The MID data set codes compromises as outcomes where the disputants agree to divide the issue between them roughly equally or agree to accept the current status quo (Jones, Bremer and Singer 1996, 180–181).

Previous analyses using the MID data set have focused on the existence of compromise as a MID outcome (Mousseau 1998), or on the presence or absence of negotiation in the dispute resolution process (Dixon and Senese 2002). The two have been isolated from each other. It is important to consider cases where disputes were *both* negotiated and resulted in a compromise. Analyzing these cases in a single model is a fairer test of the theory. For example, if the norm of bounded competition leads to mutual trust between democracies, then a negotiated end to the dispute where a target yielded, or another state was victorious in the dispute, cannot be disentangled from power politics behavior. Here, disputes may end in negotiated settlements not because of norms of trust and respect, but because more powerful states can use the threat of their superiority to make it impractical for one side to continue a dispute. While negotiating a settlement under these conditions (a yield by a target or a victory by either side) is practical, it is inconsistent with the expectations of democratic peace theory. The same problem exists for MIDs that end with imposed compromises.

The dependent variable measures instances of both negotiated settlement and compromised outcome in the dispute. In the MID data set, this occurs when the "outcome" variable has a value of "compromise" (a code of 6 in the value list) and the "settlement" variable has a value of "negotiated" (a code of 1 in the value list). I code the dependent variable as 1 when these criteria are satisfied and code all other cases as 0. With a dichotomous response variable, I fit a logistic regression to the sample.

8.4.2 Independent variables

I use the models I derived in Chapter 7 to identify those states that are at territorial peace. First, I estimate the predicted probability of conflict for each directed dyad-year from 1816 to 2000 and calculate the predicted probability of conflict based only on the territorial variables in the model.[4] I then estimated each state's highest dyadic-level probability of territorial conflict for each year. This constitutes the maximum level of territorial threat faced by the state and one of its neighbors. I define states at territorial peace as those states in the bottom 5 percent of this measure, and I lag this dummy variable one year to determine the level of territorial peace in the year prior to the dispute.

I use a dichotomous variable for three reasons. First, the democracy indicators from this literature generally identify the presence (or absence) of democracy in the state, and the territorial peace dummy variable allows for a direct comparison

---

[4] These variables include the natural log of dyad duration, the presence of an intra-state war in either the state or a neighboring state, the same colonial master for both states in the dyad, peaceful transfers, violent transfers, defense pacts with all neighbors, highest level of militarization among neighbors, either state being targeted by a territorial MID in the previous year, and the interaction of being targeted by a territorial MID and militarization.

with these variables. Second, though not true for the analyses in this chapter, there are non-linear effects across the range of the territorial threat variable for several of the victory-in-conflict models examined in the next chapter. These non-linear effects may mask the relationship between states at territorial peace and negotiation or dispute victory. Use of the dummy variable allows me to identify those state-years actually at territorial peace, rather than those states with relatively higher levels of peace (but which still face real threats to homelands).[5] This leads to my third reason: my argument implies a tipping point. Moderate levels of territorial threat still constitute threats to the state; only the elimination of those threats will also remove the international constraints placed on the leader. Therefore, the use of a dummy variable is more consistent with the theory described in Chapter 3.

I again determine the level of democracy using the Polity IV data set (Marshall and Jaggers 2002), which considers six measures of executive recruitment, political competition, and constraints on executive authority in its 11-point index. Consistent with the Polity IV project and my other analyses, I again define a state to be democratic when the Polity IV score is equal to or greater than +6.[6]

I include a control for whether the dispute involved a territorial issue, as defined by the Correlates of War Project. I code the presence of a territorial dispute when the potential initiator (State A in a MID) is attempting to change the territorial status quo with State B. All other disputes that do not satisfy this definition are coded as 0.[7] I also provide a control for contiguity. Contiguity is defined as direct contiguity using the Correlates of War scale (Stinnett *et al.* 2002). Contiguity has been long considered an important correlate of war, and I expect that this control will exert a negative influence on the likelihood of a dispute ending in a negotiated compromise (Diehl 1985; Bremer 1992, 2000).

I account for potential confounding factors in the estimates of negotiation by employing several controls. First, I identify the presence of an alliance in a dyad (Gibler and Sarkees 2004). Alliances have been linked to both democracy (Siverson and Emmons 1991; Simon and Gartzke 1996) and decreased territorial threat (Gibler and Wolford 2006). Second, I control for the capability ratio across the dyad. The capability ratio is defined as the natural logarithm of the ratio of the CINC score of State A over State B in the directed dispute-dyad.

---

[5] I discuss the curvilinear effects of this variable in the next section.

[6] The results are not sensitive to this cut point. Robustness checks using both +5 and +7 on the Polity IV scale do not create substantive changes in the results.

[7] This definition introduces some bias when both states in the dispute-dyad are revisionist, such as during "clashes." For the tests in this chapter, I include both directed dyads in these cases; however, tests using a random determination of the initiator do not differ from those presented here.

8.5 Predicting negotiated compromises

The results from my analyses using directed dispute-dyads are presented below in Table 8.1. Nevertheless, there is good reason to believe that there may be a correlation of errors between MID selection and the outcome of the MID-negotiated compromise or otherwise (Heckman 1979; Sartori 2003); the likelihood of arriving at a negotiated compromise in a dispute may influence the likelihood of a dispute occurring in the first place. However, I do not find that this is the case empirically and, therefore, present only the directed dispute-dyad results.[8]

I employ an estimation procedure that is similar to the types of analyses I presented in previous chapters. First, Model 1 provides an analysis of territorial peace on the likelihood of negotiated compromises of the dispute. The presence of territorial peace in State A does initially correlate with the likelihood of a negotiated compromise. Model 2 adds an interaction term for the level of territorial peace in State A and whether State B is contiguous. The inclusion of this interaction confirms the pacifying effect for territorial peace but also demonstrates that the effect is limited to non-contiguous dispute cases. States at territorial peace have difficulty resolving disputes with their neighbors ($p < 0.05$). This of course supports my argument that issue salience has a strong geographic component and provides empirical support for $H_{8.1}$ and $H_{8.2}$.

Models 3 and 4 provide a specification of the regime-based argument, but neither democracy score seems to matter. Democratic initiators are not more or less likely than other states to seek negotiated compromises, even if the rival state is democratic as well.[9] In the final estimation, Model 4, I combine both sets of predictors as a joint test of territory and regime type. The interpretation of this model is completely consistent with the estimation that includes the territorial peace interaction term – Model 2. Territorial peace is again associated

---

[8] For a discussion of similar Heckman models of conflict selection and negotiated compromises, see Miller and Gibler (2011).

[9] I confirmed the robustness of this result with several additional models. First, I estimated the effect of democratic initiators without the presence of the joint democracy interaction term. Neither the democratic initiator variable nor the democratic target variable was significant in this model. Second, I examined whether the results in Table 8.1 were based on the use of joint democracy as an indicator rather than the lower democracy score in the dyad. In an initial model, the lower democracy score was indeed statistically significant ($p < 0.01$) and in the expected direction – higher democracy scores in the dyad predicted negotiated compromises. However, confirming the results presented in Table 8.1, the statistically significant effect for the lower democracy score is *not* due to the presence of democracies among those states seeking negotiated compromises. Instead, both authoritarian states (lower democracy score less than -6) *and* democracies (lower democracy score greater than 6) are unlikely to seek negotiated compromises. A final multivariate model confirms this. A specification that includes the lower democracy score and its square demonstrates a curvilinear relationship as the lower democracy score is positive and statistically significant ($p < 0.01$), but the coefficient for the square of the democracy measure is negative and statistically significant ($p < 0.01$). These results are available as part of the replication data set supporting the book.

Table 8.1 *Predicting negotiation in militarized disputes, 1816–2000*

	(1)	(2)	(3)	(4)
Territorial peace variables				
Territorial peace state A	0.548*	1.020**		1.041**
	(0.263)	(0.346)		(0.349)
Territorial peace state B	0.227	0.235		0.231
	(0.264)	(0.265)		(0.268)
Territorial peace state A		−0.843*		−0.826*
× Contiguous MID		(0.419)		(0.420)
Territorial dispute	0.783***	0.765***	0.795***	0.768***
	(0.184)	(0.184)	(0.184)	(0.184)
Contiguous MID	0.388*	0.640**	0.344	0.658**
	(0.197)	(0.239)	(0.203)	(0.245)
Regime variables				
State A is democracy			0.044	0.100
			(0.242)	(0.242)
State B is democracy			−0.223	−0.144
			(0.248)	(0.249)
Both states are democratic			0.428	0.423
			(0.424)	(0.427)
Control variables				
Allied states	0.714***	0.670***	0.599**	0.632**
	(0.193)	(0.194)	(0.195)	(0.198)
Capability ratio	0.067	0.065	0.061	0.061
	(0.038)	(0.039)	(0.039)	(0.040)
Constant	−3.579***	−3.733***	−3.349***	−3.764***
	(0.181)	(0.207)	(0.204)	(0.245)
Number of observations	2,315	2,315	2,315	2,315
pseudo R^2	0.051	0.055	0.043	0.057
LR χ^2	55.85***	59.94***	46.80***	62.31***

Sample includes all directed dyads during their first year of a dispute, 1816–2000, inclusive; dependent variable is a Negotiated Compromise to the dispute.
* $p < 0.05$, ** $p < 0.01$, *** $p < 0.001$.

with negotiated compromises, and this seems mostly due to the large number of lower-salience, non-contiguous disputes experienced by these states. States at territorial peace again have great difficulty resolving disputes with their neighbors ($p < 0.05$). Regime type continues to have no effect, disproving the baseline hypothesis, $H_{8.3}$.

One surprising finding in Table 8.1 is the effect of territorial issues on the likelihood of negotiated compromises. This variable is a positive predictor of compromise in each model. I explored this result further by also estimating a separate model that included an interaction for territorial disputes between contiguous states. As expected, these types of disputes are incredibly difficult to resolve, and the interaction term is negative and statistically significant ($p < 0.003$), while the component terms of contiguity and territorial issue both remain positive and statistically significant ($p < 0.004$).[10] It would seem, therefore, that the positive coefficient for territorial issues is driven by the presence of numerous colonial and other, non-contiguous holdings; territorial issues among neighbors remain most dangerous.

Overall, the results shown in Table 8.1 provide support for my argument of the primacy of territorial issues and selections effects among disputes. States at territorial peace are more likely to seek compromise, and this is likely because the difficult-to-resolve issues have been selected out of their foreign policy agenda. Theories of democratic state behavior, meanwhile, may provide a facile link to negotiated compromises, but not in these analyses that also specify issue type. Indeed, in none of the models was regime type a statistically significant predictor of negotiated compromise. It would seem that the issues in dispute are of greater consequence.

8.6 Confirming the role of issues

While the above results provide supporting evidence that states at territorial peace are more likely to negotiate compromises to their disputes, the analyses did not necessarily provide evidence for the causal mechanism that was responsible for the relationship. Instead of states at territorial peace confronting easily resolved issues, it could still be the case that some other factor leads these states to negotiate compromises with their dispute rivals. Therefore, to confirm the differences in issue importance across states, I developed an estimate for the likelihood of conflict for each dyad in the system. This likelihood introduces variation in war-proneness across disputes in the sample, which should be strongly correlated with how difficult the issue is to resolve.

In order to generate the likelihood scores, I first estimated a general model of conflict that includes the presence of contiguity, the ratio of capabilities in the dyad, the presence of an alliance, the duration of the dyad, the years that have elapsed since the last conflict, and the temporal splines based on elapsed time. I used a sample of all directed dyads from 1816 to 2000 (though the results that I describe here are quite robust and a sample of non-directed dyads given produce

---

[10] I did not include the results of this model in Table 8.1 since the estimates for the other independent variables vary so little from those reported in Models 1 through 4.

very similar findings). Each variable in the model was statistically significant ($p < 0.001$), and each coefficient suggested a relationship consistent with the empirical literature on conflict – alliances and elapsed time since last dispute reduce the likelihood of conflict, while all other variables are positively related to conflict.

Next, I used the estimation results to calculate the predicted probabilities of conflict for each dyadic dispute-year in its first year. These predicted probabilities essentially identify the likelihood of conflict at the time a dispute occurred, based on these well-known correlates of disputes. Thus, these probabilities should provide an underlying score for how dangerous each disputed issue was, at least in terms of the factors in the general model.[11] The average predicted probability of conflict for this sample was 0.045, and the range varied from a low of less than 0.001 to a high of 0.545.

If my argument is correct, then the issues faced by states at territorial peace should be less dangerous because threats to homeland territories have been pacified. Assuming the predicted probabilities do correlate with dangerous dispute conditions, then disputes that do involve territorial peace states should have lower predicted probability of conflict scores. This is indeed the case. States free from territorial threat initiated 390 of the 2,315 disputes. The average predicted probability for these disputes was 0.029, versus a mean of 0.049 for other disputes. A difference of means test comparing these samples is statistically significant, at $p < 0.001$. According to the predicted probabilities, a dispute initiated by a state at territorial peace is likely to be half as dangerous as other types of disputes. Further, this relationship does not change if the contiguity term is omitted from the equation generating the predicted probabilities; in fact, the differences in predicted probabilities of conflict are even greater. Since the border relationship has already been modeled through the territorial peace term, contiguity adds little explanatory power, it would seem.

The average probability of conflict for disputes initiated by territorial peace states that also end in negotiated compromises is 0.033. All other negotiated compromises average conflict probabilities of 0.065, and this difference of means is again statistically significant ($p < 0.050$). Territorial peace states negotiate compromises to disputes that are, on average, half as dangerous as other disputes according to this measure.

These probabilities continue to provide strong evidence that the types of issues confronting leaders in states with settled borders are indeed different than the issues facing other leaders. That is why negotiated compromises are

---

[11] I also mimicked this procedure using likelihood of escalation to war based on the same set of factors. Again, there is no difference in the results if these escalation probabilities are used instead.

easier to find. Few factors contribute to escalation of the conflict, and this makes compromises between states more likely. These probabilities confirm the causal mechanism linking territorial peace states with a proclivity for finding negotiated compromises to their disputes.

8.7 Conclusions

This chapter provides strong evidence that the types of issues faced by states with settled borders are different from those issues confronting other states in the international system. Further, this selection effect leads to an association of territorial peace with negotiated compromise. Easier disputes make compromises easier to find.

This chapter also demonstrates that a commonly noted regularity associated with democracies may, in fact, be misunderstood. Democratic peace theory argues that mutually shared norms of nonviolent behavior explain why democracies employ peaceful conflict management techniques to terminate their disputes. However, I find little support for this norms-based argument in the data. Instead, the territorial conflict history of the initiator, the issue type, and the location of conflict best predict whether a dispute will end in negotiated compromise.

In the last chapter I demonstrated that the core of the democratic peace proposition – that democracies do not fight each other – is largely a function of a stable border peace, at least among contiguous dyads. Where borders are clearly delineated and secure, the conditions that allow for the emergence of a democracy take root, and conflict between states is less likely (see also Gibler 2007). This development path also controls the disputes that involve democracies. Their conflicts are more likely to be part of the selected sample of lesser consequence, non-contiguous, and – as this chapter demonstrates empirically – more easily negotiated disputes.

The next step in the argument is to examine how truncated issue agendas affect leader decisions to escalate conflict. With fewer constraints placed on leaders of states at territorial peace, the disputes in which these leaders do become involved should be more likely to end in victories. No longer constrained to struggle with neighbors over challenged territory, these leaders can more effectively choose the types of involvements that best fit their interests and state capabilities. Once again, rather than associating democracy with conflict victories, the real predictor is the stability of the border.

9

Territorial peace and victory in conflict

9.1 Introduction

The last two chapters demonstrate that the issues confronting states at territorial peace are quite different from the issues affecting most states. Gone are threats to the homeland, and peace with neighbors assures a selection of disputes on the foreign policy agenda that will be more easily resolved. Nevertheless, there may remain contentious issues in the international system that leaders wish to press. In this chapter, I explore how the existence of territorial peace with neighbors also affects these decisions.

Since territorial conflict with neighbors places constraints on the leader, adventurism abroad is less likely as homeland defense remains paramount. But, when those constraints are lifted following peace with neighbors, leaders are better able to choose whether to intervene in conflicts abroad. Of course, this depends upon whether the state completely demilitarized following peace with neighbors; absent a decent military, few engagements abroad will be to the state's advantage. If a capable military exists, however, leaders of territorial peace states may find issues in which intervention would be to their state's benefit, and this process of careful selection suggests a correlation between territorial peace and the likelihood of victory in these conflicts.

This extension of territorial peace theory of course challenges the notion that only democracies are thought to select well their potential rivals (Bueno de Mesquita and Siverson 1995; Bueno de Mesquita *et al.* 1999, 2003), enabling democratic leaders to emerge victorious in conflict (Lake 1992; Reiter and Stam 1998, 2003). Thus, by extending the territorial peace argument to explain additional empirical regularities associated with regime type, this chapter lays out an additional theoretical challenge to the larger body of democratic peace scholarship based on conflict selection. While some have questioned the association between democracy and victory (Desch 2008; Downes 2009), no critique of the democratic peace has subsumed these expectations within its own theoretical framework.

I believe the approach used in this chapter is also important because it highlights how state developmental histories can create spatial and temporal dependencies in the extant conflict data. These dependencies are most often ignored. International conflict is not randomly distributed across states or across time (see Goertz and Diehl 1992, for example), and processes of contagion work in ambiguous ways. I argue that these state development paths are an important predictor of when and where conflicts do and do not occur, and the evolution of states will greatly affect the conclusions of almost any study of the correlates of war.

I begin the argument by briefly outlining the studies that link conflict selection to the incentives facing democratic leaders. I then contrast these selection effects arguments with the expectations of territorial peace theory. Next, I outline a simple model of conflict selection, using mostly interaction terms to specify key differences between the territorial peace model and regime-based selection. I then present the results from tests of the argument and conclude with a discussion of the implications of this extension.

9.2 Democracy and conflict selection

Though democracies have been demonstrated to be generally more pacific than their non-democratic counterparts (Rummel 1983; Benoit 1996; Rousseau *et al.* 1996; MacMillan 2003), once in war, democracies generally emerge victorious more often than non-democratic states (Lake 1992; Reiter and Stam 1998, 2003). The theories that explain this empirical regularity typically fall into two competing explanations: war-fighting and selection effects (Reiter and Stam 1998, 2003). War-fighting theories argue that democracies fight better and harder than other types of states, while selection-effects theories suggest that democratic leaders have strong incentives to avoid costly wars that threaten their tenure.

As Reiter and Stam (2002) describe, the war-fighting argument rests on the principle that military soldiers in democracies fight better than their counterparts in authoritarian regimes. The emphasis on individualism and popular consent in democracies develops soldiers that are more loyal and trusting of their government, better equipped to demonstrate initiative in battle, and have a higher morale than soldiers deployed by other regimes. A competitive civilian authority also reinforces merit-based advancement within the military itself, and this translates into better war-fighting performance overall.

Perhaps a better argument for conflict differences across regime types turns on the likelihood of selection effects in the escalation choices of leaders.

Democracies are only likely to enter wars when the probability of winning the war is high; after all, democratic publics turn their leaders out of office following foreign policy disasters. Both Bueno de Mesquita and Siverson (1995) and Bueno de Mesquita *et al.* (1999, 2003) confirm that democratic leaders suffer more severe punishments for losing wars. Similarly, Reiter and Stam (2003) find that democracies win over 90 percent of the wars they initiate and over 60 percent of the wars in which they are targeted. While the difference across participant status slightly contradicts the claim of democratic superiority in war-fighting, democracies do win their conflicts, and this does not seem to be a chance occurrence.

Most criticism of the selection argument has focused on the particular cases that do not conform to the expectations of the theory, like the poor decision-making process that went into launching the extended US war against Iraq in 2003 (Cramer 2007). Downes (2009) offers a more systematic critique of Reiter and Stam's evidence, suggesting their analyses are not robust to slight changes in the treatment of cases and method. Further, Downes' in-depth study of United States President Lyndon Johnson's decision to escalate the Vietnam War demonstrates that domestic politics may have variegated effects on wars of choice. For Johnson, escalation of a war with a slim chance of victory was preferable to losing the ability to push forward a reform agenda at home. Thus, at least in this case, a democratic leader understood failure was likely but still escalated the conflict; moreover, the democratic leader escalated because his domestic political situation made losing the war preferable to withdrawal.

Two notable criticisms of the accountability mechanism provide additional evidence that electoral punishment may not constrain democratic leaders. Desch (2008) argues that, though painful to the leader's pride, electoral punishment for lost wars in democracies hardly outweighs the consequences of leader replacements in non-democracies, events that often include death or exile. This argument is supported by the Chiozza and Goemans (2004, Table 2) findings associating lost wars and crises with leader removal for autocracies and mixed regimes, but not for parliamentary or presidential democracies. Together, these studies provide evidence that the electoral connection may be part of a larger set of incentives that predict leader responsiveness.

9.3 Territorial peace and conflict selection

The finding that democracies tend to win their conflicts has predominantly been explained as outgrowths of the incentives facing democratic leaders. Fearing electoral challenges following failures, democratic leaders select well their conflicts and only escalate issues that are easily won. Here, I extend the territorial peace argument to suggest that this empirical association can be better understood as a product of state evolution. States tend to democratize and survive *qua* democracies in relatively safe geographic environments, and, because of this tendency of democracies to be at territorial peace, the issues that face democratic leaders seldom provoke long wars or conflicts that are difficult to win. Peace with neighbors also allows democratic leaders (or any other leader in similar circumstances) to effectively choose when to engage and when to escalate against other states in the international system. But this second point controls the relationship: all states at territorial peace should be able to choose conflicts they can win.

The model of state development I outlined in Chapter 3 has clear expectations for the variation in the occurrence and types of conflict involving states at territorial peace. First, as I demonstrated empirically in Chapter 7, states at territorial peace are not likely to fight their neighbors, especially over territorial issues. After all, resolving territorial issues was necessary to promote decentralized political power within the state. Absent threats from neighbors, states at territorial peace are more likely to be at peace generally, and any disputes that do occur are likely to be against states that are not contiguous to homeland territories.

Territorial peace also brings a change in the nature of the issues that confront the state. No longer concerned with survival in the international system, most disputes become matters of choice for the regime. Absent are the direct threats to homeland territory, which tend to be highly contentious and difficult to resolve. Instead, the territorial issues that concern the regime most often involve colonial territories and other imperialist claims, which are less salient domestically. Even less consequential are the questions of policy and regime status involving far-flung states. This is why territorial peace states often negotiate compromises, as I demonstrated in Chapter 8.[1]

---

[1] I do not explicitly test this here, but I would also argue that the distribution of issues confronting states at territorial peace will greatly influence the type of militaries that these states develop. Britain, for example, was protected by water on all sides, and as a consequence, developed a strong navy and devoted any armies it constructed to conquering territories abroad. States at territorial peace mimic the behavior of these island countries. For example, in the post-World War II period, the United States similarly stands out as a state possessive of a strong military, but again the nature of that military is different from most land-occupying forces. Surrounded by friendly neighbors and oceans, the United States has been able to involve itself, when it chooses, in conflicts abroad. This has necessitated the development of mobile, technologically advanced forces that are capable of responding to conflict issues. The army itself would likely perform rather poorly if ever asked to repress or hold territory as large as the country.

Nevertheless, there may remain issues in the international system that are either difficult to resolve or which provide advantages to the leader of the territorial peace state. Freed from the constraints of conflicts with neighbors, leaders can choose when and where to escalate these issues to conflict. Further, given the greater lattitude afforded these intervention decisions, territorial peace state leaders have a clear *ex ante* advantage in the conflict, and, therefore, should be more likely to emerge victorious after fighting starts.

The only exception to this expectation of course concerns conflicts with neighbors. As I described in Chapter 3, the nature of territorial conflict between neighbors leads to few surprises. Escalations to fight such conflicts will be quickly met with escalations in threatened neighbors, and this type of process simply renews the international constraints placed on the leader and is, therefore, likely to be avoided. Instead, conflict interventions for territorial peace states are of such a kind that they are not threatening to their immediate neighborhood. This could be due to the nature of the military forces used – air forces, navies, and/or small, quick forces for rapid deployment. Or, the leader may simply be able to convince neighbors of a common threat. In either case, this logic suggests the following hypothesis:

$H_{9.1}$: *States at territorial peace are more likely than other states to win their conflicts against non-contiguous states.*

The baseline comparison for this hypothesis is not the absence of a relationship. Instead, once again, a substantial number of studies correlate democracy with victory. According to the selection-effects argument based on regime type, leaders of democracies have greater incentives to maximize their chances of winning a dispute. This constrains democracies to only fight against much weaker than average opponents and produces the empirical regularity that democracies are more likely than other regime types to win the conflicts they initiate. My argument of course also implies a selection effect, but, instead of capability distributions affecting victory, I believe states at territorial peace have a greater ability to choose their potential targets. The differential expectations for these two arguments allow for an easy comparative test. Thus, the null hypothesis for tests in this chapter is consistent with democratic peace scholarship:

$H_{9.2}$: *Democracies are more likely to win the conflicts they initiate.*

9.4 Modeling choices and variable definition

I test the selection argument using a dependent variable that is based on the Correlates of War Militarized Interstate Dispute (MID) data set (Jones, Bremer and Singer 1996). I use Maoz's (2005) dyadic-dispute data from 1816 to 2001 as my sample.

While much of the conflict selection literature has been restricted to wars, I focus on MIDs for the simple reason that leaders do not know, *ex ante*, which disputes other leaders may escalate to the point of war. My analyses therefore examine the information available to leaders at the start of a dispute to determine whether democratic leaders are indeed especially adept at selecting conflicts that will be easily or quickly won. If the selection-effects argument is correct, then I would be analyzing a heavily biased sample if I included only wars as observations. Indeed, analyzing only wars throws out the bulk of the data for which the theory of democratic selection is applicable.[2]

This point is also important when considering a key difference between the MID and Interstate War data sets from the Correlates of War Project regarding how conflict initiations are coded. An initiator is defined with the start of actual combat in the war data set, but this is not the case for the MID data since a show of force or even a threat can begin a dispute (Sarkees and Wayman 2010, 58). Thus, for example, the Assam War of 1962 (War #160) was initiated and won by China, but the same conflict in the MID data (MID #199) was coded as initiated by India with its incursions deep into Chinese territory just a week prior to the coded start of the war (Sarkees and Wayman 2010, 154). Reiter and Stam (2002, 56) code the war as a successful initiation by a non-democracy (China) against a democracy (India). However, if I use the MID data, the same data point is coded as an unsuccessful initiation by a democracy. Perhaps one could argue that the war actually began with China's escalation of the conflict in 1962, but this argument would miss the fact that India gravely miscalculated both the likelihood of war and the likelihood of success against a powerful opponent. Of course, neither miscalculation is consistent with most theories of democratic selection. India lost a war that developed from an issue it pressed.

The second reason why the dispute data are especially important for these tests is that there are likely to be few observed differences between the territorial peace expectations and the theories of democratic war selection when the tested

---

[2] I am actually not the first to expect the democratic conflict selection argument to apply to the dispute data. Reiter and Stam (2000, 48–50) compiled a data set of directed dyads to test arguments of dispute initiation. As they write (2002, 48): "If our selection effects argument is valid, we would expect to find that the greater the chance of losing, and the more democratic a state is, the less likely it should be to initiate a militarized dispute or escalate an existing dispute to war."

sample includes wars only. Democracies are believed to choose their conflicts wisely, avoiding wars that are likely to cause heavy casualties, last a long time, or be difficult to win. In contrast, I believe all leaders would like to choose such easy wins but only states at territorial peace are actually able to select carefully their conflicts, and, since democracies are more likely than other regime types to be at territorial peace, the correlation between democracy and conflict selection makes sense. Because of this observational equivalence, I test the ability of all states to select their conflicts at earlier stages. If my argument is correct, the method of selection turns on issue and not regime type. Democracies are better able to win their wars because they have fewer territorial disputes to fight over.

Some observations from my sample are clearly consistent with this argument. For instance, the sample of all MIDs includes 26 cases in which a democracy (Polity II score of 6 or greater) initiated a dispute that reached a level of fatalities equal to war (6 on the fatality scale for the dispute). Of those cases, only 6 were wars fought by neighbors over territory. The large majority of cases – 77 percent of the total – involved other types of issues, which, according to my theory, are more prone to conflict selection by leaders. My argument would also suggest that the difference in conflict type explains the propensity for democratic victories in war, and there is again initial evidence to support this conclusion. Democratic initiators in my sample did indeed win 18 of 26 wars (or almost 70 percent), but that rate is deceptive. Democracies won only 3 of the 6 war initiations that were fought over territorial issues with a neighboring state; this is the same victory rate as flipping a coin. In other words, once the conflict issue is taken into consideration, the democratic advantage seems to disappear.[3]

9.4.1 Dependent variable

The dependent variable uses the outcome variable from the MID data set to determine all cases of MID victory by State A (a value of 1 on the outcome variable). All other types of outcomes are coded as 0. Positive coefficients suggest relationships that increase the likelihood of dispute victories by State A over State B. However, since the 0 category includes several possible values (yield, compromise, stalemate, release, etc.), negative coefficients only identify relationships that make victory for State A less likely; negative coefficients should not be interpreted as victories for State B in the dyad.

---

[3] I also wanted to ensure that my results were not determined entirely by sample selection, so I re-estimated each analysis using a selected sample of disputes that involved at least one fatality. In all cases, the additional analyses are consistent with the argument that issue selection outweighs regime type as a factor. For additional analyses, see also the analyses in, and the Web Appendix that supports, Gibler and Miller (2012).

I present analyses using only directed dispute-years. As in the analyses of negotiations in the last chapter, there are good theoretical reasons to expect a correlation of errors between MID selection and MID victory (Heckman 1979; Reed 2000; Sartori 2003), but I again do not find this to be the case empirically for these models. Nevertheless, I also estimated outcome models that jointly estimate sample selection with dispute victory; in none of these additional estimations does the selection into a dispute affect the conclusions of the outcome models presented in this chapter.

That there is no correlation of errors across the victory and selection is interesting in itself. It substantially refines both my argument and regime-based explanations of conflict victory. Democracies are supposed to select themselves into disputes that are easier to win, but the lack of correlation suggests that the choice for escalation to possible victory occurs following dispute onset (see also the logic developed in Downes' [2009] examination of the United States involvement in the Vietnam War). The same applies to those leaders released from the constraints of continual territorial conflict.

9.4.2 Independent variables

I once again identify territorial peace using estimates derived from the conflict models discussed in Chapter 7. In fact, I use the same dummy variables as before to distinguish the states with the lowest levels of territorial threat – those with conflict probabilities in the lowest 5 percent of the distribution of territorial threat.[4] Separate measures are used for the presence of territorial peace in State A and State B.

Also as before, I again define democracy as 6 or above on the Polity IV scale (Marshall and Jaggers 2002) and include in all analyses two separate dummy variables for the presence (or absence) of democracy in each state of the dyad. Experimentations with different cut-off levels for democracy (5 or 7) do not substantively change the results I report, in any of the models.

My control variables are, for the most part, common indicators used in many large-N studies of international conflict. These include the presence of contiguity, which is defined as direct land contiguity on the Correlates of War scale (Stinnett *et al.* 2002), the presence of any alliance in the dyad (Gibler and Sarkees 2004), and the capability distribution in the dyad, measured as the natural logarithm of the ratio of the Composite Index of National Capabilities (CINC) score of State A divided by the CINC score of State B (Singer, Bremer and Stuckey 1972).

---

[4] See pages 142–143 for the description of this measure.

My argument and the democratic peace arguments on conflict behavior rely mostly on interaction terms. For example, to test the argument that democracies are better than other regime types at selecting their conflicts, I include the interaction of a democratic initiator (the State A democracy dummy) and the capability ratio within the dyad. I expect this term to be positive and statistically significant if democracies are better able to select weak opponents. Similarly, my own theory suggests that states at territorial peace will not fare as well when facing neighboring states in conflict. To test this expectation, I multiply the presence of territorial peace by contiguity to create a second interaction term.

9.5 Victory in conflict

The democratic selection models contend that elected leaders select their wars well, their soldiers fight exceptionally well, and/or their governments and economies fight especially hard when involved in conflict. These explanations are all based upon the assumption that democracies are more likely than other regime types to be victorious in their conflicts. My argument considers selection to again be the product of state development path. Removal of dangerous territorial issues allows certain states, and most democracies, the ability to choose which rivals to engage. Thus, conflicts initiated by states with stable borders are more likely to be wars of choice, and wars of choice most often occur when the initiator considers victory a likely outcome.

I test these two logics with estimation procedures similar to those presented in the MID negotiation models in the last chapter. First, I estimate a basic model predicting victory in a dispute using the control variables, contiguity, the presence of a territorial issue, and whether the state was at territorial peace. As Model 1 in Table 9.1 suggests, states at territorial peace are indeed likely to win their conflicts. That is true even after controlling for the difficulty of the issue, its location, and the overall capability ratio. Model 2 adds the interaction of territorial peace and contiguity to the estimation, but the interaction provides no statistical leverage on the dependent variable and does not alter the interpretation of the other independent variables.

As I mentioned in the last chapter, the substitution of a simple territorial threat variable in Model 1 or 2 produces non-linear effects. Low levels of territorial threat behave as predicted by the territorial peace dummy variable. However, moderate levels of territorial threat are especially unlikely to garner victories, and this makes the continuous threat variable statistically insignificant at any conventional level. I confirmed that this is the case using both an estimation

Table 9.1 *Predicting victory in militarized disputes, 1816–2000*

	(1)	(2)	(3)	(4)	(5)	(6)
Territorial peace variables						
State A at territorial peace	1.012***	1.082***			1.011***	1.980***
	(0.200)	(0.233)			(0.237)	(0.404)
State B at territorial peace	−0.137	−0.130			−0.152	−0.0279
	(0.214)	(0.215)			(0.217)	(0.325)
Territorial peace (State A) × Contiguous		−0.199			−0.152	−1.382*
		(0.343)			(0.347)	(0.554)
Territorial dispute	0.751***	0.748***	0.841***	0.839***	0.800***	0.407
	(0.169)	(0.169)	(0.171)	(0.171)	(0.172)	(0.250)
Contiguous	−0.587***	−0.527**	−0.741***	−0.728***	−0.607**	−1.179***
	(0.166)	(0.196)	(0.172)	(0.174)	(0.204)	(0.289)
Regime variables						
State A is democracy			0.112	0.0409	0.107	−0.319
			(0.169)	(0.201)	(0.202)	(0.379)
State B is democracy			−1.248***	−1.240***	−1.163***	−0.618
			(0.226)	(0.227)	(0.228)	(0.337)

	Model 1	Model 2	Model 3	Model 4	Model 5	Model 6
Democracy × Capability ratio				0.0457	0.0520	0.0592
				(0.0662)	(0.0666)	(0.134)
Control variables						
Allied	0.312	0.299	0.235	0.232	0.317	0.703*
	(0.196)	(0.197)	(0.196)	(0.196)	(0.200)	(0.286)
Capability ratio	0.134***	0.134***	0.0954**	0.0803*	0.0831*	0.166**
	(0.0308)	(0.0308)	(0.0315)	(0.0383)	(0.0390)	(0.0614)
Constant	−2.758***	−2.781***	−2.230***	−2.226***	−2.523***	−1.347***
	(0.131)	(0.137)	(0.139)	(0.139)	(0.162)	(0.257)
Number of observations	2451	2451	2451	2451	2451	605
Pseudo-R^2	0.056	0.056	0.063	0.063	0.082	0.168
LR χ^2	77.21	77.55	86.91	87.38	113.2	97.17

Sample includes all directed dyads during their first year of a dispute, 1816–2001, inclusive; dependent variable is victory in MID by initiator for Models 1 through 5. Model 6 includes only fatal MID victories. * $p < 0.05$, ** $p < 0.01$, *** $p < 0.001$.

with the square of the continuous threat variable and also with a separate model that included dummy variables for various values of territorial threat. Since my dependent variable is dispute victory, I believe these non-linear effects are best explained by the many other possible outcomes that can end disputes. Low levels of territorial conflict suggest fewer homeland constraints and predict victory because the leader can choose which conflicts to dedicate state resources. Moderate levels of territorial threat allow some leader adventurism but do not allow full commitment by the state. Thus, adventurism abroad should be met with fewer victories and more stalemates and yields.

I confirmed that this is the case by re-analyzing Model 2 with two changes. First, I substituted the continuous measure of territorial threat for the territorial peace dummy. Second, I replicated the analysis on two separate samples – one of disputes with contiguous states and one with non-contiguous states. As expected, the association between moderate levels of territorial threat and lower levels of dispute victory is based almost entirely on the non-contiguous sample of disputes. There is no statistically significant effect for contiguous disputes. In a strategic setting, leaders may be unwilling to commit the necessary resources for fear of becoming vulnerable to their neighbors; too, targets are likely to know these conditions well and will hold out in the dispute in order to force stalemates or yields from the initiator. In either case, victories are unlikely for these states.

The regime variables are introduced in Models 3 and 4. Again, I use the baseline controls of capability ratio and alliance and add the presence of territorial and contiguity to the model, and I estimate one model (Model 4) with an interaction of regime type and its selection variable – in this case, capability ratio. Democracies are especially likely to choose conflicts when capability ratios favor them. However, in neither model do I find support for the argument that democracies win their disputes. Democratic initiators are not more likely to win their disputes. In fact, the standard error is greater than the estimate of the coefficient in both cases, and the same holds true for the interaction term.

Model 5 provides an estimation of victory using both the territorial threat and the regime variables. There are no substantial changes in what predicts victory in this model – territorial peace states still win their conflicts, even after controlling for regime type. Note that I do find support for regime effects among democratic targets. This variable is negative and statistically significant at $p < 0.001$ in three models. This suggests that it is difficult to win a dispute against democratic targets, but it does not necessarily imply that democratic targets are winning the disputes. Instead, conflicts targeting democracies may be more likely to end in a yield, stalemate, compromise, or release, or they could signal the joining of an ongoing war. The estimate only implies that victories are unlikely against democratic targets.

The final model restricts the cases to disputes with fatalities only. Since military deaths have occurred in these cases, the disputes themselves should be of higher intensity than most other disputes. In these 605 disputes, the presence of territorial peace in the initiator is again a strong predictor of victory, even after controlling for other variables. Further, the interaction term – territorial peace states fighting their neighbors – now has a negative effect on the likelihood of victory. Territorial peace states win their conflicts so long as they are not fighting their neighbors. Both these findings are of course consistent with the expectations of the theory.

9.5.1 Which disputes are fought to victory?

In the last chapter I demonstrated that, based on a model that included common predictors of conflict, the probability of a dispute was quite low when states at territorial peace initiated MIDs (see pages 146–148). Though the likelihood of conflict in the dyad-year before an average dispute was 0.045, the probability of conflict for disputes initiated by territorial peace states was 0.019. Recall also that, among disputes that ended in negotiation, the average conflict probability for territorial peace initiators was 0.033, while other negotiated cases had a conflict probability of 0.065. This variation in probabilities suggested that territorial peace states faced less-salient issues, which explains why these issues are easier to negotiate. Territorial peace states are also more likely to negotiate the most dangerous disputes on their agenda.

This easy-issue argument becomes a bit more nuanced when we examine the probabilities of conflict in the cases of dispute victories. In the 56 cases of dispute victory by territorial peace states, the likelihood of conflict is only 0.019. That is less than half the average for all disputes. It is also less than half the average for victories by other types of states, which is 0.041. *T* tests of the differences in these averages – territorial peace state victories versus all other dispute probabilities or versus dispute victories by other types of states – strongly suggest these variations are not occurring by chance. The differences in averages are even greater for disputes that have fatalities. Territorial peace initiators had 30 victories in the sample, with an average probability of conflict of 0.017; this compares to an average of 0.046 for all other fatal MIDs.

These probabilities again confirm the selection argument that freedom from territorial conflict provides. Leaders of states at territorial peace may become predatory over issues of importance to them, provoking conflicts in situations that were not likely to erupt in conflict without their active involvement. The underlying conditions in these dyad-years do not favor escalation to conflict. Nevertheless, the territorial peace initiators press an issue to their advantage, and they are able to do so because of the lack of constraints on their militaries. The other state may be unaware of the likelihood of conflict or may simply be under-prepared, weak, or unable to effectively deal with the territorial peace initiator. These patterns of dispute probabilities reinforce the idea that territorial peace applies only to agreements with neighbors. Territorial peace does not extend to non-contiguous disputes as a matter of course.

One final note – as I mentioned earlier in this chapter, I did not find the like-lihood of dispute onset and the likelihood of dispute victory to be correlated in joint estimations. The empirics suggest that victory has no effect on the likeli-hood of a dispute starting. While leaders may in fact not select their disputes based on likely outcomes, this would assume a level of ignorance incongru-ent with the idea that leaders respond to incentives. The finding also violates most theoretical treatments of international conflict. However, if we accept that leaders would, if able, at least partially select their disputes based on projected outcomes, then it seems likely that the common predictors of conflict I used in the selection model portray an incomplete model of dispute onset.

Based principally on power ratios, alliances, regime type, and proximity, current models of dispute omit the benefits of conflict that are derivative of leader interests. If states are no longer constrained by neighboring rivals, then leaders may be more likely to pursue the occasional conflicts that benefit them or their coalitions of supporters. Making other regimes more palatable to followers is just one of these concerns (Bueno de Mesquita *et al.* 2003). Leaders may want to improve world order, fight against repression, seek revenge for past actions, attempt to secure resources abroad, or pursue any other types of issues that would make them or their followers better off. There are anecdotes linking each of these rationales with conflict, but there is no systematic model that would predict dispute onset based on them. Nevertheless, victories in these conflicts would be appropriate selection criteria for leaders freed from the constraints of territorial conflict.

9.6 A note on conflict duration

A direct extension of the selection-effects argument is the expectation that democracies will try to fight wars that are expected to be short. Quick vic-tories are likely to be correlated with electoral success while longer conflicts drain society of personnel, materiel, and patience with the leadership. Bennett and Stam (1996, and later 1998) provided two of the first studies to demonstrate this relationship and found that the war-fighting advantage for democratic ini-tiators is mostly short-term. Within the first 18 months of combat operations, democratic initiators enjoy a significant advantage over their autocratic counterparts. The predicted probability of war victory for democratic initiators is 49 percent if the war lasts for one year and 6 percent if the war lasts for five years or more (Bennett and Stam 1998).

Since initiator advantages dwindle as wars persist, recent scholarship has stressed that the decision to initiate conflict should be modeled as a function of both expected duration and expected likelihood of victory. Slantchev (2004), for example, argues that conflicts start when differences persist in expectations over outcomes, but battlefield results provide information updates that force eventual convergence on a likely winner. The information gained from battle proves much more valuable to leaders than antebellum judgments of capabilities. This argument would suggest that the process of choosing easy opponents may be difficult for most leaders *ex ante*.

Slantchev (2004) also finds that conflict initiators are more likely to lose when the conflict issue is more salient to them. This follows the selection-effect logic since leaders would tend to only initiate conflicts over low-salience issues when the chances of victory are overwhelming. Important for my argument is the fact that salience is operationalized, in part, by disaggregating the issue descriptions provided by Holsti (1991), which include territory as a key component. Thus, Slantchev (2004) affirms that the success rate for initiators drops when the conflict involves territorial issues. Also important for my argument, the variable describing regime type is statistically insignificant when estimated jointly with issue salience.[5]

In separate work with Steve Miller, I confirm that territorial issues also have a strong effect on conflict duration (Gibler and Miller 2012). While I do not necessarily expect a correlation between states free from territorial threat and shorter conflicts, since there really are no regime incentives to force that type of selection process for the leader, there still remains the truncated set of foreign policy issues affecting states free from territorial threats. Leaders of states free from territorial threat have a foreign policy agenda filled with issues that are more easily resolved, and the level of difficulty in the dispute is likely to be correlated with conflict duration. We find this to be the case empirically. As in Models 3 and 4 of Table 9.1, we find little evidence of democratic leaders selecting their states into conflicts of shorter duration. Instead, democracies are less likely to fight over territorial issues or have conflicts with neighboring states, and once the issue and location of the conflict is controlled, regime type provides no information predicting conflict victory.

---

[5] Relatedly, Werner (1998) finds no effect for regime type when estimating settlement terms following conflict.

9.7 Conclusions

This chapter challenges the contention that democratic leaders strategically select their potential targets so that democracies fight conflicts they are more likely to win. In fact, I find little support for democratic selection arguments. Extending the territorial peace argument developed in Chapter 3, I outline a theory of dispute selection that is based on the development paths of states. Leaders in states that face few territorial threats from neighbors have an advantage in foreign policy because their actions are less constrained. These leaders can carefully choose which conflicts to escalate. This selection effect forces a strong correlation between lack of territorial threats to the homeland and victories in conflict abroad.

This confounding process of state development may also explain why democracies have been thought to be more capable war-fighters – once controls for contiguity and the presence of a territorial issue are added to the model, the effects of regime type on conflict victory are rendered statistically meaningless. This argument of course provides an additional challenge to the larger democratic peace project. While much attention has been paid to the observation that democracies do not fight each other, few if any of the challenges to the democratic peace have been extended to the many corollary findings based on the incentives faced by democratic leaders. Here, however, I have provided a unified theory that explains both the observation of peace between democracies and also the variation in dispute selection and the chances for victory.

I have tried to highlight the advantages of paying close attention to state development paths in order to understand consequent conflict behavior. The conflict literature tends to treat all dyadic relationships as equal, missing the fact that rivalries and alignments change over time. Also missing are the effects that conflict has on the development of the state. Democracies and peace cluster in space and time for a reason, and this affects the types of disputes various regimes will likely face. Understanding state development patterns is an important next step for correlation-based studies of cross-sectional conflict data.

10

Final thoughts

10.1 Summary of findings

Territorial peace theory is broad and applicable to many different literatures. I have used the theory to explain important changes in domestic institutions, such as the rise of militarized states, the likelihood of party polarization across countries, and how both of these changes affect the number of veto players able to check the power of the leader. I have also used the argument to describe how domestic political behavior becomes centralized when a state is threatened and how these attitudes aid the centralization process. With changes in both the behavior and institutions of the state documented, I then explained how state centralization altered leader incentives and constraints during international conflict. All of these mechanisms have previously remained isolated fields of study that were, to varying degrees, plagued by inconsistent results. However, treated comprehensively, as interrelated processes, strong and consistent findings confirm the over-arching theory and its many implications. I use this chapter to review the empirical support for the process of state development and change described by territorial peace theory. I also discuss several key issues that these analyses raise.

10.1.1 Territorial threat and domestic politics

I argued that territorial threats to the state are more likely than other types of threats to be salient to targeted publics. I found support for this argument in several different places. First, the average individual is less likely to be tolerant of individuals in minority groups when the state is targeted by territorial threats. Mere participation in conflict does not have an effect; neither does being targeted by non-territorial issues. Only the targeting of the state by territorial threats causes individuals to be less politically tolerant of minority group members

165

of society. This finding demonstrates the importance of the territorial issue for the average individual. The finding also provides some comparative context for the strength of the issue's salience since the addition of threat to a basic model of political tolerance eliminates the statistical significance of regime type. Isolation from threat seems to be better than democracy at predicting the liberalness of the average member of society. This is why Israel is much less tolerant than other democracies, like the United States, New Zealand, and Australia. Island states and settled borders allow individuals to respect tolerance in relative safety.

Since political tolerance is one of the fundamental values of liberal democracy, these findings demonstrate well the salience of territorial issues for the average individual in a context that is of critical importance for the development of the political regime. Without liberal values, the legitimacy of democracy becomes more difficult to establish or maintain. Thus, this reaction of intolerance among the public provides some early evidence that the type of government in a state depends at least in part on the threat environment of that state.

Territorial threats were also much more likely to establish and grow large, standing armies. An average territorial dispute immediately increases army personnel in a targeted state by over 114,000 troops. Non-territorial disputes match this personnel growth only by year five of the dispute; the first year of a non-territorial dispute provoked fewer than 500 troops in the targeted state. This differential explains why territorial disputes will be associated with states that have large, standing armies. It also provides a potential explanation for why territorial disputes tend to recur. It is difficult to dismantle a standing army once built; the process is slow and further complicated by strategic considerations of mutual demobilization. Thus, once a large army is built in one state, that army serves as a threat that also encourages the building of armies in neighboring states. Each army then serves as a lingering threat that encourages the maintenance of rivalry.

For my purposes, the personnel increases again provide confirmation of the salience of territorial issues with the general public. The difference between responses to territorial and non-territorial disputes is stark. I believe this is because territorial threat provokes greater fear in the average individual since the effects of the threat are more likely to affect them directly. This is consistent with the assumption that the public favors policies that protect the state from immediate threats, even if this might increase the ability of the elites to repress in the future. After all, a good deal of myopia is needed to believe that increasing state power in such a way does not increase the ability of any regime to repress.

The effects of territorial conflict on repression are nuanced, but, in all cases, the average citizen can expect more repression following state involvement in territorial disputes. This is true regardless of how the government decides to deal with both the state and the rival – whether through more minimal increases in army personnel or by pursuing a policy of mass conscription. In all cases, repression eases immediately during the conflict, as the government's power is directed toward the rival; then, as troops return, government repression increases by one-quarter to one-third its original rate.

The power of the military can be directly felt with repression. However, even this measure is likely to under-estimate the standing army's true political strength. Knowing that repression is likely, and knowing that government elites are likely to turn to the military if necessary, domestic group bargaining in the shadow of a militarized, territorially targeted society becomes more difficult for opposition forces. As my analyses demonstrate, opposition groups overwhelmingly support the leading party when the state is targeted by territorial issues. Opposition groups represent their fearful constituencies and also probably fear the growing political power of the leading party.

Almost all leaders are likely to prefer an easier environment to implement their policies, and the pliant opposition caused by territorial threat presents a unique opportunity. Unable to challenge the leader effectively, opposition groups are unlikely to challenge the government as the executive is made institutionally more powerful. Ceding authority to the leader is done for expediency, to better fight the territorial threat from abroad. The domestic political situation of a supportive public and a strong military also mutes any serious opposition to the leader. In the end, territorial threats lead to centralized public opinion, a centralized party system, centralized institutions, and, subsequently, an increasingly repressive state.

10.1.2 Territorial peace and international conflict

Part III of the book assessed the implications of centralization following territorial threat on both the relationship between regime type and conflict and also the foreign policy agenda of the state. First, I demonstrated that what we know as a democratic peace may in fact be a territorial peace. As above, territorial threats to the state lead to centralization of the polity. Territorial threats are also more dangerous, conflict-prone, and likely to recur. Combined, this implies that the absence of territorial threats will be associated with both decentralized states and peace, and, therefore, that the democratic peace is a product of what can perhaps better be called a territorial peace.

Previously, I have focused on geographic salients to identify the international borders least likely to be challenged – borders that follow clear geographic markers are more generally easier to identify and easier to bargain upon (Gibler 2007). In this book, however, I identified territorial threat using several behavioral indicators: the age of the border, civil and international wars, territorial transfers, defense pacts, militarization, and territorial disputes and claims. Once these behavioral indicators of the presence (or absence) of threat were added to a simple model of conflict onset among contiguous states, the statistical significance of joint democracy disappeared. This was true in every model analyzed.

Moving beyond regime type as an explanation, the implications of the territorial threat and conflict relationship are important. First, the presence of territorial issues with contiguous neighbors is likely to overwhelm the foreign policy agenda of the state. Constrained by these territorial threats, leaders have little ability to choose the international issues they wish to escalate. The salience of the territorial issue with their public makes protection from the threat a requirement for the leader, and adventurism beyond dealing with the rival becomes impossible.

However, when a state is at territorial peace with its neighbors, the issue agenda of the state changes. Gone are the difficult-to-resolve issues and the constraints placed on the leader by the public. Leaders of states at territorial peace have greater freedom to choose the issues they wish to escalate, and, without territorial issues on the agenda, negotiation and compromise are more likely. As my analyses demonstrate, the type of regime has little effect on whether leaders can negotiate compromises to disputes or win the disputes in which they are involved. Instead, non-contiguous, non-territorial issues provide the easiest compromises because their salience with the public and with leaders is low. That democracies have been selected out of these issues explains the now common association between liberal regimes and negotiation and compromise. Similarly, without territorial issues constraining the state, leaders may choose favorable situations to press their and their state's interests and withdraw or avoid those crises which they will likely lose. This is why states at territorial peace are more likely to win their disputes; it also again explains the association of democracy with victories in conflict. Once we understand that territorial issues affect the level of centralization in the state, it becomes clearer that regime type affords minimal leverage in predicting regularities in the distribution of conflict and cooperation. The constraints placed on leaders by territorial issues, and the absence of those constraints, provides a better portrait of the states likely to fight and win or compromise.

10.2 Additional issues raised by this book

The introductory chapter outlined several issues raised by the book, including the importance of second-image-reversed theories, issue-based theories of international relations, and the role of regime type. In this final section of the book, I return again to these themes by highlighting three sets of related implications from territorial peace theory. The role of regime type, predation, and issue evolution may all take on new meaning in light of the findings associated with territorial peace theory.

10.2.1 Regime type and international relations

When both peace and democracy are symptoms of the stabilization of the territorial status quo, the world should look differently than standard treatments of the democratic peace often see it, and this model holds promise for pointing inquiry in that direction. We need not remain dependent on variations of regime-based theories. Instead, more leverage can be had by re-imagining the world in terms of issues and the constraints those issues place upon leaders.

I have already demonstrated that the presence or absence of territorial issues best explains conflict onset and whether a state wins a conflict or negotiates a compromise. Extending the argument to other findings, I would also expect to find that states at territorial peace will find it easier to ally and cooperate with each other when needed. Indeed, what we know as neo-liberal institutionalism may mostly be limited to those states resting securely in their regions. The selection effect in their foreign policy agendas controls this. With fewer contentious issues, cooperation in other areas becomes much easier. This may be why we witness greater integration, trade, and movement across settled borders. States at territorial peace are also more likely to concern themselves with system governance and isses of coordination – like trade and the environment – or normative concerns such as human rights.

Alliances, another more specialized form of cooperation, are somewhat different. Mostly dedicated to cooperation during times of crisis, democracies will often have little need for formal military alliances. When alliances are signed, however, the nature of the treaty will be of a different sort. Rather than preparing for defense of the homeland, these alliance treaties are more likely to outline the specifics necessary for cooperation among signatories. Or, powerful democracies may be pushing their interests abroad. In either case, institutionalization is likely because the goal of the alliance is long-term cooperation between the democracy and its alliance partner. This logic explains why democratic alliances tend to endure – with few issues threatening or even challenging the cooperative alliances, there really is no reason to end the cooperation begun by the treaty.

The selection effect explanation also controls why states at territorial peace are unlikely to have spatial rivalries and arms races with neighboring states. Settled borders imply little need for arming. There are also, by definition, few if any threats from neighbors against states at territorial peace. The logic of settled borders limits arming and rivalries to threats against non-neighbors and states in other regions, but there will be few territorial peace states that can actually engage abroad. Territorial peace requires little militarization after all, and few leaders will be able to build their forces substantially without external threats to their state. One exception may be major states that have or had colonies since these states have previously established infrastructures for relations with the colony; this preparation tends to lower the capability costs of both cooperation and contention between the states. Of course, these few cases are truly exceptions. Rarely will the world witness two states at peace with their respective neighbors that are also both capable and willing to engage each other. In fact the world has witnessed only one such case – the Cold War between the United States and the Soviet Union, and I discuss this case in more detail in the next section.

10.2.2 Territorial peace at home and predation abroad

Today's United States is the beneficiary of an exceptionally peaceful regional environment. Neither Canada nor Mexico, its only two neighbors, has been a rival in war with the United States for over 150 years, and large expanses of ocean have separated American homeland territories from its rivals abroad. If my argument is correct, this regional peace has encouraged both political decentralization and democracy in America's political development. Nevertheless, this same territorial peace has co-existed with an American foreign policy that has been exceptionally interventionist in other regions, especially over the last decade. Indeed, in the last ten years alone, the United States has fought wars with Afghanistan and Iraq and has fought more limited engagements in Libya, Yemen, Pakistan, and several other countries.

The high level of military engagement experienced recently by the United States seems incongruent with a state that is at peace, but there is a difference between peace and stability at home and interests abroad. Freed from local threats, those states that are militarily capable can involve themselves abroad without fear of opportunism by regional rivals. Regional rivals tie down the capabilities of the state to the region; but, without regional rivals, leaders may engage on issues abroad.

At least two other states have experienced territorial peace at home and pursued active foreign policies abroad. The United Kingdom, for example, has always enjoyed well-defined, island borders, and few states on the Continent possessed the capabilities necessary to occupy the state, at least until World War II. This isolation from other major states gave the United Kingdom great latitude to pursue those foreign policies that advanced its empire, while also avoiding or negotiating those issues that would be difficult to win. Indeed, the strong, hegemonic leadership associated with *Pax Brittannica* in the nineteenth century really described a system in which the most powerful state faced few if any threats to its homeland.

Similarly, the Soviet Union was essentially at territorial peace following World War II. Only the United States had enough capabilities to threaten the Soviets, and that threat was demobilizing quickly and American forces were mostly oceans away. The Soviets had also established a sphere of influence in Eastern Europe, and more limitedly to its south, so that any attempts to conquer the homeland would be slowed, destroying only the Soviets' satellite states. This distanced the core territory of Russia from any threats abroad.

The territorial peace experienced by Soviet Russia was short-lived since the rise of China provided a significant threat to its core territories, especially after China's rapprochement with the United States in the 1970s. Domestically, the decentralizing forces of this limited period of peace were ultimately incapable of overcoming the long history of czarist oppression, economic backwardness, and political centralization that followed the many attacks on Russian territories. Nevertheless, the security from neighboring threats gave Stalin the ability to contend liberally abroad, with few or no constraints on foreign policy emanating from the Soviets' neighbors.

Seen from this perspective, the Cold War becomes a system of two states at territorial peace in their regions that were also able to engage each other on almost any issues outside their own regions. In this system the two states tried to press their advantage when able and withdrew when crises proved untenable. Costly wars were avoided principally out of choice, not because of norms or nuclear weapons or other forms of deterrence. There was a heavy status quo bias to most situations, and superior forces on the ground in each particular crisis would dictate winners, losers, and those likely to compromise. This logic implies that Cold War interests were not derivative of divisions produced by differences in democracy and authoritarianism or capitalism and communism. Rather, the Cold War began and was maintained because two powerful states had few rivals that could threaten their homeland territories.

This type of international system was unique and will probably remain so for the foreseeable future. In today's system, only the United States has regional peace at home and the ability to extend its capabilities abroad. Perhaps the best chance for a contender to the United States rests in Europe. However, though wealthy and territorially settled, the continent remains relatively weak militarily and still divided politically. Alternately, a rising China may prove able to thwart American policies in Asia itself, but there is little reason to suspect that China has either the capabilities to remove the potential threat posed by its Russian neighbor or the willingness to make a lasting peace in the region that would include Russia, India, and other potential rivals. Further, if China were to resolve its border issues, then peace with neighbors may open the country to the processes of decentralization, assuming of course a requisite rise in wealth, a middle class, and the factors that contribute to democratization.

Finally, notice in this explanation of large, system-level events that democracy provides little purchase over why the Cold War started or why the United States remains interventionist after the Soviet Union's demise. A normative explanation of democratic peace cannot really explain why the Soviet Union would often compromise on issues or establish norms of behavior with the United States (Gaddis 1986). Most democratic peace theories would expect no prolonged peace between the two states and, finally, are unable to explain the interventionism of the United States in the last decade (Russett 2005). However, if both peace and conflict become functions of the distribution of territorial issues across regions, then peace at home and aggressiveness abroad make sense for militarily powerful states. This is true regardless of whether democracy is present in either state.

10.2.3 Issue evolution in the system

Development has mostly been considered an economic problem as poverty and inequality are thought to best be eradicated with the proper mix of welfare, trade, and property rights policies. Or, when discussions turn political, democracy and the elimination of repression are proffered as best answers for developing countries. However, if both democracy and repression are endogenous – even in part – to the security environment of the state, then the nature of development takes on an international, highly political dimension. Settled borders and settled regions may have to arrive prior to the establishment of any sustainable form of democracy or any government that respects its citizens.

Let me put this a bit differently. The research I have discussed here demonstrates that issues matter and vary considerably across dyads and regions. An important implication of this argument is that there will be substantial spatial and temporal variation in the level of conflict and types of regimes that populate the international system at any given time. In other words there is a definite reason that certain regions have become peaceful and democratic while other regions remain replete with centralized states mired in various forms of conflict. That reason is based at least in part on border security.

Practically, the systematic variation in issues and regime types implies differences in what I consider to be *political* development. Settling the distribution of borders changes the nature of politics in the region. Established democracies – those states most likely to be at territorial peace – will not face the same types of issues as new states or states in dyads with continually contested borders. These states have evolved in peaceful regions, and this is why democracies tend to cluster. Also clustering, however, are unsettled regions and areas with contested borders; if the analyses presented here are correct, military buildups, intolerance, and political centralization will cluster together in time and space as well. These politically developing regions remain dominated by contentious territorial issues.

This type of systematic variation in issues is also important methodologically because, as a field, we have become dependent upon cross-sectional, time-series analyses of dyadic data. But, if issue types vary systematically and control both regime type and conflict, then this introduces substantial omitted variable bias into any large-N study of conflict. King (2001) essentially argues this point when examining the failure to account for variations in hostility levels across dyads – a form of issue-salience variation. As King argues, any peaceful years between, for example, India and Pakistan are not exchangeable with the peaceful years between the US and Canada, without first accounting for the level of hostility that exists in each dyad. Relationships in the territorially settled region of North America will be much different from those in central and south Asia, and this will affect the variables commonly used to predict conflict.

This conclusion about political (or territorial) development has far-reaching implications for many current foreign policy practices. For example, leaders of the United States, Britain, and other influential democracies continue to emphasize peace and democratization abroad, thinking that this political solution will aid development and provide relief from repression. However, neither may hold without firm, settled borders. Worse, the policies of economic development that are offered may themselves be hijacked by the centralizing tendencies associated with responses to territorial threats in insecure regions.

This reasoning suggests an even greater emphasis should be placed on peace in territorial disputes – between Israel and its neighbors, Iraq and Iran, Afghanistan and Pakistan, the Spratly Islands, and the myriad other ongoing territorial conflicts. Rather than maintaining democracy and wealth as solutions for conflict and development, territorial dispute resolution should come first. There may be many types of state development in the world. By focusing only on wealth and regime type, we are likely to miss the importance of settled borders and security in the international political system.

References

Alker, H.R. and F.L. Sherman. 1986. *International Conflict Episodes, 1945–1979*. University of Michigan, Ann Arbor: Inter-University Consortium for Political and Social Research. Data file and codebook.

Allee, T.L. and P.K. Huth. 2006. "Legitimizing Dispute Settlement: International Legal Rulings as Domestic Political Cover." *American Political Science Review* 100(2): 219.

Altemeyer, B. 1996. *The Authoritarian Specter*. Cambridge, MA: Harvard University Press.

Ambrosio, T. 2001. *Irredentism: Ethnic Conflict and International Politics*. Westport, Co: Praeger Publishers.

Babst, D.V. 1964. "Elected Governments: A Force for Peace." *The Wisconsin Sociologist* 2: 9–14.

——— 1972. "A Force for Peace." *Industrial Research* 14(4): 55–58.

Baker, W.D. and J.R. Oneal. 2001. "Patriotism or Opinion Leadership?: The Nature and Origins of the 'Rally Round the Flag' Effect." *Journal of Conflict Resolution* 45: 661–687.

Beck, N., J.N. Katz and R. Tucker. 1998. "Taking Time Seriously: Time-Series-Cross-Section Analysis with a Binary Dependent Variable." *American Journal of Political Science* 42(4): 1260–1288.

Ben-Yehuda, H. 2004. "Territoriality and War in International Crises: Theory and Findings, 1918–2001." *International Studies Review* 6(4): 85–106.

Bennett, D.S. and A.C. Stam III. 1996. "The Duration of Interstate Wars, 1816–1985." *American Political Science Review* 90(2): 239–257.

——— 1998. "The Declining Advantages of Democracy: A Combined Model of War Outcomes and Duration." *Journal of Conflict Resolution* 42(3): 344–366.

Benoit, K. 1996. "Democracies Really Are More Pacific (in General): Reexamining Regime Type and War Involvement." *Journal of Conflict Resolution* 40(4): 636–657.

Berrebi, C. and E.F. Klor. 2008. "Are Voters Sensitive to Terrorism? Direct Evidence from the Israeli Electorate." *American Political Science Review* 102(3): 279–301.

Boix, C. 2003. *Democracy and Redistribution*. New York, NY: Cambridge University Press.

Boix, C. and S.C. Stokes. 2003. "Endogenous Democratization." *World Politics* 55(4): 517–549.

Braithwaite, A. 2005. "Location, Location, Location... Identifying Conflict Hot Spots." *International Interactions* 31(4): 251–272.

Brass, P.R. 1997. *Theft of an Idol: Text and Context in the Representation of Collective Violence*. Princeton University Press.

Braumoeller, B.F. 2004. "Hypothesis Testing and Multiplicative Interaction Terms." *International Organization* 58(4): 807–820.

Brecher, M. and J. Wilkenfeld. 1997. *A Study of Crisis*. University of Michigan Press.

Bremer, S.A. 1992. "Dangerous Dyads: Conditions Affecting the Likelihood of Interstate War, 1816–1965." *Journal of Conflict Resolution* 36(2): 309–341.

    1993. "Democracy and Militarized Interstate Conflict, 1816–1965." *International Interactions* 18(3): 231–249.

    2000. Who Fights Whom, When, Where, and Why? In *What Do We Know About War?*, ed. John A. Vasquez. Lanham, MD: Rowman & Littlefield, pp. 23–36.

Brody, R.A. and C.R. Shapiro. 1989. "A Reconsideration of the Rally Phenomenon in Public Opinion." *Political Behavior Annual* 2: 77–102.

Brubaker, R. 2004. Ethnicity, Migration, and Statehood in Post Cold War Europe. In *The Fate of the Nation-state*, ed. M. Seymour. Montreal: McGill Queen's University Press, pp. 357–374.

Brubaker, R. and D.D. Laitin. 1998. "Ethnic and Nationalist Violence." *Annual Review of Sociology* 24(1): 423–452.

Bueno de Mesquita, B. and D. Lalman. 1994. *War and Reason: Domestic and International Imperatives*. Yale University Press.

Bueno de Mesquita, B. and R.M. Siverson. 1995. "War and the Survival of Political Leaders: A Comparative Study of Regime Types and Political Accountability." *American Political Science Review* 89(4): 841–855.

Bueno de Mesquita, B., A. Smith, R.M. Siverson and J.D. Morrow. 2003. *The Logic of Political Survival*. Cambridge, MA: MIT Press.

Bueno de Mesquita, B., J.D. Morrow, R.M. Siverson and A. Smith. 1999. "An Institutional Explanation of the Democratic Peace." *American Political Science Review* 93(4): 791–807.

Butterworth, R.L. and M.E. Scranton. 1976. *Managing Interstate Conflict, 1945–74: Data with Synopses*. Pittsburgh: University Center for International Studies.

Byrk, A. and S. Raudenbush. 1996. Hierarchical Linear Modeling: Applications and Data Analysis Methods. Thousand Oaks, CA: Sage Publications.

Carter, D.B. and H.E. Goemans. 2011. "The Making of the Territorial Order: New Borders and the Emergence of Interstate Conflict." *International Organization* 65(2): 275–309.

Carter, D.B. and C.S. Signorino. 2010. "Back to the Future: Modeling Time Dependence in Binary Data." *Political Analysis* 18(3): 271–292.

Chan, S. 1984. "Mirror, Mirror on the Wall... Are the Freer Countries More Pacific?" *Journal of Conflict Resolution* 28(4): 617–648.

Chandler, D.P. 1999. *Voices from S-21: Terror and History in Pol Pot's Secret Prison*. University of California Press.

Chiozza, G. and H.E. Goemans. 2004. "International Conflict and the Tenure of Leaders: Is War Still Ex Post Inefficient?" *American Journal of Political Science* 48: 604–619.

CIA. 2009. *Central Intelligence Agency World Factbook*. Central Intelligence Agency.

Colaresi, M. 2004. "When Doves Cry: International Rivalry, Unreciprocated Cooperation, and Leadership Turnover." *American Journal of Political Science* 48(3): 555–570.

Colaresi, M.P. and W.R. Thompson. 2005. "Alliances, Arms Buildups and Recurrent Conflict: Testing a Steps-to-War Model." *Journal of Politics* 67(2): 345–364.

Colaresi, M.P., K.A. Rasler and W.R. Thompson. 2007. *Strategic Rivalries in World Politics: Position, Space and Conflict Escalation*. Cambridge University Press.

Coplin, W.D. and J.M. Rochester. 1972. "The Permanent Court of International Justice, the International Court of Justice, the League of Nations, and the United Nations: A Comparative Empirical Survey." *American Political Science Review* 66(2): 529–550.

Coser, L. 1956. *The Functions of Social Conflict*. New York: Free Press.

Cramer, J.K. 2007. "Militarized Patriotism: Why the US Marketplace of Ideas Failed Before the Iraq War." *Security Studies* 16(3): 489–524.

Dafoe, A. 2011. "Statistical Critiques of the Democratic Peace: Caveat Emptor." *American Journal of Political Science* 55(2): 247–262.

Dahl, R.A. 1991. *Democracy and its Critics*. Yale University Press.

Darby, W.E. 1904. *International Tribunals*. 4th edn. London: J.M. Dent.

Davenport, C. 1995. "Assessing the Military's Influence on Political Repression." *Journal of Political and Military Sociology* 23(1): 119–144.

2007. *State Repression and the Domestic Democratic Peace*. Cambridge University Press.

Davis, D.W. and B.D. Silver. 2004. "Civil Liberties vs. Security: Public Opinion in the Context of the Terrorist Attacks on America." *American Journal of Political Science* 48(1): 28–46.

Davis, J.A. 1975. "Communism, Conformity, Cohorts, and Categories: American Tolerance in 1954 and 1972–73." *American Journal of Sociology* 81(June): 491–513.

DeRouen, K.R. Jr. 1995. "The Indirect Link: Politics, the Economy, and the Use of Force." *Journal of Conflict Resolution* 39(4): 671–695.

2000. "Presidents and the Diversionary Use of Force: A Research Note." *International Studies Quarterly* 44(2): 317–328.

Desch, M.C. 1996. "War and Strong States, Peace and Weak States?" *International Organization* 50(2): 237–268.

2002. "Democracy and Victory: Why Regime Type Hardly Matters." *International Security* 27(2): 5–47.

2008. "America's Liberal Illiberalism: The Ideological Origins of Overreaction in US Foreign Policy." *International Security* 32(3): 7–43.

Diehl, P.F. 1985. "Contiguity and Military Escalation in Major Power Rivalries, 1816–1980." *Journal of Politics* 47(4): 1203–1211.

Dixon, W.J. 1993. "Democracy and the Management of International Conflict." *Journal of Conflict Resolution* 37(1): 42–68.

1994. "Democracy and the Peaceful Settlement of International Conflict." *American Political Science Review* 88(1): 14–32.

Dixon, W. and G. Goertz. 2005. Weakest Links, Compensability and the Liberal Peace: A Note on Measurement Validity. In *Social Science Concepts: A User's Guide*, ed. Gary Goertz. Princeton University Press.

Dixon, W.J. and P.D. Senese. 2002. "Democracy, Disputes, and Negotiated Settlements." *Journal of Conflict Resolution* 46: 547–571.

Donald, H. 1985. *Ethnic Groups in Conflict*. Berkeley; Los Angeles; London: University of California Press.

Downes, A.B. 2009. "How Smart and Tough are Democracies? Reassessing Theories of Democratic Victory in War." *International Security* 33(4): 9–51.

Doyle, M.W. 1986. "Liberalism and World Politics." *American Political Science Review* 80(4): 1151–1169.

Duch, R.M. and J.L. Gibson. 1992. "'Putting Up With' Fascists in Western Europe: A Comparative, Cross-Level Analysis of Political Tolerance." *The Western Political Quarterly* 45(1): 237–273.

Duchacek, I.D. 1970. *Comparative Federalism – The Territorial Dimension of Politics*. New York: Holt, Rinehart & Winston.

Epstein, D.L., R. Bates, J. Goldstone, I. Kristensen and S. O'Halloran. 2006. "Democratic Transitions." *American Journal of Political Science* 50: 551–569.

Erikson, R.S., M.B. MacKuen and J.A. Stimson 2002. *The Macro Polity*. New York: Cambridge University Press.

Farber, H.S. and J. Gowa. 1997. "Common Interests or Common Polities? Reinterpreting the Democratic Peace." *Journal of Politics* 59(2): 393–417.

Fearon, J.D. 1994. "Domestic Political Audiences and the Escalation of International Disputes." *American Political Science Review* 88(3): 577–592.

Fearon, J.D. and D.D. Laitin. 2003. "Ethnicity, Insurgency, and Civil War." *American Political Science Review* 97(1): 75–90.

Feldman, S. and K. Stenner. 1997. "Perceived Threat and Authoritarianism." *Political Psychology* 18(4): 741–770.

Friedberg, A.L. 1988. *The Weary Titan*. Princeton University Press.
  2000. *In the Shadow of the Garrison State: America's Anti-statism and its Cold War Grand Strategy*. Princeton University Press.

Gaddis, J.L. 1986. "The Long Peace: Elements of Stability in the Postwar International System." *International Security* 10(4): 99–142.

Gartzke, E. 2007. "The Capitalist Peace." *American Journal of Political Science* 51(1): 166–191.

Geller, D.S. 2000. Material Capabilities: Power and International Conflict. In *What Do We Know About War?*, ed. J.A. Vasquez. Lanham, MD: Rowman & Littlefield Publishers, Inc., pp. 259–280.

Gelpi, C. 1997. "Democratic Diversions: Governmental Structure and the Externalization of Domestic Conflict." *Journal of Conflict Resolution* 41(2): 255–282.

Ghobarah, H.A., P. Huth and B. Russett. 2003. "Civil Wars Kill and Maim People Long after the Shooting Stops." *American Political Science Review* 97(2): 189–202.

Ghosn, F., G. Palmer and S.A. Bremer. 2004. "The MID3 Data Set, 1993–2001: Procedures, Coding Rules, and Description." *Conflict Management and Peace Science* 21(2): 133.

Gibler, D.M. 1996. "Alliances that Never Balance: The Territorial Settlement Treaty." *Conflict Management and Peace Science* 16(1): 75–97.

1997. "Control the Issues, Control the Conflict: The Effects of Alliances that Settle Territorial Issues on Interstate Rivalries." *International Interactions* 22(4): 341–368.

2007. "Bordering on Peace: Democracy, Territorial Issues, and Conflict." *International Studies Quarterly* 51(3): 509–532.

2011. "Teritorial Issues, Audience Cost, and the Democratic Peace: The Importance of Issue Science." Working Paper. University of Alabama.

Gibler, D.M. and A. Braithwaite. N.d. "Territorial Hot Spots: Assessing the Relationship between Conflict and Democracy in the Region." Working Paper. University of Alabama.

Gibler, D.M. and S.V. Miller. 2012. "Quick Victories? Territory, Democracies and Their Disputes." *Journal of Conflict Resolution*. Working Paper. University of Alabama.

Gibler, D.M. and K.A. Randazzo. 2011. "Testing the Effects of Independent Judiciaries on the Likelihood of Democratic Backsliding." *American Journal of Political Science* 55(3): 696–709.

Gibler, D.M. and M. Reid Sarkees. 2004. "Measuring Alliances: The Correlates of War Formal Interstate Alliance Data Set, 1816–2000." *Journal of Peace Research* 41(2): 211–222.

Gibler, D.M. and J. Tir. 2010. "Settled Borders and Regime Type: Democratic Transitions as Consequences of Peaceful Territorial Transfers." *American Journal of Political Science* 54(4): 951–968.

Gibler, D.M. and S. Wolford. 2006. "Alliances, Then Democracy: An Examination of the Relationship between Regime Type and Alliance Formation." *Journal of Conflict Resolution* 50(1): 129–153.

Gibler, D.M., M.L. Hutchison and S.V. Miller. in press. "Individual Identity Attachments and International Conflict: The Importance of Territorial Threat." *Comparative Political Studies*. Unpublished Manuscript. University of Alabama.

Gibson, J.L. 1992a. "Alternative Measures of Political Tolerance: Must Tolerance be 'Least-Liked'?" *American Journal of Political Science* 36(2): 560–577.

1992b. "The Political Consequences of Intolerance: Cultural Conformity and Political Freedom." *American Political Science Review* 86(2): 338–356.

1998. "A Sober Second Thought: An Experiment in Persuading Russians to Tolerate." *American Journal of Political Science* 42(3): 819–850.

2004. *Overcoming Apartheid*. New York: Russell Sage Foundation.

2006. "Enigmas of Intolerance: Fifty Years after Stouffer's Communism, Conformity, and Civil Liberties." *Perspectives on Politics* 4(01): 21–34.

Gibson, J.L. and R.M. Duch. 1993. "Political Intolerance in the USSR: The Distribution and Etiology of Mass Opinion." *Comparative Political Studies* 26(3): 286.

Gibson, J.L. and A. Gouws. 2003. *Overcoming Intolerance in South Africa: Experiments in Democratic Persuasion*. Cambridge University Press.

Gibson, J.L., R.M. Duch and K.L. Tedin. 1992. "Democratic Values and the Transformation of the Soviet Union." *Journal of Politics* 54(2): 329–371.

Gleditsch, K.S. 2002. *All International Politics is Local: The Diffusion of Conflict, Integration, and Democratization.* University of Michigan Press.

Gleditsch, K.S. and M.D. Ward. 1997. "Double Take." *Journal of Conflict Resolution* 41(3): 361.

Goddard, S.E. 2006. "Uncommon Ground: Indivisible Territory and the Politics of Legitimacy." *International Organization* 60(1): 35–68.

Goemans, H. 2006. Territoriality, Territorial Attachment, and Conflict. In *Territoriality and Conflict in an Era of Globalization*, ed. M. Kahler and B. Walter. Cambridge University Press.

Goertz, G. 1994. *Contexts of International Politics.* Cambridge University Press.

Goertz, G. and P.F. Diehl. 1992. "The Empirical Importance of Enduring Rivalries." *International Interactions* 18(2): 151–163.

Goodall, J. 2000. *Through a Window: My Thirty Years with the Chimpanzees of Gombe.* New York: Mariner Books.

Gourevitch, P. 1978. "The Second Image Reversed: The International Sources of Domestic Politics." *International Organization* 32(4): 881–912.

Gurr, T. 1986. *Persisting Patterns and Emergent Structures in a Waning Century.* New York: Praeger, pp. 149–168.

Hassner, R.E. 2010. "Indivisible Territory and the Politics of Legitimacy: Jerusalem and Northern Ireland by Stacie E. Goddard (Cambridge University Press, 2009)." *Journal of Politics* 72(4): 1256–1258.

Heckman, J.J. 1979. "Sample Selection Bias as a Specification Error." *Econometrica* 47(1): 153–161.

Henisz, W.J. 2002. "The Institutional Environment for Infrastructure Investment." *Industrial and Corporate Change* 11(2): 355.

Hensel, P.R. 1994. "One Thing Leads to Another: Recurrent Militarized Disputes in Latin America, 1816–1986." *Journal of Peace Research* 31(3): 281–297.

1996. "Charting a Course to Conflict: Territorial Issues and Interstate Conflict, 1816–1992." *Conflict Management and Peace Science* 15(1): 43–73.

2000. Territory: Theory and Evidence on Geography and Conflict. In *What Do We Know About War?*, ed. J. Vasquez. Lanham, MD: Rowman & Littlefield, pp. 57–84.

2011. *The Evolution of Territorial Claims and Armed Conflict between Neighbors.* Montreal, Quebec: International Studies Association.

Hensel, P.R., S. McLaughlin Mitchell, T.E. Sowers and C.L. Thyne. 2008. "Bones of Contention." *Journal of Conflict Resolution* 52(1): 117.

Heston, A., R. Summers and B. Aten. 2002. "Penn World Table." Center for International Comparisons at the University of Pennsylvania.

Hetherington, M. and E. Suhay. 2011. "Authoritarianism, Threat, and Americans' Support for the War on Terror." *American Journal of Political Science* 55(3): 546–560.

Hetherington, M.J. and J.D. Weiler. 2009. *Authoritarianism and Polarization in American Politics.* Cambridge University Press.

Hintze, O. 1975. Military Organization and State Organization. In *The Historical Essays of Otto Hintze*, ed. Felix Gilbert. New York, NY: Oxford University Press. Originally published in 1906.

Holsti, K.J. 1991. *Peace and War: Armed Conflicts and International Order, 1648–1989*. Cambridge University Press.

Huddy, L., S. Feldman, C. Taber and G. Lahav. 2005. "Threat, Anxiety, and Support of Antiterrorism Policies." *American Journal of Political Science* 49(3): 593–608.

Hutchison, M.L. 2011a. "Territorial Threat and the Decline of Political Trust in Africa: A Multilevel Analysis." *Polity* 43(4): 432–461.

2011b. "Territorial Threats, Mobilization, and Political Participation in Africa." *Conflict Management and Peace Science* 28(3): 183–208.

Hutchison, M.L. and D.M. Gibler. 2007. "Political Tolerance and Territorial Threat: A Cross-National Study." *Journal of Politics* 69(1): 128–142.

Huth, P.K. 1998. *Standing Your Ground: Territorial Disputes and International Conflict*. University of Michigan Press.

Huth, P.K. and T.L. Allee. 2002. *The Democratic Peace and Territorial Conflict in the Twentieth Century*. Cambridge University Press.

Inglehart, R. 1997. *Modernization and Postmodernization: Cultural, Economic, and Political Change in 43 Societies*. Princeton University Press.

James, P. 1987. "Conflict and Cohesion: A Review of the Literature and Recommendations for Future Research." *Cooperation and Conflict* 22(1): 21.

James, P. and S. Rioux. 1998. "International Crises and Linkage Politics: The Experiences of the United States, 1953–1994." *Political Research Quarterly* 51(3): 781.

Jervis, R. 1978. "Cooperation under the Security Dilemma." *World Politics: A Quarterly Journal of International Relations*, pp. 167–214.

Joffe, J. 1990. Tocqueville Revisited: Are Good Democracies Bad Players in the Game of Nations? In *The New Democracies: Global Change and US Policy*, ed. Brad Roberts. Cambridge, MA: MIT Press, pp. 123–134.

John, A. 1989. *Animal Behavior: An Evolutionary Approach*. Sunderland, MA: Sinauer.

Jones, D.M., S.A. Bremer and J.D. Singer. 1996. "Militarized Interstate Disputes, 1816–1992: Rationale, Coding Rules, and Empirical Patterns." *Conflict Management and Peace Science* 15(2): 163–213.

Kam, C.D. and D.R. Kinder. 2007. "Terror and Ethnocentrism: Foundations of American Support for the War on Terrorism." *Journal of Politics* 69(2): 320–338.

Kant, I. 1796. *Project for a Perpetual Peace: A Philosophical Essay*. London: Vernor and Hood.

Keefer, P. and D. Stasavage. 2003. "The Limits of Delegation: Veto Players, Central Bank Independence, and the Credibility of Monetary Policy." *American Political Science Review* 97(3): 407–423.

Kinder, D.R. and C.D. Kam. 2009. *Us Against Them: Ethnocentric Foundations of American Opinion*. University of Chicago Press.

King, G. 2001. "Proper Nouns and Methodological Propriety: Pooling Dyads in International Relations Data." *International Organization* 55(2): 497–507.

Kocs, S.A. 1995. "Territorial Disputes and Interstate War, 1945–1987." *Journal of Politics* 57: 159–175.

Kornprobst, M. 2008. *Irredentism in European Politics: Argumentation, Compromise, and Norms*. Cambridge University Press.

Kuenne, R.E. 1989. "Conflict Management in Mature Rivalry." *Journal of Conflict Resolution* 33(3): 554.

Kugler, J. and D. Lemke. 1996. *Parity and War: Evaluations and Extensions of the War Ledger*. University of Michigan Press.

Lai, B. and D. Reiter. 2005. "Rally 'Round the Union Jack? Public Opinion and the Use of Force in the United Kingdom, 1948–2001." *International Studies Quarterly* 49(2): 255–272.

Lake, D.A. 1992. "Powerful Pacifists: Democratic States and War." *American Political Science Review* 86(1): 24–37.

Lemke, D. 2002. *Regions of War and Peace*. Cambridge University Press.

Levine, E.P. 1971. "Mediation in International Politics." *Peace Research Society (International) Papers* 17(1): 23–43.

Levy, J.S. 1988. "Domestic Politics and War." *Journal of Interdisciplinary History* 18(4): 653–673.

Lian, B. and J.R. Oneal. 1993. "Presidents, the Use of Military Force, and Public Opinion." *Journal of Conflict Resolution* 37(2): 277–300.

Lipset, S.M. 1959. "Some Social Requisites of Democracy: Economic Development and Political Legitimacy." *American Political Science Review* 53(1): 69–105.

Lowi, T.J. 1972. "Four Systems of Policy, Politics, and Choice." *Public Administration Review* 32(4): 298–310.

MacMillan, J. 2003. "Beyond the Separate Democratic Peace." *Journal of Peace Research* 40(2): 233–243.

Mansfield, E.D. and J.L. Snyder. 1995. "Democratization and the Danger of War." *International Security* 20(1): 5–38.

    2002. "Democratic Transitions, Institutional Strength, and War." *International Organization* 56(2): 297–337.

    2005. *Electing to Fight: Why Emerging Democracies Go to War*. Cambridge, MA: MIT Press.

Maoz, Z. 2005. "Dyadic MID Data Set (Version 2.0)." http://psfaculty.ucdavis.edu/zmaoz/dyadmid.html. Accessed April 16, 2012.

    2010. *Networks of Nations: The Evolution, Structure, and Impact of International Networks, 1816–2001*. Vol. XXXII. Cambridge University Press.

Maoz, Z. and N. Abdolali. 1989. "Regime Types and International Conflict, 1816–1976." *Journal of Conflict Resolution* 33(1): 3–35.

Maoz, Z. and B. Russett. 1992. "Alliance, Contiguity, Wealth, and Political Stability: Is the Lack of Conflict among Democracies a Statistical Artifact?" *International Interactions* 17(3): 245–267.

    1993. "Normative and Structural Causes of Democratic Peace, 1946–1986." *American Political Science Review* 87(3): 624–638.

Marshall, M.G. and K. Jaggers. 2002. "Polity IV Project: Political Regime Characteristics and Transitions, 1800–1999." University of Maryland, Center for International Development and Conflict Management.

Mayhew, D. 1974. *The Electoral Connection*. New Haven, CT: Yale University.

McGinnis, M.D. and J.T. Williams. 1989. "Change and Stability in Superpower Rivalry." *American Political Science Review* 83: 1101–1123.

Meernik, J. 2000. "Modeling International Crises and the Political Use of Military Force by the USA." *Journal of Peace Research* 37(5): 547.

Melander, E. 2005. "Political Gender Equality and State Human Rights Abuse." *Journal of Peace Research* 42(2): 149.

Merritt, R.L. and D.A. Zinnes. 1991. Democracies and War. In *On Measuring Democracy*, ed. A. Inkeles. New Brunswick, NJ: Transaction.

Miller, S.V. and D.M. Gibler. 2011. "Democracies, Territory, and Negotiated Compromises." *Conflict Management and Peace Science* 28(3): 261.

Mitchell, S. McLaughlin and B.C. Prins. 1999. "Beyond Territorial Contiguity: Issues at Stake in Democratic Militarized Interstate Disputes." *International Studies Quarterly* 43(1): 169–183.

Mondak, J.J. and M.S. Sanders. 2003. "Tolerance and Intolerance, 1976–1998." *American Journal of Political Science* 47(3): 492–502.

Moore, B. 1966. *Social Origins of Dictatorship and Democracy: Lord and Peasant in the Making of the Modern World*. London: Allen Lane The Penguin Press.

Morgan, T.C. and S. Howard Campbell. 1991. "Domestic Structures, Decisional Constraints and War." *Journal of Conflict Resolution* 35: 187–211.

Mousseau, M. 1998. "Democracy and Compromise in Militarized Interstate Conflicts, 1816–1992." *Journal of Conflict Resolution* 42(2): 210–230.

2000. "Market Prosperity, Democratic Consolidation, and Democratic Peace." *Journal of Conflict Resolution* 44(4): 472–507.

Mueller, J.E. 1973. *War, Presidents and Public Opinion*. New York, NY: Wiley.

1994. *Policy and Opinion in the Gulf War*. University of Chicago Press.

North, D.C. and B.R. Weingast. 1989. "Constitutions and Commitment: The Evolution of Institutions Governing Public Choice in Seventeenth-Century England." *The Journal of Economic History* 49(4): 803–832.

Nunn, C.Z., H.J. Crockett and J.A. Williams 1978. *Tolerance for Nonconformity: A National Survey of Americans' Changing Commitment to Civil Liberties*. San Francisco: Jossey-Bass.

Olson, M. 1993. "Dictatorship, Democracy, and Development." *American Political Science Review* 87(3): 567–576.

Oneal, J.R. and J. Tir. 2006. "Does the Diversionary Use of Force Threaten the Democratic Peace? Assessing the Effect of Economic Growth on Interstate Conflict, 1921–2001." *International Studies Quarterly* 50(4): 755–779.

Ostrom, C.W. and B.L. Job. 1986. "The President and the Political Use of Force." *American Political Science Review* 80(2): 541–566.

Owsiak, A. 2012. "Signing Up for Peace: International Boundary Agreements, Democracy, and Militarized Interstate Conflict." *International Studies Quarterly* 56: 51–66.

Paasi, A. 1996. *Territories, Boundaries, and Consciousness: The Changing Geographies of the Finnish-Russian Boundary*. New York: Wiley.

Parker, S.L. 1995. "Towards an Understanding of 'Rally' Effects: Public Opinion in the Persian Gulf War." *Public Opinion Quarterly* 59(4): 526.

Peffley, M. and R. Rohrschneider. 2003. "Democratization and Political Tolerance in Seventeen Countries: A Multi-level Model of Democratic Learning." *Political Research Quarterly* 56(3): 243.

Poe, S.C. and C.N. Tate. 1994. "Repression of Human Rights to Personal Integrity in the 1980s: A Global Analysis." *American Political Science Review* 88(4): 853–872.

Poe, S.C., C.N. Tate and L.C. Keith. 1999. "Repression of the Human Right to Personal Integrity Revisited: A Global Cross-national Study Covering the Years 1976–1993." *International Studies Quarterly* 43(2): 291–313.

Przeworski, A. 2000. *Democracy and Development: Political Institutions and Well-being in the World, 1950–1990.* Cambridge University Press.

Przeworski, A. and F. Limongi. 1997. "Modernization: Theories and Facts." *World Politics* 49(2): 155–183.

Przeworski, A., M. Alvarez, J.A. Cheibub and F. Limongi. 1996. "What Makes Democracies Endure?" *Journal of Democracy* 7(1): 39–55.

Quinlivan, J.T. 1995. "Force Requirements in Security Operations." *Parameters* 25: 1995–1996.

Ralston, J.H. 1929. *International Arbitration from Athens to Locarno.* Stanford University Press.

Rasler, K. 1986. "War Accommodation, and Violence in the United States, 1890–1970." *American Political Science Review* 80(3): 921–945.

Rasler, K.A. and W. Thompson. 1989. *War and State-Making: The Shaping of Global Powers.* Boston, MA: Unwin Hyman.

   2004. "The Democratic Peace and a Sequential, Reciprocal, Causal Arrow Hypothesis." *Comparative Political Studies* 37(8): 879–908.

Raymond, G.A. 1994. "Democracies, Disputes, and Third-Party Intermediaries." *Journal of Conflict Resolution* 38(1): 24–42.

   1996. "Demosthenes and Democracies: Regime-Types and Arbitration Outcomes." *International Interactions* 22(1): 1–20.

Reed, W. 2000. "A Unified Statistical Model of Conflict Onset and Escalation." *American Journal of Political Science* 44(1): 84–93.

Reiter, D. and A.C. Stam. 1998. "Democracy and Battlefield Military Effectiveness." *Journal of Conflict Resolution* 42(3): 259–277.

   2002. *Democracies at War.* Princeton University Press.

   2003. "Understanding Victory: Why Political Institutions Matter." *International Security* 28(1): 168–179.

Rogowski, R. 1990. *Commerce and Coalitions: How Trade Affects Domestic Political Alignments.* Princeton University Press.

Rousseau, D.L., C. Gelpi, D. Reiter and P.K. Huth. 1996. "Assessing the Dyadic Nature of the Democratic Peace, 1918–88." *American Political Science Review* 90(3): 512–533.

Roy, A.B. 1997. "Intervention across Bisecting Borders." *Journal of Peace Research* 34(3): 303–314.

Rueschemeyer, D., E.H. Stephens and J.D. Stephens. 2000. "Capitalist Development and Democracy." *Sociological Worlds: Comparative and Historical Readings on Society*, p. 243.

Rummel, R.J. 1983. "Libertarianism and International Violence." *Journal of Conflict Resolution* 27(1): 27–71.

Russett, B.M. 1993. *Grasping the Democratic Peace.* Princeton University Press.

   2005. "Bushwhacking the Democratic Peace." *International Studies Perspectives* 6(4): 395–408.

Russett, B.M. and J.R. Oneal. 2001. *Triangulating Peace: Democracy, Interdependence, and International Organizations.* New York: WW Norton & Company.

Sahlins, P. 1989. *Boundaries: The Making of France and Spain in the Pyrenees.* University of California Press.

Saideman, S.M. 1997. "Explaining the International Relations of Secessionist Conflicts: Vulnerability Versus Ethnic Ties." *International Organization* 51(4): 721–753.

2001. *The Ties That Divide: Ethnic Politics, Foreign Policy, and International Conflict*. New York: Columbia University Press.

Sarkees, M.R. and F. Wayman. 2010. *Resort to War*. Washington, DC: CQ Press.

Sartori, A.E. 2003. "An Estimator for Some Binary-Outcome Selection Models without Exclusion Restrictions." *Political Analysis* 11(2): 111–138.

Schelling, T.C. 1960. *The Strategy of Conflict*. Cambridge, MA: Harvard University Press.

Schmitter, P.C. and T.L. Karl. 1991. "What Democracy Is... and Is Not." *Journal of Democracy* 2(3): 75–88.

Senese, P.D. 1996. "Geographic Proximity and Issue Salience: Their Effects on the Escalation of Militarized Interstate Conflict." *Conflict Management and Peace Science* 15(1): 133–161.

2005. "Territory, Contiguity, and International Conflict: Assessing a New Joint Explanation." *American Journal of Political Science* 49(4): 769–779.

Senese, P.D. and J.A. Vasquez. 2003. "A Unified Explanation of Territorial Conflict: Testing the Impact of Sampling Bias, 1919–1992." *International Studies Quarterly* 47(2): 275–298.

2008. *The Steps to War: An Empirical Study*. Princeton University Press.

Shamir, M. 1991. "Political Intolerance among Masses and Elites in Israel: A Reevaluation of the Elitist Theory of Democracy." *Journal of Politics* 53(4): 1018–1043.

Shamir, M. and T. Sagiv-Schifter. 2006. "Conflict, Identity, and Tolerance: Israel in the Al-Aqsa Intifada." *Political Psychology* 27(4): 569–595.

Sherif, M., O.J. Harvey, B.J. White, W.R. Hood and C.W. Sherif. 1961. *Intergroup Conflict and Cooperation: The Robbers Cave Experiment*. Norman, OK: University Book Exchange.

Simmel, G. 1955. *Conflict and the Web of Group Affiliations* (translated by K.H. Wolff and R. Bendix). New York: Free Press.

Simmons, B.A. 1999. *A Road Map to War: Territorial Dimensions of International Conflict*. Vanderbilt University Press, pp. 205–237.

2006. Trade and Territorial Conflict: International Borders as Institutions. In *Territoriality and Conflict in a Era of Globalization*, ed. M. Kahler and B.F. Walter. Cambridge University Press.

Simon, M.W. and E. Gartzke. 1996. "Political System Similarity and the Choice of Allies: Do Democracies Flock Together, or Do Opposites Attract?" *Journal of Conflict Resolution* 40(4): 617–635.

Singer, J.D., S.A. Bremer and J. Stuckey. 1972. Capability Distribution, Uncertainty, and Major Power War, 1820–1965. In *Peace, War and Numbers*, ed. B. Russett. Beverly Hills, CA: Sage Publications, Inc.

Siverson, R.M. and J. Emmons. 1991. "Birds of a Feather: Democratic Political Systems and Alliance Choices in the Twentieth Century." *Journal of Conflict Resolution* 35(2): 285–306.

Skjelsbaek, K. 1986. "Peaceful Settlement of Disputes by the United Nations and Other Intergovernmental Bodies." *Cooperation and Conflict* 21(3): 139–154.

Slantchev, B.L. 2004. "The Principle of Convergence in Wartime Negotiations." *American Political Science Review* 97(4): 621–632.

Small, M. and J.D. Singer. 1976. "The War-Proneness of Democratic Regimes, 1816–1965." *Jerusalem Journal of International Relations* 1(4): 50–69.

Smith, A.D. 1981. *The Ethnic Revival*. Cambridge University Press.

Snyder, J. 2000. *From Voting to Violence: Democratization and Nationalist Conflict*. New York: Norton.

State System Membership List, v2008.1. 2008. http://correlatesofwar.org. Accessed April 16, 2012.

Stein, B. and D. Arnold. 2010. *A History of India*. Vol. IX. New York: Wiley-Blackwell.

Stinnett, D.M., J. Tir, P. Schafer, P.F. Diehl and C. Gochman. 2002. "The Correlates of War Project Direct Contiguity Data, Version 3." *Conflict Management and Peace Science* 19(2): 58–66.

Stouffer, S.A. 1955. *Communism, Conformity, and Civil Liberties*. New York: Doubleday & Company.

Stuyt, A.M. 1972. *Survey of International Arbitration*. Leiden: A.W. Sijthoff.

Sullivan, J.L., J. Piereson and G.E. Marcus. 1993. *Political Tolerance and American Democracy*. University of Chicago Press. Originally published in 1982.

Sullivan, J.L., M. Shamir, P. Walsh and N.S. Roberts. 1985. *Political Tolerance in Context*. Boulder, CO: Westview Press.

Sullivan, J.L., P. Walsh, M. Shamir, D.G. Barnum and J.L. Gibson. 1993. "Why Politicians Are More Tolerant: Selective Recruitment and Socialization among Political Elites in Britain, Israel, New Zealand and the United States." *British Journal of Political Science* 23(1): 51–76.

Tajfel, H. 1981. *Human Groups and Social Categories*. Cambridge University Press.

Thies, C.G. 2005. "War, Rivalry, and State Building in Latin America." *American Journal of Political Science* 49: 451–465.

Thompson, W.R. 1995. "Principal Rivalries." *Journal of Conflict Resolution* 39(2): 195. 1996. "Democracy and Peace: Putting the Cart before the Horse?" *International Organization* 50(1): 141–174. 2001. "Identifying Rivals and Rivalries in World Politics." *International Studies Quarterly* 45(4): 557–586.

Thompson, W.R. and R. Tucker. 1997. "A Tale of Two Democratic Peace Critiques." *Journal of Conflict Resolution* 41(3): 428–454.

Tilly, C. 1985. War Making and State Making as Organized Crime. In *Bringing the State Back In*, ed. P.B. Evans, D. Rueschemeyer and T. Skocpol. New York, NY: Cambridge University Press, pp. 169–191.

Tir, J., P. Schafer, P.F. Diehl and G. Goertz. 1998. "Territorial Changes, 1816–1996: Procedures and Data." *Conflict Management and Peace Science* 16(1): 89.

Toft, M.D. 2003. *The Geography of Ethnic Violence*. Princeton University Press.

Tsebelis, G. 2002. *Veto Players: How Political Institutions Work*. Princeton University Press.

Tuan, Y.F. 1991. "Language and the Making of Place: A Narrative-Descriptive Approach." *Annals of the Association of American Geographers* 81(4): 684–696.

Vasquez, J.A. 1993. *The War Puzzle*. Vol. XXVII. Cambridge University Press.

1995. "Why Do Neighbors Fight? Proximity, Interaction or Territoriality?" *Journal of Peace Research* 32(3): 277–293.

1996. "The Causes of the Second World War in Europe: A New Scientific Explanation." *International Political Science Review* 17(2): 161.

2009. *The War Puzzle Revisited*. New York, NY: Cambridge University Press.

Vasquez, J.A. and D.M. Gibler. 2001. "The Steps to War in Asia, 1931–1945." *Security Studies* 10(3): 1–45.

Vasquez, J.A. and M.T. Henehan. 2001. "Territorial Disputes and the Probability of War, 1816–1992." *Journal of Peace Research* 38(2): 123–138.

Vasquez, J.A. and B. Valeriano. 2010. "Classification of Interstate Wars." *Journal of Politics* 72(2): 292–309.

Vayda, A.P. 1976. *War in Ecological Perspective*. New York: Plenum.

Verba, S. and G. Almond. 1963. *The Civic Culture: Political Attitudes and Democracy in Five Nations*. Princeton University Press.

Vincent, J. 1987. "Freedom and International Conflict: Another Look." *International Studies Quarterly* 31(1): 103–112.

Wallace, M.D. 1979. "Arms Races and Escalation." *Journal of Conflict Resolution* 23(1): 3.

Waltz, K.N. 1967. *Foreign Policy and Democratic Politics: The American and British Experience*. London: Little, Brown.

Wayman, F.W. 1996. Power Shifts and the Onset of War. In *Parity and War*, ed. Jacek Kugler and Douglas Lemke. University of Michigan Press, pp. 145–162.

Weede, E. 1984. "Democracy and War Involvement." *Journal of Conflict Resolution* 28(4): 649–664.

Weeks, J.L. 2008. "Autocratic Audience Costs: Regime Type and Signaling Resolve." *International Organization* 62(1): 35–64.

Werner, S. 1998. "Negotiating the Terms of Settlement: War Aims and Bargaining Leverage." *Journal of Conflict Resolution* 42(3): 321–343.

Wilson, E.O. 1975. *Sociobiology: The Modern Synthesis*. Harvard University Press.

World Development Indicators. 2009. The World Bank.

Zaller, J. 1993. "The Converse-McGuire Model of Attitude Change and the Gulf War Opinion Rally." *Political Communication* 10: 369–388.

Ziegenhagen, E.A. 1986. *The Regulation of Political Conflict*. Westport, CT: Praeger.

Index

Afrobarometer, 67
Allee, Todd, 16, 19, 122, 127, 131
Argentina, 82
authoritarianism, support for, 73–74

Boix, Carles, 75–77
Bueno de Mesquita, Bruce, 17, 113,
   123, 151

Cambodia, 82
Chile, 82
China, 171–172
   Assam War with India (1962), 154
Cold War, 98
   explanation of, 171–172
   political centralization and, 100, 106
Coser, Lewis, 29, 50, 54, 62, 91

democracy
   diversionary use of force and, 91–92
   independent judiciaries and, 106–107
   political tolerance, 51, 64
   rally effects and, 68, 91–92
   territorial issues as predictor of, 125–127
   types of issues and, 17, 140, 146–148
democratic peace, 112–114
   alliances and, 169
   conflict selection and, 150–151, 154–155
   electoral accountability and, 71
   normative explanations of, 112–113,
     136–138, 172
   spuriousness of, 123–124, 128–133
   structural explanations of, 113
   victory in conflict and, 150–151,
     154–155

democratization, 4
   territorial threats and, 36–39
Diehl, Paul, 20

ethnocentrism, 72–73

Germany, West, 81
Gleditsch, Kristian, 90, 108, 114, 116
Goertz, Gary, 20, 67
Great Britain, 39, 81, 171

Hensel, Paul, 11, 20, 22, 117, 123
Huth, Paul, 12, 14, 16, 19, 22, 31, 50, 53, 108,
   122, 127, 131

India, 38
   Assam War with China (1962), 154
   Kashmir, 1
Israel, 38
   political tolerance in, 51
issue evolution in international system,
   172–174

Lipset, Seymour, 36

Malaysia, 81

negotiated compromises
   operationalization of, 141–142
   predicting, 144–146
Nigeria, 67
non-democracies
   rally effects in, 92–95

opposition parties, 90–101

Pakistan, 38
  Kashmir, 1
political tolerance, 60–65
  cross-country variation in, 51–52

Rasler, Karen, 22, 75
realism, 4

Schelling, Thomas, 117–119
selectorate theory, 17, 89, 93, 95, 113, 123, 151
Simmel, Georg, 29, 50, 54, 62, 91
Soviet Union, 171–172

territorial issues
  conflict-proneness, 10–12
  decolonization and, 120
  democratic peace and, 43–44
  economic value of, 27–28
  ethnicity, identity, and, 12–13
  geography and, 117–119
  MID data and, 18–19, 58–59, 79
  recurrent conflict and, 11, 40–42, 75
  rivalries and, 20
  strategic territory, 14
  symbolic nature of, 12–13
  territorial claims and settlements, 19–20
  territorial transfers, 121, 127, 132
territorial peace, 167–168
  conflict duration and, 162–163
  conflict onset and, 128–133
  conflict selection and, 44, 151–163
  conflict victory and, 157–162
  explanations for democratic peace,
    114–117, 169–170
  negotiated compromises and, 139–141,
    144–146
  operationalization of, 142–143, 156

rivalries and, 170
types of issues and, 140, 146–148, 152–153,
  161–162, 168
territorial threats
  democracy and, 36–39
  domestic strength of military and, 39–40
  foreign policy constraints and, 42–43
  group definition and, 29, 50–51
  individuals and, 26–31, 66–67, 71–74
  MID "hot spots" as measure of, 133
  operationalization of, 21–23, 58–59, 79, 97,
    117–123, 132–133
  opposition parties and, 96–101
  political centralization and, 35–40, 95,
    101–106, 165–167
  political tolerance and, 53–54, 62–65
  rally effects and, 68
  repression and, 34–35, 74–88
  salience of, 2, 17–23, 28–31, 40–43, 65–68,
    71–73, 75, 80–81, 92, 96, 100–101, 104,
    108, 116, 136, 138, 144–145, 163, 166,
    168, 173
  socialization and attachments, 28–29
  standing armies and, 32–34, 74–88
Thompson, William, 20–22, 116

United States, 39, 81, 170–172
  political tolerance in, 51–52

Vasquez, John A., 9–10, 34, 50, 53, 59, 65, 70,
  108, 117, 121
  Steps-to-War theory, 14–16
veto players, 101–106
victory in conflict, *see* democratic peace,
    conflict selection; territorial peace,
    conflict selection
  operationalization of, 155–156

World Values Survey, 54–57, 63, 66, 67